J. C. Queiroz

# Brazil: A Frontier of High-Yield Investment Opportunities

Brasília (in Brazil)

2025

**International Cataloguing-in-Publication Data (CIP)**
**(Câmara Brasileira do Livro, SP, Brazil)**

Queiroz, J. C.

Brazil: a frontier of high-yield investment opportunities / J. C. Queiroz. -- 1. ed. -- Brasília, DF: Ed. by the Author, 2025.

ISBN 978-65-01-54748-0

1. Brazil - Socioeconomic development. 2. Economy – Brazil. 3. Investments – Brazil. 4. Opportunity. 5. Strategic planning.

I. Title.

25-281308 CDD-332.6781

**Indexes for systematic catalog:**

1. Brazil : Investments : Administration : Economy 332.6781

Eliane de Freitas Leite - Librarian - CRB 8/8415

# Summary

# Preface

Brazil. For the foreign investor, few words evoke such a broad and contradictory spectrum of images. On one side, the vibrant postcard of carnival, football, and contagious joy. On the other hand, alarming headlines about currency volatility, political instability, and a complexity that borders on the indecipherable. It is a country often relegated to the category of "exotic risk" or, at best, the eternal "country of the future" — a future that always seems to be postponed.

This book, like a vaccine against stereotypes aimed at the skeptical investor, was born out of a deep unease with this superficial view. Its goal is to present a Brazil that exists beyond the headlines, a country that, upon closer examination, reveals a coherent internal logic, remarkable resilience, and a range of opportunities that most are unaware of.

Throughout my life, I have witnessed the paradox of a country of continental dimensions, endowed with extraordinary natural and human wealth, being consistently ignored or misunderstood by global capital. I have seen an agricultural powerhouse that feeds the world, a financial market that has developed unique sophistication to navigate volatility, and an innovation ecosystem that flourishes precisely by creating solutions to its own chronic challenges. I have realized that the "Brazil risk," which scares so many, is, for those willing to understand it, the very source of above-average returns.

To guide you on this expedition, I have structured the work as a progressive journey. In the initial chapters, we deconstruct stereotypes and present the "map" of Brazil, diving into its history, culture, and the paradoxes that define it. Next, we open the "engine room," detailing the functioning of the financial market, the importance of the interest rate (Selic[1]), exchange rate dynamics, and key assets. With this knowledge in hand, we head to the field, analyzing key sectors of the economy—from global agribusiness and energy to the fintech revolution and the vast consumer market. Finally, we connect theory to practice, discussing portfolio strategy building, risk management, and concrete paths to invest.

This journey as an author, the desire to share this vision with the world, for a long time seemed like a distant ambition, constrained by language barriers. I am grateful for technological evolution, which has democratized communication and allowed me to translate a lifetime of observations and analyses into a guide that, I hope, can serve as a bridge for the foreign investor.

I invite you, dear reader, to dive into these pages not as a tourist seeking confirmations, but as an explorer seeking understanding. Let informed curiosity guide your exploration. This book will not offer you a smooth journey; Brazil rarely does. What it promises is a grounded perspective, a new lens through which complexity transforms into opportunity. The

---

[1] "Selic (Brazil's benchmark interest rate)".

true frontier of value is not in a place without risks, but in a place where risks are well understood.

The expedition to the real Brazil begins now.

# Introduction

In a world where developed markets are increasingly correlated and returns are becoming scarce, the global investor is compelled to look toward new frontiers in search of value and diversification. In this context, Brazil emerges not merely as another emerging market but as a universe of complexity and potential. However, for most, the country remains an enigma, shrouded in headlines about crises and a volatility that seems unpredictable. This book was written to serve as the antidote to that perception. Its mission is to provide the skeptical investor with a detailed map and an analytical compass to navigate the Brazilian territory, transforming noise into signal and complexity into competitive advantage.

The relevance of this work is anchored in the current global context. Brazil is a strategic and irreplaceable player in at least three of the major investment theses of the 21st century: food security, as the world's largest exporter of a vital set of commodities; energy transition, with one of the cleanest electricity matrices on the planet and a leading role in the green revolution; and digital innovation at scale, where chronic social problems act as a catalyst for the emergence of fintechs and startups that are reshaping entire sectors. Ignoring Brazil is, therefore, ignoring a central piece in the puzzle of the future global economy.

To conduct this analysis, the methodology employed is both analytical and immersive. We start with an approach that combines quantitative data extracted from official sources such as the National Treasury, B3, CVM, and company reports, with a deep qualitative analysis of the historical, political, and cultural context that shapes the business environment. The book functions as an analytical funnel, guiding the reader from the broader panorama to the most granular details of investment.

The structure of the book was designed to reflect this journey of discovery:

Chapters 1 and 2: Deciphering Brazil. We begin our expedition by deconstructing stereotypes. We present the country in its proper proportions, revisit its economic cycles, and offer a manual to understand the DNA of volatility, the "Brazil Cost", and how diversity and inequality become drivers of innovation.

Chapters 3, 4, and 5: The Economy and Its Engines. With the map in hand, we delve into the heart of the economy, analyzing its three major engines: the commodity superpower, the strength of domestic consumption, and the rising new digital economy. Next, we open the "engine room" of the financial market, explaining the role of institutions, the dominance of the Selic rate, and the assets where the game takes place. Finally, we explore the key sectors where value hides, from agribusiness to banks, from energy to retail.

Chapters 6, 7, 8, and 9: From Strategy to Action. The final part of the book is eminently practical. We discuss how to build a portfolio aligned with different risk profiles, how to manage the critical variables of political and exchange rate risk, and detail the operational paths for foreign investors to allocate their capital, whether from home (via ETFs and ADRs) or directly on B3. As a bonus, we offer in-depth guides on investing in government bonds and a complete overview of the 50 largest companies listed on the Brazilian stock exchange.

The following pages are an invitation to go beyond the superficial. By the end of this reading, you will have the tools necessary to replace the fear of uncertainty with a structured understanding of risks and opportunities. If you are ready to decipher one of the most fascinating and rewarding markets in the world, this book is your starting point.

The journey begins now.

# Chapter 1 — Brazil Beyond Stereotypes: An Introduction for the Foreign Investor

Imagine a country where the same soil is home to untouched tropical forests, densely populated urban centers, highly productive agricultural regions, and a cultural diversity that borders on the unclassifiable. A country that is, at the same time, an agricultural powerhouse, a strategic energy player, and a social laboratory in constant turmoil. That country is Brazil. And understanding it, especially from the perspective of a foreign investor, requires not only data, but context — and a good dose of humility.

## 1.1. Brazil in Numbers and Proportions

Brazil is the largest country in South America and the fifth largest in the world in terms of territorial extension. With an area of over 8.5 million square kilometers, it has continental dimensions that make it almost a continent within a continent. Its population exceeds 215 million inhabitants, making it the sixth most populous country in the world.

This scale has direct implications for investors. The Brazilian domestic market, despite being uneven, is one of the largest and most dynamic in emerging markets. In 2023, Brazil's nominal GDP exceeded US$2 trillion, placing the country among the ten largest global economies. In 2024, GDP grew by 3.4% compared to the previous year, so that the Brazilian economy maintained its growth trajectory, driven by domestic demand, especially household consumption and the resumption of investments. The country is also the world's largest exporter of commodities such as soybeans, coffee, sugar, beef and iron ore — products that help balance external accounts, even in times of crisis.

## 1.2. A History of Cycles and Breaks

The Brazilian economy has developed in a cyclical manner, often dependent on external shocks. In the 20th century, the country went through phases of accelerated industrialization, hyperinflation, economic stabilization plans, redemocratization and structural reforms. These ups and downs shaped a society accustomed to volatility — and a financial market that, to a certain extent, learned to operate with it.

The introduction of the Plano Real in 1994 marked a turning point. Four-digit inflation was brought under control, the currency gained relative stability, and the country opened up to foreign investors with greater legal certainty and integration into global markets. Since then, Brazil has enjoyed a stable democratic regime, although permeated by recurring political tensions.

Brazil currently operates under an inflation targeting regime, with several strong agencies influencing economic policies, such as the Central Bank of Brazil, the National Monetary Council, and the Ministry of Finance, which are closely monitored by the Federal Legislative Branch, through a specialized technical audit and compliance body, the Federal Court of Auditors, responsible for issuing a preliminary opinion on government accounts, which are assessed annually by the National Congress.

The National Monetary Council (CMN) is the highest body of the National Financial System (SFN) and is responsible for formulating currency and credit policy. Its objective is the stability of the currency and the economic and social development of the country.

The members of the CMN meet once a month to deliberate on matters such as guiding the application of financial institutions' resources; facilitating the improvement of financial institutions and instruments; ensuring the liquidity and solvency of financial institutions; and coordinating monetary, credit, budgetary and internal and external public debt policies.

This Council is chaired by the highest executive of the Central Bank of Brazil, and is composed of several government authorities, such as the President of the Securities and Exchange Commission, the Executive Secretary of the Ministry of Planning and Budget, the Executive Secretary of the Ministry of Finance, the Secretary of the National Treasury of the Ministry of Finance, the Secretary of Economic Reforms of the Ministry of Finance, the Secretary of Economic Policy of the Ministry of Finance, in addition to Directors of the Central Bank of Brazil.

The Central Bank of Brazil can be understood as the Federal Reserve, for the sake of simplicity. The Monetary Policy Committee of the Central Bank of Brazil (Copom/Bacen)), in turn, is the body responsible for setting the basic interest rate for the economy, the Selic. In addition, Copom defines the guidelines and instruments of monetary policy, seeking to maintain currency stability and control inflation.

The main inflation index is the so-called Broad Consumer Price Index (IPCA). Since 2018, the CMN has implemented a gradual strategy to reduce the inflation target, with annual cuts of 0.25 percentage points. This initiative seeks to align Brazilian parameters with those of other economies, strengthening the credibility of the country's monetary policy.

In the last three years (2022 to 2024), the annual inflation target set for the country was 3.5%, 3.25% and 3.0%, respectively, with a tolerance margin of +-1.5 percentage points, corresponding to the target ceiling of 5.0%, 4.75% and 4.5%, respectively. The IPCA was measured, in the same period, at 5.79%, 4.62% and 4.83%, so that there was a small extrapolation of the ceiling in the years 2022 and 2024.

The year 2022 corresponds to a cyclical year. Federal and state elections took place during this year, a time when there is high public spending on the electoral process and adjacent areas, in which the Executive and Legislative branches, without a shadow of a doubt, use the public budget directly and indirectly as a way to interfere in the economy.

The monetary policy implemented by the Central Bank uses the short-term basic interest rate (Selic) as the main instrument to control the Broad National Consumer Price Index (IPCA), defined as a parameter for meeting the inflation target. Here is a brief history of the basic interest rate practiced in Brazil:

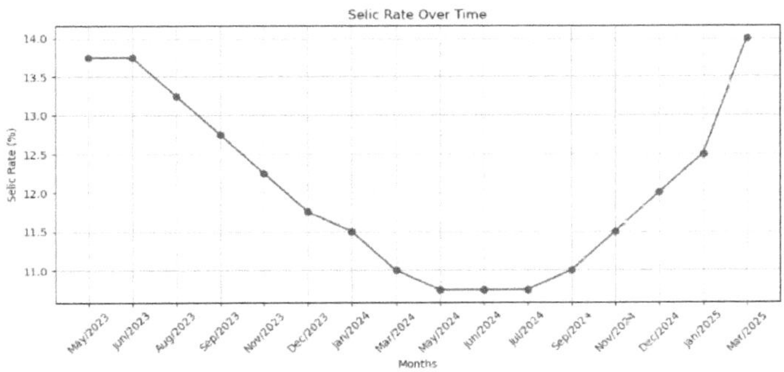


Source: Central Bank of Brazil.

Interest rate policy is closely linked to inflation, not only in Brazil but also worldwide. Specifically speaking of Brazil, among the factors that have put pressure on inflation are the increase in food prices – influenced by the drought, the exchange rate and commodities –, inflation in services, driven by a buoyant labor market (which sustained demand and put pressure on costs), a market that will show low unemployment levels in 2025, and specific shocks in industrial goods and regulated prices.

According to the Central Bank, previous increases are still reflected in new contracts and economic agents anticipate adjustments due to expectations of high inflation. In addition, companies, with production capacity close to its limit, choose to raise prices instead of expanding production.

Fiscal policy also has an influence. The Monetary Policy Committee (Copom), in its 267th meeting, highlighted the importance of harmony between fiscal policy and monetary policy, warning that fiscal uncertainty and the increase in targeted credit raise the neutral interest rate, reducing the power of monetary policy and increasing the cost of disinflation.

All of this is reflected in a double-digit interest rate, although it has to face inflation of around 5% per year, opening up space for good returns on fixed income, if exchange rate parameters are maintained, creating opportunities for foreign investors to apply resources through the purchase of federal public bonds, many of which are indexed to the interest rate or inflation plus a gain, as will be seen below.

## 1.3. A Present, Sometimes Heavy State

The Brazilian state has a significant presence in the economy, whether through state-owned companies such as Petrobras and Banco do Brasil, or through heavy regulation and a tax burden that exceeds 33% of GDP. Bureaucracy and the slowness of the judicial system are real obstacles — and are frequently cited by foreign investors as points of concern.

At the same time, the country has reasonably developed institutional mechanisms for control and transparency. The Fiscal Responsibility Law (2000), the autonomy of the Central Bank (2021), and the actions of audit courts and the Public Prosecutor's Office provide a certain degree of institutional stability that is not common in all emerging markets.

Despite this, in 2024, according to data from official Brazilian bodies, the General Government Gross Debt (which involves the debt of all Brazilian local governments, at the federal, state and municipal levels) and the Federal Public Debt grew as a proportion of GDP in relation to 2023.

This increase reflects the predominance of upward factors (interest charges, primary deficit and fiscal pressures) over containment elements, such as economic growth and expenditure reduction.

The Central Government's primary deficit fell from R$264.5 billion in 2023 to R$45.3 billion in 2024. Even so, the General Government's Gross Debt maintained an upward trajectory, reaching R$9.032 billion, compared to R$8.079

billion in 2023, increasing by R$952.6 billion, equivalent to 2.7% of GDP.

This movement is mainly due to nominal interest incorporated into the debt stock.

Also contributing, to a lesser extent, were the exchange rate devaluation – which increased the value of the external debt – and the net issuance of government bonds. It is also worth considering the increase in the share of securities indexed to the Selic (Special Settlement and Custody System), which makes the cost of debt more sensitive to the basic interest rate, on the Brazilian side, constituting an investment opportunity for individuals, companies with high net cash, and institutional and foreign investors.

Despite these data, there are mechanisms for risk management and internal controls of the federal public debt. To ensure that the objectives of public debt management are achieved, the National Treasury Secretariat (STN) maintains risk management and internal control structures and processes, in accordance with the responsibilities assigned by the applicable risk management and control policies and methodologies.

Despite this scenario, it is important to mention that the volume of Brazil's international reserves has remained at over 300 billion dollars (330 billion in 2024).

This factor, combined with a relatively stable exchange rate of around BRL 5.50 for each dollar, has contributed to the country's sustainability and credibility in terms of attracting investment. The exchange rate has shown slight increases in recent months as a result of a modest recovery in the competitiveness of Brazilian exports in 2025, compared to previous years.

## 1.4. Social Contradictions and Cultural Diversity

It is impossible to understand Brazil without considering its profound inequalities. Income concentration is historic, and public services such as health, education and transportation still leave much to be desired in many regions. Urban violence and high levels of informality in the labor market also weigh on the business environment.

On the other hand, the country is extremely diverse — ethnically, religiously, linguistically and culturally. This plurality is reflected in a vibrant, creative, entrepreneurial and adaptable society. Socially impactful startups, inclusive *fintechs* and technology-centric business models have emerged precisely from the attempt to overcome these challenges.

Brazil is divided into 5 regions: North, Northeast, Central-West, Southeast and South.

The North Region is the largest in territorial extension, covering a vast area of the Amazon Rainforest.

- **The following states are in this region:** Acre (AC), Amapá (AP), Amazonas (AM), Pará (PA), Rondônia (RO), Roraima (RR) and Tocantins (TO).

- **Economic Potential:** It is the lungs of the world, with its immense forest and mighty rivers such as the Amazon, which boosts plant extraction (timber, rubber, açaí) and mineral extraction (iron ore, bauxite, gold). Fishing is vital, and the Manaus Free Trade Zone (AM) stands out in the electronics and computer industries, attracting investment. Hydroelectric power generation is also a strong point.
- **Social and Cultural Characteristics:** The population has strong ties to indigenous peoples and riverside culture, with events such as the Parintins Festival (AM). The cuisine is rich in fish and Amazonian fruits. There is a great challenge in reconciling economic development with environmental preservation and the rights of traditional communities.
- **Consumption and Per Capita Income:** Per capita income in the North Region is usually among the lowest in the country, reflecting socioeconomic challenges and the concentration of wealth in specific areas. Consumption is often linked to essential goods and products from the region.

Known for its **beautiful beaches**, tropical climate and rich popular culture, the Northeast Region is one of the cradles of Brazilian history.

- **Includes the states of:** Alagoas (AL), Bahia (BA), Ceara (CE), Maranhão (MA), Paraíba (PB), Pernambuco (PE), Piauí (PI), Rio Grande do Norte (RN) and Sergipe (SE).

- **Economic Potential:** Tourism is the country's major economic driver, attracting millions of visitors to its beaches and historic cities. Agriculture is strong, with emphasis on sugar cane, tropical fruits (irrigated fruit growing hub) and cocoa. The naval and petrochemical industries (Bahia), textiles and footwear, and the growing production of wind and solar energy are also important.
- **Social and Cultural Characteristics**: A region of great cultural diversity, with a strong African influence, lively June festivals, frevo in Pernambuco and *axé* in Bahia. It presents a great social and climatic disparity, from the humid coast to the semi-arid interior, where drought is a historical challenge.
- **Consumption and Per Capita Income:** Per capita income in the Northeast has grown in recent years, driven by economic development and social programs, but it still presents rates below the national average. Consumption is greatly influenced by local characteristics and the growth of tourism.
- The Central-West Region is the heart of Brazilian agribusiness, with vast areas of crops and livestock farming. It is where the federal capital, Brasília, is located.
- **States:** Goiás (GO), Mato Grosso (MT), Mato Grosso do Sul (MS) and Distrito Federal (DF).
- **Economic Potential:** Agribusiness is the driving force of the economy, with large-scale production of

soybeans, corn, cotton and beef. The logistics infrastructure for transporting production (railways and highways) is crucial. The service sector is strong in the Federal District, and ecological tourism in the Pantanal and Bonito (MS) is gaining prominence.

- **Social and Cultural Characteristics:** A region marked by the backlands culture and rural way of life. The presence of Brasília brings a unique cultural and political dynamism. In the Federal District, all Brazilians mix, forming a cultural diversity, critical thinking, values and the complexity of Brazil. The city is planned, with incredible architectural complexes and wide roads, with landscaping of a first world country. It contrasts with the outskirts just a few kilometers away. The Pantanal is a biome of unparalleled beauty, with an extremely rich biodiversity and Pantanal communities with a strong connection to the environment.
- **Consumption and Per Capita Income:** Per capita income in the Central-West is one of the highest in the country, driven by the government center and agricultural activities in the other states. In agricultural states, income is more dependent on agribusiness cycles, but consumption reflects the greater purchasing power generated by this sector, which produces many millionaires. The Federal District, the only one without agricultural characteristics, has a large middle class, formed by politicians, highly educated public servants, and technology and service

activities, made available to this public and the Brazilian government.

The Southeast Region is the most populous and industrialized in Brazil, being the country's main economic center. According to the 2022 Demographic Census of the Brazilian Institute of Geography and Statistics, the Southeast Region of Brazil has 84,840,113 inhabitants.

It remains the most populous region in the country, with around 41.8% of the Brazilian population.

- **States:** Espírito Santo (ES), Minas Gerais (MG), Rio de Janeiro (RJ) and São Paulo (SP).
- **Economic Potential:** A hub of diversified industry (automotive, steel, petrochemical, textile), advanced services (financial, technology) and commerce. The state of São Paulo is the economic engine of this region, and is home to the largest financial center in the country. Rio de Janeiro stands out for its oil, tourism and industry, but also has a significant contribution to financial market institutions. Minas Gerais has a strong mining, agribusiness and vehicle assembly industry. It has several industrial hubs and once had a semiconductor industry. Steel companies also have their place. Espírito Santo is a state with strong tourism and has ports, oil and gas production.
- **Social and Cultural Characteristics:** A region of great cultural diversity, with the urban effervescence of São Paulo, the carnival and natural beauty of Rio de Janeiro, and the historical and culinary richness of

Minas Gerais. It is home to the largest cities in the country, with challenges such as urban mobility, social inequality and violence.

- **Consumption and Per Capita Income:** Per capita income in the Southeast is the highest in Brazil, which drives a high level of consumption, especially of durable goods and services. Access to products and technologies is easier, and the consumer market is the largest in the country.
- The Southern Region is the smallest in terms of territorial extension, but stands out for its subtropical climate and strong European influence.
- **States:** Paraná (PR), Rio Grande do Sul (RS) and Santa Catarina (SC).
- **Economic Potential:** Diversified agriculture (soybean, wheat, corn, grapes), livestock and industry (automotive, textile, furniture, food) are very strong. The technology and innovation sector has grown, especially in Santa Catarina. Tourism, with the mountains of Rio Grande do Sul and Santa Catarina, beaches and cities with European heritage, is also an economic pillar.
- **Social and Cultural Characteristics:** Strong influence of European immigration (Germans, Italians, Poles, Ukrainians), visible in the architecture, cuisine and typical festivals (Oktoberfest). The subtropical climate allows for four well-defined seasons, with snowfall in

some cities in winter. The region is known for its high levels of human development and quality of life.

- **Consumption and Per Capita Income:** Per capita income in the South Region is among the highest in Brazil, with good purchasing power and access to goods and services. Consumption reflects economic diversity and European cultural influence.

Brazil is a country of many diverse peoples. The cultural trait that most unites this population is precisely the miscegenation between whites, blacks and Indians, under a single, broad, vast, continental territory, and that speaks the same Portuguese language, different from the traditional language coming from Portugal, spoken in other continents where that European state played a colonizing role, given its own accent, and often a different vocabulary, the result of the contribution of the *Brazilianization* of the indigenous people, the Africans and the Europeans who colonized it.

Make no mistake — Brazil is a dormant powerhouse. The climate is not too arid or too cold, which helps agricultural production. The land is fertile. There is plenty of water, with a wealth of minerals of all kinds. And a considerable population.

## 1.5. An Imperfect But Resilient Democracy

Since redemocratization in 1985, Brazil has held regular and peaceful elections. Despite institutional crises and polarized discourses that have gained space in public debate, institutions — such as the Supreme Federal Court, Congress and the Superior Electoral Court — have managed to guarantee democratic continuity.

The press is free and active, civil society is articulate, and citizen participation is growing, especially among the younger generations. In other words, despite all its imperfections, Brazil has demonstrated its ability to preserve its democratic foundations in adverse contexts.

For a foreign investor, it is crucial to understand that the Brazilian electoral system is robust and transparent, with mechanisms that guarantee its integrity and credibility.

Elections in Brazil are based on solid democratic pillars. Voting is universal, which means that all Brazilian citizens over the age of 18 (and optional for those aged 16-17, over 70 and illiterate) have the right to participate in the electoral process, regardless of their social class, gender, race or religion.

The periodic nature of elections ensures the alternation of power and the constant renewal of mandates, with fixed dates for federal, state and municipal elections, generally every four years alternating with two-year periods between federal and municipal elections.

Finally, the secret ballot is a fundamental right guaranteed by the Constitution. Each voter casts his or her vote in secret, without any form of tracking or identification that could link his or her vote to a specific candidate, protecting freedom of choice and avoiding external pressure.

One of the distinguishing features of the Brazilian electoral system is the use of electronic voting machines. Since 1996, Brazil has used this system, which replaced paper voting, which was notorious for fraud and slow counting. The electronic voting machine is a device that:

- Ensured speedy counting: Results are processed and released within a few hours of the polls closing, a stark contrast to the previous long manual process.
- Reduced the chance of fraud: The electronic system was designed with multiple layers of security, including advanced encryption, reinforced physical seals and systems that only work on the equipment itself. The software is developed and audited by experts and regulatory entities.
- It is extensively audited: Before and during elections, several public security tests (PSTs) and audits are carried out, such as verifying the authenticity of the systems and auditing electronic voting in a transparent manner. Representatives of political parties, the Public Prosecutor's Office, the Armed Forces, and universities have access to the source code of the ballot boxes in advance for inspection purposes.

It is important to emphasize that, despite occasional misinformation, the Superior Electoral Court (TSE) reiterates the infallibility of the electronic system against large-scale fraud. Audits and the absence of proven cases of tampering with results confirm the solidity and reliability of Brazilian electronic voting machines.

The Brazilian electoral process is closely followed by extensive coverage from the press, both nationally and internationally. Major media outlets send teams to cover the campaigns, the debates and, of course, the day of the vote and the counting of the results. This constant monitoring contributes to the transparency of the election.

In addition, elections in Brazil are monitored and monitored by international organizations, such as the Organization of American States (OAS), the Inter-American Union of Electoral Organizations (UNIORE) and other electoral observer missions. These observers issue detailed reports on the conduct of the election, and historically, Brazilian elections have received positive evaluations regarding their fairness and reliability.

his external oversight, combined with the robustness of the electronic voting system and the democratic principles that govern the process, guarantees the Brazilian electoral system solid international credibility. This provides an environment of predictability and political stability, essential elements for the confidence of foreign investors.

Brazil demonstrates, in each electoral cycle, its commitment to democracy and the integrity of its institutions, which is a positive factor for attracting investments and the country's development.

## 1.6. Brazil in the World

On the international stage, Brazil has an ambiguous role. It is a regional power and a key country in environmental issues, given its presence in the Amazon. It is also an active member of the BRICS, the G20 and the UN. Despite this, the country suffers from a sometimes erratic foreign policy, oscillating between diplomatic prominence and occasional isolation.

From a geoeconomic perspective, Brazil represents a pole of relative stability in South America. Its strategic position, with abundant resources and diversified production capacity, makes it a relevant destination for investors seeking exposure to commodities, energy transition and emerging domestic consumption.

Brazil defies simplistic classifications. While it offers real risks — political, economic, social and exchange rate — it also represents a frontier of opportunities. Its complexity may be daunting at first glance, but it is precisely in this complexity that its greatest asset lies: the possibility of above-average returns for those willing to understand the terrain.

In the next chapters, we will delve deeper into the specifics of the economic environment, the functioning of the local financial market, and the most promising sectors for the foreign investor who seeks, above all, to understand before investing.

# Chapter 2: Deciphering Brazil – A Handbook for the Skeptical Investor

You probably carry around two ideas about Brazil. The first is the postcard version: lush beaches, carnival, soccer and contagious joy. The second is the one from the headlines of financial newspapers: political instability, exchange rate volatility, fiscal crises and legendary bureaucracy. Both versions are real, but dangerously incomplete.

The purpose of this book, and especially this chapter, is not to sell you the postcard version, nor to confirm your worst fears. The purpose is to give you a map of the terrain. Brazil is not a country for amateurs, but it generously rewards those who dedicate themselves to understanding it. The complexity that frightens the average investor is, for the informed investor, the main source of alpha.

Let's start by debunking some myths and putting together an honest portrait of one of the most fascinating and challenging emerging markets in the world.

## 2.1. The Illusion of a "Country": Understanding Scale and Diversity

The first mistake a foreigner makes is to think of Brazil as a unified country. It is more useful to think of it as a continental shelf that houses different "Brazils" coexisting, often in parallel realities.

At 8.5 million square kilometers, Brazil is larger than the contiguous United States. Saying that we are going to "invest in Brazil" is as vague a statement as saying that we are going to "invest in the United States.".

High-tech agribusiness in Mato Grosso state has more in common with the American Corn Belt than with the Amazon rainforest economy in Pará.

The financial industry on Avenida Faria Lima in São Paulo operates with a sophistication that rivals London or New York, while just a few kilometers away, entire communities still struggle for access to basic sanitation.

This heterogeneity is the key to everything. It means that:

- **The risk is not uniform:** A political crisis in Brasília (this is the name of the country's capital, which is also located in a Federal District, in the geographic center of this continental country) can have different impacts on a retail company focused on the Northeast and a pulp exporter in the South.
- **The opportunity is widespread:** Disruptive innovations do not only arise in large cities. They arise from the need to solve complex local problems, such as logistics in remote areas, financial inclusion for an unbanked population or solving problems related to Brazilian entrepreneurship (examples of this are the cases of Nubank, Banco Inter, Locaweb, TOTVS, Intelbras).

- **The domestic market is a mosaic:** With over 215 million inhabitants (it is the sixth most populous country in the world), Brazil has one of the largest consumer markets on the planet. And this scale has direct implications for investors, since the Brazilian domestic market, despite being unequal, is one of the largest and most dynamic of the emerging markets. However, it is not a monolithic block. It is a patchwork of different social classes, consumption habits and regional realities. Understanding this mosaic is the secret to unlocking value.

## 2.2. The DNA of Volatility: A Story of Cycles and Resilience

For the American or European investor, accustomed to decades of low inflation and institutional stability, Brazil's economic history may seem like an action movie. The country has lived through four-digit hyperinflation, savings confiscations (impossible today due to the legal and regulatory framework), debt moratoriums and countless economic plans.

In the 20th century, the country went through phases of accelerated industrialization, hyperinflation, economic stabilization plans, *redemocratization* and structural reforms.

This is not a flaw; it is the DNA of the market. This history has shaped a unique economic culture:

1. **Corporate Resilience:** Brazilian companies that have survived this environment have learned to be agile, to

operate with high volatility and to have extremely disciplined cash management. They are not easily frightened.

2. **Sophisticated Financial Market:** Paradoxically, the instability forced the local financial market to develop hedging mechanisms, derivatives and complex interest rate strategies long before other emerging markets. The market learned to "dance with volatility". The ups and downs shaped a society accustomed to volatility.

3. **The watershed moment - The Real Plan (1994)[2]:** This was not just a stabilization plan; it was the milestone that brought Brazil into modern capitalism. By taming hyperinflation, it created a stable currency and allowed, for the first time, long-term planning, access to credit and a real opening to foreign investment. Understanding Brazil today is impossible without understanding the "before" and "after" the Real.

Since then, the country has built important institutional pillars. The Fiscal Responsibility Law (2000s), for example, imposed limits on public spending, and the recent formal

---

[2] The Real Plan was a comprehensive macroeconomic stabilization framework implemented in 1994 to halt chronic hyperinflation in Brazil. It combined a currency reform—anchoring the new Real to the U.S. dollar in its initial phase—with tight monetary policy, fiscal discipline, and institutional reforms. The plan restored price stability, enabled long-term financial planning, and laid the foundation for Brazil's modern capital markets.

autonomy of the Central Bank is a crucial step forward for the credibility of monetary policy.

Today, for example, Brazil has large monetary reserves in dollars and a very low external debt. The country is financed mainly by internal debt backed by federal government bonds, and by its own people, by the business that people do with the world, whose trade balance is strong in agriculture, oil and mining especially. However, it is an economy that turns a lot of money into services, given its demographics.

Democracy, although noisy and sometimes tense, has proven to be resilient. Thus, despite the so-called country risk, we believe that the country is undervalued by the world's major economies, especially by foreign capital. And if the West does not see the potential, there is a risk that the East, especially countries like China, Korea and Japan, will see the opportunities, putting their investors ahead of the exploration of these potentials.

## 2.3. The "Brazil Cost": Navigating Between the Heavy State and Solid Institutions

Herein lies the greatest paradox for the investor. The Brazilian State is simultaneously an obstacle and an anchor.

**The Obstacle (The famous "Brazil Cost"):**

The term “Brazil Cost” (Custo Brasil, in Portuguese) refers to the set of structural inefficiencies, bureaucratic hurdles, and hidden costs that increase the complexity and expense of doing business in Brazil. It is not a single tax or fee, but rather a combination of factors—economic, legal, logistical, and institutional—that collectively reduce competitiveness and productivity.

For foreign investors, the Brazil Cost can manifest in several ways:

**Excessive bureaucracy**: Lengthy and complex procedures to open or operate a business, obtain licenses, or navigate the legal system.

**Tax complexity**: A notoriously intricate tax code with overlapping federal, state, and municipal taxes, often requiring specialized legal and accounting support.

**Judicial inefficiency**: Slow court processes and legal uncertainty, especially in contract enforcement and regulatory disputes.

**Infrastructure bottlenecks**: Deficiencies in transportation, logistics, and port systems that increase operational costs.

**Regulatory unpredictability**: Frequent changes in rules, policies, or enforcement practices that can affect long-term planning.

Despite these challenges, Brazil also offers solid institutions, a large consumer market, and high-yield investment opportunities—especially for those who understand how to navigate the system. In fact, many successful companies have developed internal expertise and resilience precisely because of this environment.

In short, the Brazil Cost is the "entry ticket" to a complex but potentially rewarding market. For the informed investor, it is not just a risk—it is a barrier to entry that, once overcome, can become a competitive advantage.

- **Tax Burden**: With over 33% of GDP, the tax system is not only cumbersome, but also byzantinely complex, requiring specialized advice. By investing in Brazilian stocks, however, you are investing in a structure that has a legal and accounting team ready to face the challenges of Brazilian legislation.
- **Bureaucracy and Justice:** Opening a company, obtaining licenses or resolving a contractual dispute can be a slow and costly process, and is a recurring concern for direct investors. Investing through the Brazilian stock exchange, however, is an alternative to this obstacle.
- **State Presence:** The government still controls strategic companies in sectors such as oil and gas (Petrobras) and banking (Banco do Brasil), which introduces an element of political risk into the decisions of these companies. Much more so in the case of the oil company (Petrobras) than in Banco do Brasil. It should not be forgotten, however, that the oil company is a cutting-edge company in technology and deep-water oil extraction, where Brazil's largest oil reserves are located. And Banco do Brasil is a company that is over 215 years old (founded in 1808), in addition to being

located in the so-called Novo Mercado, where the levels of governance are higher, and it does not have preferred shares, only ordinary shares, with the same weight as its controllers in terms of voting rights.

**The Anchor (The Control Institutions):** Despite its problems, Brazil is not a "Wild West". The country has developed an ecosystem of counterbalances that, although imperfect, works.

The Public Prosecutor's Office has autonomy to investigate, the Courts of Auditors monitor government spending, and can adopt measures of coercion, judgment, conviction and application of penalties, and the Judiciary, although slow, is independent, with judges having constitutional guarantees for the full exercise of the magistracy, without public or private interference.

By the way, the Judiciary is currently undergoing a technological shift that tends to speed up processes. There is a judicial system based on electronic processes, petitioning via the internet, holding virtual trial sessions, using technologies provided by the most successful American BigTechs, including electronic signatures and recent use of artificial intelligence.

The press is free and combative, and civil society is increasingly active.

For the investor, this means that although the rules are complex and the game is tough, there are rules. The risk is not that of anomie, but rather that of complexity.

## 2.4. Inequality as a driver: social contradiction and innovation

It is impossible to ignore Brazil's deep social scars. Income concentration is one of the highest in the world, and the quality of public services is deficient when compared to first world countries.

However, access to healthcare is free and universal. There are programs to provide medicines at the three levels of government: federal, state and municipal. Schools are free for everyone, from childhood to university, and some are better than others (The country spans a continental scale, with five culturally and economically distinct regions). In these two aspects, there is a niche for the private market, both in healthcare and education, which is why there are also good companies that explore these activities. This reality is an unexpected source of dynamism.

Brazilian creativity flourishes in adversity. Where the State fails, entrepreneurship emerges to fill the gaps. It is no coincidence that Brazil has become one of the largest fintech hubs in the world. In a country with tens of millions of people without bank accounts, startups have created digital payment and credit solutions that have revolutionized the financial system. Logistics companies are innovating to deliver products to addresses without a formal address code. Healthcare startups (healthtechs) are using technology to make access to exams and consultations cheaper.

Investors who only see the problem of inequality miss the opportunity that arises from the solution. Brazilians' cultural diversity and ability to adapt are intangible assets of enormous value.

Brazil, as we have seen, is a country built on paradoxes. It is a global agricultural powerhouse that struggles with food insecurity in certain regions. It is a resilient democracy, but its institutions are under constant stress. It has a sophisticated market, but it operates amidst enormous social deprivations.

We do not promise a smooth investment journey in this book. There will be bumps in the road. Politics will make noise, exchange rates will fluctuate, and bureaucracy may test your patience, especially if you choose to invest directly.

What this book offers you is the thesis that, for the investor willing to go beyond the superficial, the risks are more than compensated by the opportunities. Brazil's complexity is not a defect to be avoided, but a code to be deciphered. Whoever deciphers it will find a market of continental dimensions, rich in resources, with a creative people and a growth potential that few places in the world still offer.

In the following chapters, we will leave the panoramic view and dive deep. We will analyze how the capital markets work, the particularities of the main sectors and how to put together a practical investment strategy to navigate this fascinating and rewarding territory.

Welcome to the real Brazil.

# Chapter 3: The Multi-Engine Economy: From Global Agribusiness to the New Digital Economy

In the first chapters, we established that Brazil is a mosaic of realities. Now, let us apply that same lens to its economy. Thinking of the Brazilian economy as a single entity is a mistake. It operates largely on the basis of two main engines, often at different speeds and directions: an outward-facing, robust, and traditional engine; and an inward-facing, resilient, and increasingly dynamic one.

Understanding the interaction — and sometimes disconnect — between these two drivers is the first step to sophisticated investment analysis.

Recently, a third, smaller but high-revving engine has begun to gain traction: the digital economy. Let us take each of them apart.

## 3.1 The First Mover: The Commodity Superpower

This is the most well-known face of Brazil on the global stage. The country is a force of nature when it comes to natural resources and agricultural production.

- It is the world's largest exporter of essential products such as soybeans, coffee, sugar, beef and iron ore.

- This massive production not only feeds the world and supplies global industries, but also serves as a stabilizer for the Brazilian economy itself, helping to balance external accounts, especially in times of crisis.
- With a nominal GDP that exceeded two trillion dollars in 2023, Brazil is among the ten largest economies in the world, largely driven by this export strength.

**What this means for the investor?**

1. **Direct Exposure to the Global Cycle**: Investing in companies linked to this engine is a direct bet on global growth and demand for commodities. When China grows, the demand for Brazilian iron ore increases. When the world population demands more food, Brazilian agribusiness benefits.
2. **Currency Vulnerability:** These companies' revenues are in dollars, but many of their costs are in reais. A depreciation of the real (a more expensive dollar) can dramatically increase their profit margins, making them a natural hedge against local currency weakness. The opposite is also true.
3. **Price Risk:** This sector is at the mercy of international commodity prices, which are volatile and influenced by geopolitical, climatic and macroeconomic factors beyond Brazil's control.

This engine is the basis of the economy, the source of dollars that gives the country a certain external stability. It is the part of Brazil that is fully integrated into global production chains.

## 3.2. The Second Engine: The Power of Domestic Consumption

If the first engine looks outward, the second looks inward. With a population of over 215 million, Brazil has one of the most powerful and sought-after domestic markets in the emerging world. Despite its notorious inequality, decades of (slow) social mobility and income transfer programs have created a consumer mass with enormous potential.

This engine is fueled by retail, services, construction and the financial system that serves millions of citizens and businesses

**What does this mean for the investor?**

1. **Relative Insulation:** Domestically focused companies (such as shopping malls, large retailers or healthcare companies) are less exposed to fluctuations in commodities and the global economy. Their results depend more on local consumer confidence, employment and access to credit.
2. **Sensitivity to Domestic Politics:** This sector is extremely sensitive to decisions made in Brasília. The Central Bank's interest rate policy, the minimum wage level, social programs and the general political mood

have a direct impact on Brazilians' pockets and purchasing power.

3. **The Challenge of Inequality:** The domestic market is vast, but not homogeneous. The deep concentration of income is a fact. Companies that are able to offer products and services to different income brackets, especially to the base of the pyramid, find gigantic avenues for growth.

This engine represents the resilience of the local economy. Even when the external scenario is challenging, the strength of domestic consumption can often keep the economy moving.

## 3.3. The Third Engine: Innovation Born from Chaos

Amid the inefficiencies of a bureaucratic and unequal economy, a third, more modern and agile engine has emerged: technology. Brazil is experiencing a silent revolution in sectors such as finance, agribusiness, health and education, driven by startups.

In terms of agribusiness, technology research is encouraged by the Brazilian government and is being developed with the aim of increasing productivity and reducing production costs. This role is played by the state-owned company Embrapa. However, with the success of Embrapa's discoveries, technology is being transferred to Brazilian agricultural and livestock production.

The logic is simple: every chronic problem in the country is a business opportunity.

- The concentrated and expensive banking system gave rise to one of the largest fintech scenes in the world. And these have generated a revolution in their services, due to the competitive environment.
- State bureaucracy has created a market for govtechs that simplify processes.
- The deficiencies of the public health system open space for healthtechs.

Technology-centric business models, social impact startups and inclusive fintechs are emerging precisely as an attempt to overcome the country's historical challenges. This "new economy" is perhaps the most exciting investment thesis in Brazil today, as it combines high growth potential with the solution of real problems.

## 3.4. The Operating System: Interest, Inflation and the Central Bank

If these are the drivers, monetary policy is the operating system that regulates them. Investors need to understand the almost obsessive relationship that Brazil has with inflation and interest rates. The memory of the hyperinflation of the 1980s and 1990s is still alive.

This resulted in the creation of one of the most orthodox and vigilant monetary policy regimes in the world, consolidated by two landmarks:

1. **The Real Plan (1994):** Broke the backbone of hyperinflation and stabilized the currency.
2. **Central Bank Autonomy (2021):** Gave the monetary authority the formal independence to pursue its inflation targets without direct political interference, a pillar of institutional credibility.

In practice, this means that the Central Bank of Brazil (BCB or Bacen) does not hesitate to raise the basic interest rate (Selic) aggressively to control inflation, even if this slows down the economy.

For the investor, this has a direct and fundamental consequence: Brazil is, structurally, a country with high real interest rates (nominal interest rates minus inflation).

This makes local fixed income assets extremely attractive, but it also makes credit more expensive and can slow down the engine of domestic consumption. It is possible to win on both sides, anticipating the upward or downward movements in interest rates, or investing in companies that have learned to surf both these moments, the rising and falling interest rates.

It is also possible to make money simply with the high interest rate, when allocating capital in fixed income investments or public bonds linked to the variation of the CDI (Interbank Deposit Certificate) or Selic.

### Conclusion: Putting the Puzzle Together

The Brazilian economy does not move in unison. It is a dynamic puzzle formed by the interaction of these three engines, all regulated by an operating system of high interest rates.

A successful investor in Brazil is one who can read the moment of each play. There are times when the global scenario favors the commodity engine. At other times, the strength of the domestic market prevails. And, silently, the new digital economy grows, independent of the broader macroeconomic cycles.

Understanding which engine is accelerating, which is braking, and how the Central Bank is calibrating the system is the essence of macroeconomic analysis in Brazil. In the next chapter, we will see how these forces translate into tradable assets in the local financial market: stocks, bonds, and foreign exchange.

# Chapter 4: The Machine Room – How the Brazilian Financial Market Works

In the previous chapter, we drew a map of Brazil: a territory of continental dimensions, forged in volatility and driven by paradoxes. Now that you understand the terrain, it is time to inspect the engine. The Brazilian financial market, like the country, has its own rules, rhythms and personalities. Ignoring them is the fastest path to failure.

This chapter is your guide to the engine room. We will learn about the institutions that dictate the rules, the key variable that moves all the gears (interest rates), the assets where the action happens and, crucially, how currency risk impacts every dollar you invest.

## 4.1. The Pillars of the System: B3, CVM and the Central Bank

Unlike the United States, which has multiple exchanges such as the NYSE and NASDAQ, **Brazil has consolidated its capital markets into a single, powerful entity: B3 (*Brasil, Bolsa, Balcão* – Brazil, Stock Exchange, Counter)**. It is the nerve center where virtually all trading of stocks, commodity futures, derivatives and private debt securities takes place. This centralization offers an advantage: concentrated liquidity and a single point of regulation and transparency. For investors, it means less fragmentation and greater ease in monitoring the market.

It is worth mentioning that B3 also has listed shares, as it is a publicly traded company. With no competitors in the financial market, it is a good opportunity for foreign capital investment, which can ride the wave of growth in the Brazilian capital market. The biggest risk associated with this potential investment is the installation of a second stock exchange, in competition. This situation is possible, but remote. This is because the capital market is still very small in Brazil compared to the rest of the world.

Overseeing B3 and all market participants is the **CVM (*Comissão de Valores Mobiliários* or Brazilian Securities and Exchange Commission)**. Think of it as the Brazilian SEC (Securities and Exchange Commission). Its role is to regulate, monitor and ensure market integrity, protecting investors against fraud and manipulation. Although bureaucracy can be a challenge, the existence of a regulator like the CVM is a pillar of legal certainty.

The third and perhaps most important pillar is the **Central Bank of Brazil (BCB)**. Equivalent to the Federal Reserve, the BCB has a dual mandate: to control inflation and to ensure the stability of the financial system.

Since gaining formal autonomy in 2021, its ability to make technical decisions without direct political interference has increased, representing an immense credibility factor for foreign investors. And the BCB's main tool takes us to the heart of the Brazilian market.

## 4.2. The Heart of the Market: His Majesty, the Selic Rate

In the US, investors obsessively follow the Fed's decisions on interest rates. In Brazil, this obsession is raised to a higher power. The **Selic rate** is the basic interest rate of the economy, set by the BCB every 45 days. It is the reference for all other rates, from financing a car to the cost of debt for a large company and, most importantly, the return on fixed-income investments.

Due to its history of high inflation, Brazil has become accustomed to operating with one of the highest real interest rates (after inflation is discounted) in the world. This has a fundamental consequence that foreign investors need to internalize: **Fixed Income is a powerful and ubiquitous asset class.**

While fixed income is often seen as a low-return haven in the US, in Brazil it is a fierce competitor for capital allocation. When the Selic rate is high, it is possible to obtain double-digit returns in dollars on government bonds, which are considered to have a very low risk of default. This creates a huge "opportunity cost" for the stock market. Companies need to offer very high growth potential to justify the risk, when the investor can simply "sit" in a government bond and watch their money grow.

Therefore, the first question from any analyst in Brazil is always: "What is the trajectory of the Selic rate?".

## 4.3. Where the Game Happens: Stocks, Fixed Income and the Ibovespa Trap

With the institutional scenario and the importance of Selic in mind, let us look at the main assets:

- **Stocks and the Bovespa Index (Ibovespa)**: The Ibovespa is the main index of the Brazilian stock exchange, similar to the S&P 500. However, it has a trap: it is highly concentrated. Historically, a few large companies dominate its composition, mainly in the commodities (such as mining company Vale and state-owned oil company Petrobras) and financial sectors (large banks such as Itaú, Bradesco and Santander). Brazil is a major global exporter of soybeans, coffee, sugar, oil and iron ore, and this is reflected in its main index. Therefore, buying an ETF that tracks the Ibovespa is not buying a diversified basket of the Brazilian economy; it is, to a large extent, making a targeted bet on banks and the global commodity cycle. There are other options outside the Ibovespa, whose returns are higher, and still with great liquidity. There are companies focused on infrastructure, energy, sanitation, medical services and technology, areas that lack public investment, with high long-term returns and considerable margins.
- **The King of Fixed Income:** As mentioned, this is the preferred universe of local investors. The federal

government offers its bonds through a digital platform called Tesouro Direto, allowing individuals to invest directly. The main ones are Tesouro Selic (post-fixed, which follows the basic interest rate) and Prefixados and IPCA+ (which pay a fixed rate or a rate plus inflation variation). For the investor, understanding this dynamic is crucial, as it dictates the flow of capital in the country.

- **Real Estate Investment Trusts (FIIs):** Similar to American REITs, FIIs are funds that invest in real estate projects (shopping malls, office buildings, logistics warehouses, agricultural land, residential housing). They are traded on the stock exchange like shares and distribute monthly income exempt from income tax to individuals, which has made them extremely popular.

## 4.4. The Critical Variable: Navigating Currency Risk

For those of you who hold your assets in dollars, euros or any other foreign currency, any investment in Brazil has two sources of return (or risk): the performance of the asset itself (in BRL) and the exchange rate variation (BRL vs. Dollar, for example). You may have a spectacular gain on a Brazilian stock, but if the Real depreciates sharply against the Dollar, especially, your gain may be reduced or even wiped out when converted back to your currency.

The Brazilian currency, the Real (BRL), is notoriously volatile. It is influenced by the global appetite for risk (in times of crisis, investors flee emerging currencies), by the prices of the commodities that the country exports and, of course, by the domestic political and fiscal scenario.

An investment strategy for Brazil that does not include an outlook on the exchange rate is incomplete. Some investors choose to hedge (currency protection), while others accept volatility as part of the game, seeking gains both in the asset and in the possible appreciation of the currency. There is no right answer, but ignoring the question is a gross error.

In particular, we do not have the correct answer regarding exchange rate risk, since only with a crystal ball can we predict what the exchange rate will be like in the future. However, in the medium and short term, it can be said that exchange rate risk appears to be low, except for the global impacts of wars that have been planned or are underway in Europe and the Middle East, or climate catastrophes that may eventually affect South America.

If you are worried about the exchange rate, do this: invest the amount of money you feel comfortable with. Seen from a country with a strong currency, Brazil seems too cheap to ignore.

## 4.5. Demystifying the gains provided by Fixed Income in Brazil

For the American or European investor, accustomed to interest rates that flirted with zero for more than a decade, the idea of obtaining double-digit returns on government bonds considered low risk may sound like an anomaly, or even “too good to be true.” However, in Brazil, this is not an anomaly; it is the fundamental logic of the system, shaped by decades of fighting inflation.

**Understanding this logic is the first step to unlocking one of the most attractive and consistent investment opportunities in the country**.

### 4.5.1. The Bottom Line: Why Interest Rates Are So High?

He answer lies in history. Brazil experienced a period of hyperinflation that left deep scars on the country's economic psyche. To control this inflation and maintain currency stability, the Central Bank of Brazil (BCB) has historically used its main tool, the Selic rate, **much more aggressively** than its peers in developed countries.

This means that the BCB needs to offer a positive and attractive "real interest rate" (nominal interest rate minus inflation). This real interest rate is the real premium paid to investors for investing their money in the country. While in many countries the objective of fixed income is simply to preserve capital, in Brazil the objective is to significantly remunerate capital, serving as a pillar of profitability for any portfolio.

### 4.5.2. Treasury Direct: The Gateway to Sovereign Wealth

The Brazilian government has created an online platform called *Tesouro Direto*, which allows any investor (including foreigners, through a local brokerage firm) to purchase federal government bonds in a simple and transparent manner.

These bonds are the basis of fixed income and are divided into three main categories, each with a different strategic function.

a) The Pillar of Liquidity and Security: *Tesouro Selic (LFT)*

How it works: This security pays exactly the variation of the Selic rate during the period. Its yield is daily and closely follows the basic interest rate. Crucially, its market price hardly fluctuates, which makes it an asset with very low market risk. At the time of writing this book, the annual return on this security is around 15%. Although it may already be at the peak of the interest rate curve, it is known that the downward movement of this rate is much slower than the upward movement, precisely because of the effects on economic activity, which remains buoyant even in times of high interest rates in Brazil. Brazilians, unlike other people in developed countries, are not very scared by interest rates. The immediacy of the Brazilian people makes it more important for the consumer to know how much they pay each month than how much it will cost. This is the logic of local thinking. Therefore, it is important to know whether the installment will fit into the budget. Consumption follows this logic.

Reasoning for foreign investors: Think of the Tesouro Selic as a high-yield savings account or a turbocharged money market fund. It is the ideal place to keep your portfolio's cash, your opportunity reserve to buy other assets in times of decline, or simply to have a solid and predictable profitability base. If you decide to withdraw your capital from the country, it will take no more than 3 days. All you have to do is redeem the bond, make the exchange and repatriate the funds to your country.

In a scenario with the Selic rate at 10% per year, for example, this security acts as a "floor" for your entire strategy in Brazil. Any other higher-risk investment must, by definition, offer a potential return significantly higher than this 10% to justify the allocation. The same reasoning should be applied to the current rate.

At these amounts, it is difficult to find companies capable of outperforming an investment like this with very low risk, unless the long-term goal is achieved. In the long term, profitable Brazilian companies, with recurring profits in scenarios of high or low interest rates, are capable of beating interest rates. But it is necessary to study each asset carefully. There are at least thirty companies on the Brazilian stock exchange with this profile alone and, because they are profitable, they pay good dividends. Therefore, the return on these assets must consider not only the evolution of the stock price, but also the return on profits and dividends.

b) The Directional Bet: *Tesouro Prefixado (LTN)*

How it works: This bond "locks in" a fixed interest rate at the time of purchase (for example, 11.5% per year) until maturity. If market expectations for future interest rates fall, the price of this bond rises, generating capital gains in addition to the contracted rate. The reverse is also true.

Reasoning for the foreign investor: This is an instrument for the investor who has a macroeconomic view. If you believe that the Central Bank has been successful in controlling inflation and that the next move will be to cut the Selic rate, buying a Treasury Prefix allows you not only to guarantee a high interest rate for several years, but also to profit from the appreciation of the security. It is a sophisticated way of betting on the improvement of the Brazilian economic scenario. It requires continuous macroeconomic assessment, in addition to considering seasonalities, including an assessment of the political and institutional field.

c) The Protector of Heritage: *Tesouro IPCA+ (NTN-B)*

How it works: This is perhaps the most powerful low-risk instrument for the long term. It pays a fixed real interest rate (the "+", for example, 5.5% per year) plus the variation in official inflation for the period (the IPCA).

Reasoning for the foreign investor: For those who fear that Brazilian inflation may erode their returns, this bond is the definitive solution. It offers a guarantee, given by the government, that your purchasing power will not only be maintained, but will grow at a real and predictable rate. It is the perfect asset for those investing with a focus on retirement or very long-term goals. It eliminates the main uncertainty of investing in an emerging market – inflation risk – transforming it into a component of your return.

In all these investments, never disregard the exchange rate.

### 4.5.3. Beyond the Government: The World of Private Credit Linked to the CDI

The CDI (Interbank Deposit Certificate) is a rate that is closely linked to the Selic rate, serving as a reference for private debt. Many bonds issued by banks (CDBs, LCIs, LCAs) or companies (Debentures) pay a percentage of the CDI (e.g.: "110% of the CDI").

Reasoning for the foreign investor: After building a solid base in government bonds, the investor can seek an "extra" return on private credit.

When buying a bond that pays 110% of the CDI, you are receiving the basic interest rate (practically the Selic rate) plus a premium. This premium compensates for the credit risk – the risk that the bank or issuing company will not honor the payment.

To mitigate this risk in bank issues, Brazil has the FGC (Credit Guarantee Fund), which works like the American FDIC, insuring investments up to a certain limit per CPF/CNPJ per institution (BRL 250,000). This makes the search for a "spread" over the CDI a calculated and quite popular risk strategy.

In short, allocation to fixed income in Brazil is not a purely defensive decision. It is a strategic move that allows the investor:

- ✓ Establish a high profitability floor (Tesouro Selic).
- ✓ Speculate on the direction of interest rates and economic policy (Tesouro pré-fixado - Treasury Prefix).

- ✓ Protect yourself structurally from inflation, ensuring real gains (Tesouro IPCA+).
- ✓ Seek additional risk premiums in the private credit market (Securities linked to the CDI).

For the foreign investor, mastering these concepts means transforming one of Brazil's greatest perceived "risks" – its historical macroeconomic instability – into a diversified and robust source of returns.

**Ready for Analysis?**

You now know the pillars that support the market (B3, CVM, BCB), the gravitational force of the Selic rate, the composition (and pitfalls) of the main indexes and the critical importance of exchange rate risk.

This engine room may seem complex, but it is logical. It is a system shaped by the need to survive and thrive in a highly volatile environment, resulting in a financial market that is more resilient and sophisticated than many imagine.

With this technical knowledge in hand, we are finally ready to do what we came here to do: look for opportunities. In the next chapter, we will put on our boots and visit the construction sites of the Brazilian economy, analyzing the most promising sectors – from agribusiness to technology – and identifying where the true value may be hidden.

Excellent. With the map and the operations manual in hand, it is time to "put on our boots" and explore the territories where value is effectively generated. This chapter will abandon theory to focus on the drivers of the real economy, showing our skeptical investor where the concrete opportunities lie and, as always, the associated risks.

We continue the journey.

# Chapter 5: Where Value Hides – Key Sectors of the Brazilian Economy

If the previous chapters gave you a map of Brazil and a manual for how its market operates, this is the field guide. Here, we will analyze the major drivers of the Brazilian economy. The goal is not to provide an exhaustive list, but rather to offer an analytical lens so that you, the investor, can understand the internal logic of the most relevant sectors and identify where your investment thesis best fits.

Each sector is a microcosm of Brazil, reflecting its strengths and contradictions. Some are consolidated global powers; others are frontiers of innovation born out of necessity. Let us explore them.

## 5.1. The World's Farm: Agribusiness and Commodities

It is impossible to talk about the Brazilian economy without starting with agribusiness. This is not the primary sector of a developing country; it is one of the most sophisticated and efficient platforms for food and fiber production on the planet.

Brazil is an agricultural powerhouse and the world's largest exporter of a range of vital commodities, such as soybeans, coffee, sugar, beef and orange juice, as well as a giant in iron ore and oil.

The Investment Thesis: Investing in Brazilian agriculture is betting on the most fundamental thesis of all: the world needs to eat. With a growing global population and arable land constraints in other parts of the world, Brazil's productive capacity is a strategic long-term asset. Efficiency comes from the combination of a favorable climate, cutting-edge technology (precision agriculture, genetically modified seeds) and a constantly improving supply chain.

How to Expose Yourself: Exposure goes far beyond buying land. The capital market offers animal protein companies (JBS, Marfrig, BRF), sugar and ethanol producers (Raízen, São Martinho), logistics companies (Rumo) and input companies (BrasilAgro, Agrogalaxy, Kepler Weber, Raízen, SLC Agrícola, São Martinho, Boa Safra, and Três Tentos). Companies such as M. Dias Branco, Camil, Josapar, in the food sector, sell products of agricultural origin.

Other interesting companies are Vale (mining – VALE3), PRIO (Oil, PRIO3), Petrobras (PETR3; PETR4, Oil, Gas, Derivatives and Energy), PetroReconcavo (RECV3), as well as Cosan (CSAN3), Ultrapar (UGPA3), Vibra Energia (VBBR3), Enauta (ENAT3) and 3R Petroleum (RRRP3).

No company mentioned here represents a recommendation to buy or sell, but it deserves to be studied by the financial investor, using fundamental analysis, graphical, multiples, or own valuation techniques.

Furthermore, a rapidly expanding market is that of Fiagros (Investment Funds in Agro-Industrial Production Chains), which operate in a similar way to FIIs and allow direct investment in financing the harvest.

Risks to Monitor:

*Global Cycle:* Prices are dictated by the international market and the strength of the dollar. A slowdown in China, for example, directly impacts Brazilian exporters.

*Climate:* Extreme weather events are an inherent risk of the activity.

*ESG (Environmental, Social and Governance):* International pressure on deforestation, especially in the Amazon, is the main reputational and, increasingly, financial risk. Foreign investors must know how to differentiate sustainable producers from predatory practices.

## 5.2. The Steamroller and the Challengers: Banks and the Financial Sector

The financial sector in Brazil is an interesting story. On one side, we have some of the largest and most profitable banks in the world. The history of high interest rates has allowed giants such as Itaú (ITUB3; ITUB4), Bradesco (BBDC3; BBDC4) and Santander (SANB11) (together with the state-owned Banco do Brasil – BBAS3) to build true fortresses, with return on equity (ROE) that would be the envy of any American or European banker..

The Investment Thesis (Incumbents): Investing in large banks is a bet on the Brazilian economy itself, but with a safety cushion. They are so systemic and diversified that they act as a proxy for the country's GDP, paying robust and consistent dividends. It is the conservative and resilient choice.

The Investment Thesis (Challengers): Extreme concentration and high service fees have created the perfect opportunity for disruption. Driven by technology and consumer frustration, inclusive fintechs and digital banks (such as Nubank, Inter and XP) have emerged to attack the inefficiencies in the system. They have offered fee-free products, improved user experience and access to credit for millions of people previously ignored by big banks.

The Investor's Dilemma: The choice here is classic: the stability and dividends of the "champions" or the exponential growth (with greater risk) of the "challengers"? Fierce competition is forcing large banks to modernize, while fintechs face the challenge of becoming profitable in a scenario of higher interest rates. Banco Inter and XP, both traded on the Nasdaq, seem to have come out ahead in terms of fintechs, emerging as companies that already have the trust of Brazilians for multiple facets of their operations, from banking itself, to issuing cards, credit and financing, and making investments by their account holders. Traditional banks have received over the years the trust and admiration of Brazilians who have higher capital, including companies, given the security they represent.

## 5.3. The Double Face of Energy: Oil and the Green Revolution

Brazil is a strategic player in the global energy scene, but it lives a fascinating duality.

*The Oil Powerhouse*: Thanks to its gigantic pre-salt reserves, Brazil has become one of the ten largest oil producers in the world. The main investment vehicle here is Petrobras (PETR3 or PETR4), the state-owned company. Investing in it means having exposure to a world-class asset, but also accepting a significant level of political risk, since the company's decisions can be influenced by government guidelines (such as fuel pricing policy). Obviously, because it is a state-owned company, this scenario of political risk is inherent to a country with a culture that is still precarious when it comes to corruption, as evidenced by the Lava Jato scandal of the Federal Police, the largest corruption scandal in the Brazilian government, involving large construction companies, the government and public employees of the state-owned company involved, notably its board of directors. But this scenario, at least in the past, served to raise the company's governance levels. The losses were absorbed and the company became stronger.

*The Vanguard of Clean Energy:* Paradoxically, Brazil also has one of the cleanest electricity grids on the planet, thanks to its abundance of water, wind and solar resources. The country is a natural leader in the energy transition. The opportunities here are immense, ranging from wind and solar power generation companies to the entire chain of green hydrogen and biofuels. For investors focused on ESG and long-term trends, this is perhaps the most promising sector.

In this sector, we find generation, transmission and distribution companies, in addition to the oil companies already mentioned. Some of the main ones are: Eletrobras (ELET3), Cemig (CMIG4), CPFL Energia (CPFE3), Neoenergia (NEOE3), Equatorial (EQTL3), Engie Brasil (EGIE3), Taesa (TAEE11), COPEL (CPLE3; CPLE6) and Auren Energia (AURE3).

Once again, this is not a buy or sell recommendation.

## 5.4. The Sleeping Giant: Retail and Domestic Consumption

With a GDP of over two trillion dollars and a population of over 215 million people, the Brazilian domestic market is a colossus. The retail and consumer sector is the most direct way to bet on the social and economic advancement of Brazilians.

*The Investment Thesis:* The bet is simple: with falling unemployment and rising incomes, people will consume more. The sector ranges from large supermarket chains and department stores to pharmaceutical retail and, mainly, e-commerce. Internet and smartphone penetration is very high, but e-commerce still has a long way to go to reach the maturity of markets such as the US or China, representing a clear opportunity for growth.

*Risks to Monitor:* This sector is extremely sensitive to domestic economic cycles. Consumer sentiment is directly affected by inflation, interest rates (which make credit more expensive) and confidence in politics. In addition, the country's deep inequality means that performance can vary dramatically between companies focused on high-income consumers and those focused on the base of the pyramid. In this sector, with the exception of pharmaceutical retail, there is a high probability of impacts on the online sales policies of large Chinese retailers. To this end, it is worth studying case studies such as Renner, Casas Bahia and Magalu to get an idea.

**Conclusion: Putting the Puzzle Together**

As we have seen, the Brazilian economy is not monolithic. It is a mosaic of robust and diversified sectors. Brazil is at once a global farm, a sophisticated financial hub, a dual energy powerhouse and a gigantic consumer market.

Your task as an investor is not to find the "best" sector, but rather to understand the workings of each one and see how they align with your own strategy and risk tolerance. Are you a value investor looking for dividends and stability? The big banks, the electricity sector and the infrastructure development sector may be your place. Are you looking for exponential growth and comfortable with volatility? Fintechs and technology companies may be your bet. Are you looking for a long-term macro thesis? Agribusiness, the mining and oil sector and the energy transition are the frontiers.

Now that we know the terrain, the market, and the key sectors, the next step is practical. How do we effectively build a portfolio? How do we systematically manage political and regulatory risks? In the next chapter, we will discuss building a Brazilian investment portfolio and strategies for navigating the uncertainties that will inevitably arise.

With pleasure. We have reached the most practical chapter of our journey. After understanding the country, how the market works, and the key sectors, the natural question is: "What now? How do I turn this knowledge into a real investment strategy?".

This chapter aims to answer that question, serving as a bridge between analysis and action.

# Chapter 6: Building the Strategy – Portfolio Construction and Risk Management

So far, our expedition through Brazil has been analytical. We have unraveled the cultural and economic map, inspected the engine room of the financial market, and identified the main construction sites of the economy. Now, the work becomes personal. It is time to take these pieces and build something that serves your goals.

There is no "perfect" portfolio for Brazil. The ideal strategy will depend on your appetite for risk, your time horizon, and your own view on the theses we have discussed.

The goal of this chapter or this book is not to make recommendations, but rather to provide mental models and practical tools so that you can build your own strategy in a conscious and disciplined way.

## 6.1. What is your Brazil? Three Investor Profiles

To simplify the approach, we can think of three archetypes of investors looking at Brazil. See which one you fit into the most.

**The Traditionalist (Focus on Value and Income)**

This investor is attracted by the scale of the Brazilian economy and its established companies. He is not looking for the next stock market "rocket", but rather resilient companies, leaders in their sectors, that pay consistent dividends and trade at multiples that would be considered cheap in developed markets.

Central thesis: Buy high-quality assets at a "complexity discount".

Sector Focus: Large banks, electricity sector (due to predictable revenue and dividends), sanitation and insurance companies. Avoids state-owned companies with high political risk.

Typical Allocation: Strong concentration in blue chip stocks, complemented by fixed income securities linked to inflation (Treasury IPCA+) to protect purchasing power in the long term.

Mindset: "I am buying a stake in solid businesses that have proven their ability to navigate Brazil's crises. Volatility is the price I pay for a good entry point.".

## 6.2. The Optimist (Focus on Growth and Innovation)

This investor sees Brazil beyond commodities and banks. He is attracted by the dynamism of the domestic market, the digital transformation and the capacity for innovation that is emerging to solve the country's chronic problems.

Central Thesis: Bet on Brazil's convergence with more developed economies through technology and the growth of the new middle class.

Sector Focus: Fintechs, e-commerce retail, software companies (yes, they exist in Brazil), healthcare startups (healthtechs) and companies linked to the energy transition.

Typical Allocation: Greater weight in growth stocks, including small caps with high potential. May keep part in cash or short-term fixed income (Treasury Selic) to take advantage of market declines to buy more.

Mindset: "Brazil's problems are actually the biggest business opportunities. I want to invest in companies that are building the country's future.".

## 6.3. The Macro Player (Focus on Cycles and Exchange)

This is the most sophisticated investor, who thinks from the top down. His strategy is less focused on individual companies and more on major economic cycles. He closely follows the decisions of the Central Bank, fiscal policy in Brasília and the global commodities scenario. This requires a lot of study and reading, with daily monitoring of Brazilian finances, the political environment, exchange rates and the trade balance.

Central Thesis: Generate returns by anticipating and positioning oneself correctly in the major waves of the Brazilian market (cycles of high and low interest rates, appreciation and depreciation of the Real).

Sector Focus: Its allocation is dynamic. It may be long in companies that export commodities when it foresees a global rise and a strong dollar. Months later, if it believes in a cycle of falling interest rates, it may migrate to shares of domestic companies (retail, construction) that benefit from cheaper credit. With a focus on the macro and attentive to public policies, it also invests in the infrastructure sector. The country is large and needs transportation to distribute production and for the internal movement of people and goods.

Typical Allocation: Uses a wide range of assets, including interest rate futures, dollar, indexes and stocks. Fixed income is a strategic tool, not just a safe haven.

Mindset: "The company is secondary; the macro scenario is everything. In Brazil, the wind blows stronger than the sailor's skill."

## 6.4. The Essential Tool: Political and Regulatory Risk Management

Regardless of your profile, you will have to deal with the "Brazil risk". Political noise is constant and bureaucracy is a fact of life. Ignoring it is naive; panicking at every headline is unproductive. The professional approach is to manage it.

*Distinguish Signal from Noise:* The daily political debate in Brasília is mostly noise. Learn to focus on the signals: bills that change fiscal fundamentals (such as the Fiscal Responsibility Law), changes in the governance of state-owned companies or concrete threats to the autonomy of the Central Bank. These are the events that matter.

*Diversification is your Best Defense:* Avoid concentrating all your capital in a single sector that is highly dependent on government decisions. Having a portfolio that mixes exporters (less sensitive to domestic risk) with companies linked to domestic consumption can cushion shocks.

*Invest in Governance:* Companies with good corporate governance, transparent management and low debt tend to be more resilient during political crises. They depend less on "favors" from Brasília and more on their own competence.

## 6.5. The Dollar in the Room: Strategies for Exchange Rate Risk

As we discussed, for the dollarized investor, the exchange rate is half the equation. There are three main approaches:

1. *No Hedge (Accept the Risk):* The simplest strategy. You invest and accept the volatility of the Real, betting that, in the long term, the appreciation of your assets will outweigh any possible depreciation of the currency. It is suitable for those with a very long time horizon (10+ years).

2 *Full or Partial Hedging (Neutralize Risk)*: Using derivative instruments (such as dollar futures contracts) to lock in the exchange rate. This protects your dollar assets from a depreciation of the Real, but it comes at a cost and also eliminates potential gains if the Real appreciates.

3. Natural Hedge (Risk Avoidance): The most elegant strategy. Invest in companies that have revenues in dollars, such as large commodity exporters (agribusiness, mining, pulp

– there are excellent publicly traded companies in the latter two sectors). When the Real depreciates, the profits of these companies (converted into Reais) increase, which tends to increase the value of their shares, naturally offsetting the exchange rate loss in your portfolio.

**Conclusion: Patience, the Supreme Virtue**

Building an investment portfolio in Brazil is an exercise in strategy, but its execution is a test of patience. The market will test your conviction with unexpected crises and sharp volatility.

Brazil rarely rewards immediacy. Investment theses, whether value, growth or macro, take time to mature. The country has been through countless crises and has demonstrated a remarkable ability to bounce back, often stronger and more sophisticated, as it did after the introduction of the Plano Real in 1994, which tamed hyperinflation and stabilized the economy.

The successful investor is not the one who tries to predict the next crisis, but the one who builds a portfolio robust enough to survive it. The complexity and risk that drive so many investors away are, for those who have done their homework, the main source of opportunity.

Once you have put your strategy together, the final step is execution. In our final chapter, we will discuss practical ways for foreign investors to allocate their capital in Brazil, from the simplest of vehicles to direct investment.

Excellent. This is the final chapter of our journey. After understanding the country's mentality, the mechanics of its market, the promising sectors and how to design a strategy, there is only one question left: how exactly can a foreign investor put their capital to work in Brazil?

This chapter is the practical guide to execution. It details the entry points, from the simplest to the most complex, and concludes our conversation with a final reflection on Brazil's role in a global portfolio.

# Chapter 7: From Strategy to Action – How to Invest and the Final Frontier

Our expedition has reached its decisive stage. We have covered Brazil from end to end: from its complex history to its vibrant economy, from the corridors of the financial market to the fields of agribusiness. You have learned to decipher its signals, to respect its risks and to identify its opportunities. With a strategy in mind, it is time to open the toolbox and turn the plan into action.

The questions now are eminently practical. What are the investment vehicles available? What are the advantages and disadvantages of each? And how, finally, can we position ourselves to capture the value we have identified?

## 7.1. The Shortest Path: Investing "Without Leaving Home" (ETFs and ADRs)

For investors seeking exposure to Brazil in a simple and quick way, without the need to open accounts abroad or deal with currency conversion, the American market offers two excellent tools.

- **ETFs (Exchange-Traded Funds):** These are exchange-traded funds that replicate a market index. The best known is the **EWZ (iShares MSCI Brazil ETF)**, that follows the main Brazilian stock index.

  - **Advantages:** With a single purchase order from your American broker, you acquire a diversified basket of the largest companies in Brazil. It is simplicity at its best.
  - **Disadvantages:** You are "hostage" to the composition of the index. As we have seen, the main Brazilian indices are very concentrated in commodities and banks. If your investment thesis is focused on technology or healthcare, for example, EWZ may not be the ideal vehicle. You have no control over the individual companies within the fund.

- **ADRs (American Depositary Receipts):** An ADR is a certificate, traded in the US, that represents shares of a foreign company. The largest and most liquid Brazilian companies have ADRs listed on the NYSE or NASDAQ. Examples include Petrobras (PBR), mining company Vale (VALE), Itaú bank (ITUB) and beverage giant Ambev (ABEV).
  - **Advantages:** Allows you to choose specific companies (stock picking), aligning the investment directly with your thesis. If you believe in the financial sector, you can buy the ADR of a bank; if you bet on commodities, you buy the ADR of a mining company.
  - **Disadvantages:** The selection is limited. Only a few dozen Brazilian companies have ADRs. The

entire universe of small caps, FIIs and mid-sized companies is left out.

## 7.2. The Deep Dive: Investing Directly in B3

For investors who want total control over their portfolio and unrestricted access to all the assets that the Brazilian market offers – from shares in small companies to fixed income securities and real estate funds – the way to go is direct investment.

- **The Process:** A foreign investor needs to open an account through a specific regulatory process (known as a "Foreign Domiciled Account"). This is usually done through Brazilian brokerages that have specialized service desks for international clients. The process involves filling out forms and submitting documents, but it has become significantly more streamlined in recent years, especially since everything can be done online.
- **Advantages:** Full access. You can build the exact portfolio you designed in the appropriate chapter of this book, buying any stock, FII, Treasury Direct bond or other asset listed on B3. You have granular control over your strategy.

**Disadvantages:** Greater complexity and cost. Requires dealing directly with the exchange rate to send and repatriate funds, in addition to local brokerage and custody fees, if operating through traditional banks. Such brokerage fees are non-existent at many brokerages, and at some fintechs. Requires a greater commitment in terms of time and administration, but no different than operating on the NYSE or NASDAQ.

## 7.3. Beyond the Open Market: Private Equity and Venture Capital

For institutional or ultra-high net worth investors seeking the highest potential returns, there is the world of private investment.

- **The Innovation Frontier:** This is where we invest directly in startups and privately held companies. If you are excited about the idea of fintechs and technology solving Brazil's chronic problems, the Venture Capital universe is where the action takes place.
- **Advantages:** Potential for exponential returns, investing in companies before they become known to the general public.
- **Disadvantages:** Extremely high risk, total lack of liquidity (capital is "locked" for many years) and a huge entry barrier, requiring large capital and, more importantly, an extremely qualified local network of contacts.

# Chapter 8 (Bonus): Investing in Brazilian Government Bonds Like a Brazilian

## 8.1. Understanding the Federal Public Securities issued by Brazil

Brazil's public debt is currently largely financed by the issuance of government bonds, known as National Treasury Bonds.

Their creation was intended to provide individuals with conditions that are as advantageous as those offered by financial institutions when negotiating such bonds in traditional auctions for purchase and sale, while also allowing the country to be financed by its citizens.

For these bonds, there are two basic types of remuneration: pre-fixed and post-fixed..

According to the website www.tesourodireto.com.br, we present the definitions and characteristics of these titles (you can explore the website, which is in Portuguese, using online translation tools and learn more about it).

### 8.1.1. Prefixed Securities

You know exactly the return you will receive on the maturity date. For each bond unit, the gross amount to be received on maturity is BRL 1,000.00.

Because they have a predefined return, their yield is nominal. This means that it is necessary to discount inflation to obtain the real return on the investment.

In this modality, there are two bonds available:

• *Tesouro Prefixado (LTN)*

Treasury Prefix. Bonds with a defined return (fixed rate) at the time of purchase.

Payment method: at maturity.

With this bond, you will receive the amount invested plus the return on the maturity or redemption date

• *Tesouro Prefixado com juros semestrais (NTN-F)*

Treasury Prefix with semi-annual interest. Bonds with fixed profitability, plus interest defined at the time of purchase.

Payment method: semi-annually (interest) and at maturity (principal).

This bond pays interest every six months. This means that you receive the income throughout the investment period.

### 8.1.2. Post-Fixed Securities:

The amount received on the due date depends on the basic interest rate (Selic) or inflation (IPCA). Thus, the return on the investment is made up of a rate predefined at the time of purchase of the security plus the variation of one of these two rates (also called indexes).

In this modality, there are three titles available:

- Tesouro Selic (LFT):

Tesouro Selic (LFT). Securities with daily profitability linked to the basic interest rate of the economy (Selic rate).

Payment method: upon maturity.

- Tesouro IPCA+ com Juros Semestrais (NTN-B):

IPCA+ Treasury with Semiannual Interest (NTN-B). Security with profitability linked to the variation of the IPCA plus the interest defined at the time of purchase.

Payment method: semiannual (interest) and at maturity (principal).

- Tesouro IPCA+ (NTN-B Principal):

IPCA+ Treasury (NTN-B Principal). Security with profitability linked to the variation of the IPCA plus the interest defined at the time of purchase. There is no semi-annual interest coupon payment.

Payment method: at maturity.

This security also offers real profitability, but makes the payment in a single installment, at the end of the investment. It is one of the preferred securities of pension funds.

- Tesouro Educa+ (NTN-B1):

Security with profitability linked to the variation of the IPCA plus the interest defined at the time of purchase. The objective of this security is to accumulate resources to provide a monthly income to finance education, such as the payment of university tuition fees.

Payment method: Monthly income.

This security offers real profitability, corrected for inflation (IPCA), ensuring the preservation of purchasing power over time. After the accumulation period, the security begins to pay a monthly income for a period of 5 years, helping to cover educational costs.

- Tesouro RendA+ (NTN-B1):

Security with profitability linked to the variation of the IPCA plus the interest defined at the time of purchase. The objective of this security is to accumulate resources to provide an extra income during retirement.

Payment method: Monthly income.

This security offers real profitability, corrected for inflation (IPCA), ensuring the preservation of purchasing power over time. After the accumulation period, the security begins to pay a monthly income for a period of 20 years, complementing the investor's public pension. It is an alternative for investors who save for retirement, but do not want to be tied to pension funds or private pension plans..

## 8.2. Fees

There are two fees for Tesouro Direto. One is charged by your financial institution and the other is charged by B3 for services rendered. However, several financial institutions and brokerages, in order to attract clients, do not charge trading fees for these securities. Therefore, the investor only pays the fees charged by B3.

**Custody fee collection**

The custody fee of 0.2% per year is calculated on the value of the securities and provisioned daily in the investor's position from the settlement of the purchase transaction, on D+1. This fee is charged pro rata for Treasury Selic, Treasury IPCA and Treasury Prefixado securities, and is charged in the following cases:

1. In advance sale: You purchased a Treasury Selic bond and decide to sell it before the maturity date. In this case, the custody fee accumulated up to the date of sale will be deducted from the amount you receive.

2. At maturity of the position: You purchased a Treasury Prefixado 2026 bond. If you hold the bond until this date, the accumulated custody fee will be deducted from the amount you will receive at maturity.

3. In custody events (interest payments): You purchased a Treasury IPCA 2035 bond with semi-annual interest. With each interest payment, the custody fee accumulated up to that date will be deducted from the interest you receive.

Important: For Tesouro Selic, there will be no custody fee for amounts up to BRL 10,000.00 per CPF (approximately

USD $1,800). Above this amount, the fee will only be charged on excess!

**Fee charged by the Financial Institution:**

The rate charged by the Financial Institution is freely agreed upon with the investor. Tesouro Direto provides a ranking of the rates charged by each Institution on its website. You can use this information to check with your bank or brokerage firm what is being charged.

The rate may be annual, the most common type, or per transaction. For clarification regarding payment, contact your Financial Institution.

**Differentiated rate for *Tesouro Educa+* and *Tesouro RendA+*:**

The custody fee will only be charged on early redemptions or monthly receipts. If you hold the bond until maturity and the amount received is within the exemption limit, there will be no fee charged.

***Tesouro Educa+*:**

B3 Custody Fee Charging Table for Advance Sales:

| Prazo até saída (anos) | | |
|---|---|---|
| Data início vigência | Data final vigência | Taxa sobre valor vendido (a.a.) |
| 0 (Anos) | 7 (Anos) | 0,50% |
| 7 (Anos) | 14 (Anos) | 0,20% |
| 14 (Anos) | Até vencer | 0,10% |

Source: Tesouro Direto website[3]

[3] Decoding the table: "Prazo até saída (anos)" = Deadline until exit (years); "Data início vigência" = Start date of validity; "Data final vigência"

For investors who hold their bonds until the maturity date, the exemption applies to monthly income of up to four minimum contracts. Amounts exceeding this limit will pay a fee of 0.10% per year on the excess.

***Tesouro RendA+:***

B3 Custody Fee Charging Table for Advance Sales:

| Prazo até saída (anos) | | |
|---|---|---|
| Data início vigência | Data final vigência | Taxa sobre valor vendido (a.a.) |
| 0 (Anos) | 10 (Anos) | 0,50% |
| 10 (Anos) | 20 (Anos) | 0,20% |
| 20 (Anos) | Até vencer | 0,10% |

Source: Tesouro Direto website[4]

For investors who hold their bonds until the maturity date, the exemption applies to monthly incomes of up to six minimum wages. Amounts exceeding this limit will be subject to a fee of 0.10% per year on the excess.

## 8.3. How to invest in Public Bonds in Tesouro Direto

To purchase government bonds through Tesouro Direto, you must have an account with an authorized financial institution, whether a bank or a brokerage firm.

---

= End date of validity; Anos = Years; "Taxa sobre o valor vendido" = Rate on the value sold (p.a.); "Até vencer" = Until maturity.

[4] Decoding the table: "Prazo até saída (anos)" = Deadline until exit (years); "Data início vigência" = Start date of validity; "Data final vigência" = End date of validity; Anos = Years; "Taxa sobre o valor vendido" = Rate on the value sold (p.a.); "Até vencer" = Until maturity.

You can open an account with Tesouro Direto through the TD quick registration process or through your brokerage firm or bank. In the case of non-resident foreigners, this must be done through a financial institution or brokerage firm in Brazil. Contact the institution of your choice and provide the requested information and documents. Nowadays, you don't even need to leave your home to do this; most brokerage firms do this process entirely online!

Once your account is created, you will receive a temporary password sent by B3 to the email address provided. The first time you access the account, the system will ask for a new password that must contain between 8 and 16 digits, with letters, numbers and special characters such as: ! @ # $ % / * - + ?

This password allows access to the exclusive area of the Tesouro Direto website, where investment and redemption operations are carried out, as well as balance and statement inquiries, etc. However, this information is also available on the website or app of the financial institution with which you operate.

If you want to change your registration information, you must request the change from your Financial Institution and submit the requested documentation. You can change your email address and password yourself, directly on the Tesouro Direto platform.

Depending on the policy of your bank or brokerage firm, investments can only be made on their respective websites, but access to the exclusive area of the Tesouro Direto website remains available for additional queries. Invest using PIX or transfer the money to the chosen Financial Institution.

We recommend that readers deepen their knowledge by accessing official information from the following websites:

- https://www.gov.br/empresas-e-negocios/pt-br/invest-export-brasil/investir/guias/GuiaLegal.pdf

- https://www.b3.com.br/pt_br/regulacao/investimento-estrangeiro/

- https://www.tesourodireto.com.br/conheca/bancos-e-corretoras.htm

**Opening hours**

Investments and withdrawals can be made on business days, during business hours, from 9:30 a.m. to 6:00 p.m., Brasília time zone, with prices and rates in effect at the time of the transaction.

From 6:00 p.m. to 5:00 a.m., on weekends or holidays, the prices and rates displayed on the Tesouro Direto website are for reference only. You can make investments and withdrawals, but the market opening prices and rates of the next business day will be considered.

On business days, from 5:00 a.m. to 9:30 a.m., the system is under maintenance.

For additional queries, you can access the Tesouro Direto website at any time.

It is worth remembering that, for your greater security, investments and withdrawals may be suspended throughout the day, ensuring that the prices and rates of the bonds are always aligned with market parameters.

**Suspension period**

As of August 17, 2018, the National Treasury Secretariat (STN) began allowing requests for investments and/or redemptions during periods of market suspension.

These transactions must be made directly in the exclusive area of the Tesouro Direto website.

The prices and rates of securities traded on Tesouro Direto are based on the rates traded on the secondary market for government securities and are generally updated three times a day.

It is also important to know that, in times of volatility, these rates may be quite different from Tesouro Direto rates, making the prices for investments and redemptions incompatible with those practiced on the market.

In these cases, the National Treasury Secretariat suspends negotiations to update the prices and rates of the securities to current levels.

The investments and redemptions included in the suspension periods will be made when the market reopens at the new prices and rates announced by STN, without exceeding the value expressed in the act of investment and/or redemption.

**How much does it cost to invest and withdraw?**

The investment price of government bonds is calculated based on the market rates on the purchase settlement date.

When you redeem a government bond early, the price is calculated by the National Treasury by applying another rate, called spread, to the purchase price in the case of early redemption.

Buying and selling prices are available at Bond Price and Rate Table. The National Treasury may change the price of the bonds offered at any time.

If you are purchasing securities at the time of the price change, you will receive a notification with the updated prices, and you will be able to confirm or cancel the transaction.

**Treasury Direct investment methods**

After registering, there are three ways to invest in Tesouro Direto:

1. Directly on the Tesouro Direto website/app: you access the Portal do Investidor and negotiates its public securities;
2. Directly on your Financial Institution's website/app: if the Financial Institution is an integrated agent, that is, its website is integrated with Tesouro Direto's, you can invest and redeem government bonds through its website, in real time and with the same prices and rates as Tesouro Direto;

3. Your Financial Institution does it for you: in this case, you authorize your Institution to negotiate the public securities on your behalf.

Don't forget to contact your Financial Institution to find out what options they offer!

**What are the application and redemption limits?**

Traditional investments in Tesouro Direto must be multiples of 0.01 bond or 1% (one percent) of the value of a bond.

When investing, you can choose to enter the financial value or the number of bonds you wish to purchase. If you enter the value, the Tesouro Direto system will automatically adjust it to the closest value that represents a number of bonds multiple of 0.01, already discounting the service fees charged. You can confirm the purchase or change the values entered again until you reach the amount you wish to invest.

The maximum investment limit per person is R$2,000,000.00 (two million reais) per month (approximately USD $360,000). This limit should be considered for the portfolio of securities acquired by the person during the month, and not for each security separately.

In the months of maturity and interest payment of bonds previously acquired from Tesouro Direto and still in your portfolio, you can invest in more bonds, using your limit of R$2,000,000.00, plus the redemption value and interest of the bonds.

This limit is flexible if you choose to reinvest your resources, making a reinvestment (here, you can only choose a single type of bond to invest in and you can do so in full or in part up to 1 day before the bond's maturity, in the case of redemption reinvestment, or the payment of the next coupon, in the case of coupon reinvestment) or traditional purchase within the maturity month of your previous investments.

**Liquidation**

Settlement is the final stage of the investment and redemption process, in which the transfer of ownership of the security and the payment/receipt of all money involved takes place.

**Investment Settlement**

he investment in Tesouro Direto will be registered in your name and available in your statement after settlement in the market, according to the following rule:

- Application made on business days (from 0:00 to 18:00): from 18:00 on the 1st business day after the application request;
- Application made on weekdays (from 6:00 p.m. to midnight), weekends or holidays: from 6:00 p.m. on the 2nd business day;

During the period between the date of the application request and the date on which the securities appear on your statement, you can check the investment settlement stage by consulting protocols in the exclusive area of the Tesouro

Direto website. While the investment is not finalized/settled, your statement displays the status "In settlement".

**Redemption Settlement**

The money from the redemption of your investment will be available at the Financial Institution according to the following rule:

- Redemption made on weekdays (from 9:30 am to 1:00 pm): from 1:00 pm on the same day of redemption;
- Redemption made on business days (from 1:00 p.m. to 6:00 p.m.): from 1:00 p.m. on the first business day after the redemption request;
- Redemption scheduling (from 6:00 pm to 5:00 am, weekends and holidays): from 1:00 pm on the 1st business day.

**Payment of interest coupon and redemption at maturity**

The amount corresponding to the payment of the interest coupon and the redemption of the security, due to its maturity, will only be available at your Financial Institution from 1:00 p.m. on the same day of payment. The date and time of deposit into your account depend on the opening hours of your Financial Institution.

**How to redeem**

The National Treasury guarantees daily liquidity for your government bonds purchased through Tesouro Direto. This means that you can redeem your investments at any time.

From 9:30 a.m. to 6:00 p.m. on business days, redemptions will be processed at the prices and rates available at the time of the transaction. From 6:00 p.m. to 5:00 a.m. and on weekends and/or holidays, redemptions will be settled at the opening prices and rates of the following business day.

To benefit investors, Tesouro Direto uses the FIFO (first in, first out) model, thus paying the lowest possible rate within your stock of bonds.

For securities that pay semi-annual interest – Tesouro IPCA+ with Semi-Annual Interest (NTN-B), Tesouro IGPM+ with Semi-Annual Interest (NTN-C) and Tesouro Prefixado with Semi-Annual Interest (NTN-F) – the redemption option will be suspended 2 (two) business days before the payment of these periodic flows.

It is worth remembering that government bonds are repurchased by the National Treasury at market prices on the date of the transaction.

If you hold the bonds until the maturity date, you will receive the return value defined at the time of purchase, regardless of the price variations of the bond during the investment. However, if you make an early redemption, the National Treasury will repurchase the bond based on the market value. In other words, the return on the investment may be different from that agreed upon at the time of purchase, depending on the price of the bond at the time of redemption.

## 8.4. Taxes

The taxes charged on operations carried out in Tesouro Direto are the same as those levied on fixed income operations, such as investment funds and CDBs: the Tax on Financial Operations (IOF), for redemptions of the investment in less than 30 days, and the Income Tax (IR), with a regressive rate depending on the term of the investment, as follows:

- i. 22.5% for investments with a term of up to 180 days;
- ii. 20% for investments with a term of 181 days to 360 days;
- iii. 17.5% for investments with a term of 361 days to 720 days;
- iv. 15% for investments with a term of over 721 days.

The Brazilian Legislative Branch is currently discussing the possibility of changing this set of rates to a single rate of 17.5%. However, discussions on taxes have been met with resistance from the Brazilian parliament, especially as we move towards the middle of the electoral term.

Taxes are levied on financial income obtained from early redemption, on the payment of interest coupons (the Tax on Financial Transactions - IOF does not apply to interest coupons; only IR) and on the maturity of bonds. The IOF is a regulatory tax. It has a very low incidence rate, but it can be changed at any time by the Federal Executive Branch itself.

The days for the purposes of levying income tax are counted from the settlement date. Therefore, with regard to interest coupons, the income tax rates provided for will be applied, with the term counted from the date of commencement of application.

In 2018, the National Treasury reported that the counting of the term of financial investments for the purposes of calculating income tax withheld at source provided for in article 1 of Law No. 11,033/04 and in article 46 of Normative Instruction RFB No. 1,585/14 ("IRRF"), levied on income produced by Treasury Direct public securities, must be carried out considering the settlement dates of the investment and redemption operations.

## 8.5. Where to check Balances and Statements

You can check balances and statements on your government bonds at any time. Simply access the exclusive area of the Tesouro Direto website, click on the CONSULT option in the TOP MENU and select the CONSOLIDATED STATEMENT item. The statement/balance reflects the market price of the bonds. Therefore, if there is a drop in the prices traded on the market, the balance decreases and, if there is an appreciation of the bond, the balance increases. The value of the bond is updated considering these variations and according to the value at which it is traded on the secondary market at that time (this procedure is known as marking to market).

Between the investment date and the maturity date, the price of the bond may vary depending on market conditions and expectations regarding the behavior of future interest rates. An increase in the market interest rate in relation to the rate that was applied causes a drop in the price of the bond, while a decrease in the interest rate has the opposite effect.

This is the same mechanism as investment funds, which mark their assets to market based on the determination of the Securities and Exchange Commission (CVM), the regulatory body of the securities market.

If you hold the bonds until the maturity date, you will receive the amount corresponding to the profitability defined at the time of investment, regardless of the variations in the price of the bond during the investment. In the case of early redemption, the National Treasury repurchases the bond based on its market value. In other words, the return on investment may be different from that agreed upon at the time of purchase, depending on the price of the bond at the time you decide to redeem it.

# Chapter 9 (Bonus): The 50 largest companies listed on the Brazilian stock exchange

In a dynamic and constantly evolving economic scenario, the 50 largest companies listed on B3, Brazil's stock exchange, represent the vanguard of corporate power and wealth generation in the country. Analyzing data from 2024, we have compiled a comprehensive list that not only ranks these companies by their market value, but also delves into their business models, financial performance and historical trajectory.

The top of the ranking is marked by the strong presence of companies from the commodities, financial and energy sectors, reflecting the Brazilian economic matrix. *Vale* and *Petrobras*, global mining and oil giants, respectively, compete for the top positions, driven by international demand for their products. The financial sector, represented by *Itaú Unibanco*, *Bradesco* and *Banco do Brasil*, demonstrates its solidity and capillarity in the national economy.

The following analysis details each of the 50 largest companies, providing a complete overview of how they generate cash, their main brands, net income and revenue in 2024, as well as profitability indicators such as Return on Equity (ROE) and operating margin. Information on their operations in the foreign market, the time they have been listed on the stock exchange and the date of foundation complement the overview, offering a historical and corporate governance perspective.

## 9.1. The 50 Giants of B3: An X-ray of the Largest Companies in Brazil by Market Value

This topic presents a detailed and multifaceted analysis of the 50 largest companies listed on B3, classified by market value, but is not exhaustive. The analysis goes beyond a simple listing, delving at least a little into the business models, financial performance, brand positioning and international footprint of each corporation.

To ensure data integrity and accuracy, all financial metrics refer to the full and audited fiscal year of 2023, since consolidated data for 2024 is not yet fully available. The goal is to provide a strategic reference document for investors seeking to understand the fundamental structure of the Brazilian corporate elite.

Nothing presented here represents a recommendation to buy or sell Brazilian assets. It is worth remembering that these companies have investor relations websites, where information is updated at all times. B3's governance model and CVM's regulatory provisions ensure transparency for publicly held companies, and it is on the websites of these companies and B3 that investors will find sufficient material for their own analyses with a view to making investments.

It is worth noting that B3 currently has more than 400 publicly traded companies listed. Try accessing the B3 website to find out about each one: www.b3.com.br.

## 9.1.1. The Two Pillars of the Brazilian Economy at B3

Analysis of the composition of the top of B3 reveals a notable concentration in two macroeconomic sectors: **Financial Services and Commodities & Basic Materials**.

Together, companies in these two segments represent an overwhelming share of the total market value of the 50 largest companies, establishing themselves as the twin pillars on which Brazil's capital economy rests.

The prominence of the financial sector is driven by the concentrated nature of the banking industry and a high interest rate environment (SELIC) that has historically supported robust margins.

In parallel, the commodities sector, led by mining, oil and gas, and pulp giants, acts as the engine of the country's trade balance, directly connecting the performance of the Brazilian stock exchange to the dynamics of the global economy and exchange rate fluctuations.

The services and technology sector stands out next. Among the companies, there is one in the industrial sector that has developed like a black diamond, in the south of the country, which is respected and admired nationally by national investors and analysts, and which also gains international appreciation.

### 9.1.2. Performance Snapshot (FY2023)

Collectively, the 50 companies analyzed in this report represent the vanguard of Brazil's economic power.

The combined market value of these corporations constitutes the majority of the Ibovespa, and their financial performance serves as a barometer for the health of the national economy.

In fiscal year 2023, these companies demonstrated a formidable profit-generating capacity, albeit with significant heterogeneity across sectors.

Metrics such as Return on Equity (ROE) and operating margins vary dramatically, reflecting fundamentally different business models – from the high-margin, high-cyclicality operations of commodity exporters to the more stable but highly competitive business models of domestic retail.

### 9.1.3. Exporting Powers vs. Domestic Champions

A clear strategic division emerges: on one side, the exporting powers, whose revenues are predominantly dollarized and whose destinations are tied to global markets.

Companies such as Vale, Petrobras and Suzano are prime examples, acting as major generators of foreign exchange for Brazil.

On the other side, there are the domestic champions, whose operations and success are intrinsically linked to the health of consumption, credit and consumer confidence in Brazil.

Financial institutions such as Itaú Unibanco and Bradesco, and retail giants such as Ambev and Lojas Renner, embody this group.

Understanding this duality is essential to decipher the risks and opportunities inherent in investing in the Brazilian capital market.

### 9.1.4. Master Data Table of the 50 Largest Companies on B3

The following table consolidates key corporate and financial data for the top 50 companies listed on B3, sorted by market value based on data from fiscal year 2024.

This tool serves as a central data repository for quick screening and comparative analysis, allowing readers to identify trends and outliers across multiple dimensions before delving deeper into qualitative profiles.

**Table: B3 Top 50 - Key Financial and Corporate Data (Fiscal Year 2024)**

| Rank | Company | Ticker | Market value (US$ Billions) | Sector | Listing Date on B3 | Foundation | Exporter Status | Sales Revenue 2024 (US$ Billion) | EBITDA Margin (%) | ROE 2024 (%) | Net profit 2024 (US$ Billion) |
|---|---|---|---|---|---|---|---|---|---|---|---|
| 1 | Petrobras | PETR4 | 81.7 | Oil, gas and biofuels | 1957 | 1953 | Yes | 91.4 | 35.26% | 10% | 7.5 or<br>19.4 *no exclusive events |
| 2 | Itaú Unibanco | ITUB4 | 71.68 | Financial | 1944 | 1924 | - | 60.96 | - | 20,77% | 7.66 |
| 3 | Vale | VALE3 | 41.44 | Mining | 1943 | 1942 | Yes | 37.45 | 34.94% | 15.28% | 5.53 |
| 4 | Ambev | ABEV3 | 38.9 | Non-cyclical consumption | 1999 | 1999 | Yes | 16.26 | 32.34% | 14.64% | 2.7 |

| Rank | 5 | 6 | 7 | 8 | 9 | 10 |
|---|---|---|---|---|---|---|
| Company | WEG | BTG Pactual | Bradesco | Banco do Brasil | Itaúsa | Santander |
| Ticker | WEGE3 | BPAC11 | BBDC4 | BBAS3 | ITSA4 | SANB11 |
| Market value (US$ Billions) | 31.69 | 37.59 | 29.75 | 22.2 | 21.52 | 20.03 |
| Sector | Industrial Goods | Financial | Financial | Financial | Financial holding | Financial |
| Listing Date on B3 | 1971 | 2012 | 1946 | 1906 | 1966 | 2009 |
| Foundation | 1961 | 1983 | 1943 | 1808 | 1966 | 1982 |
| Exporter Status | Yes | - | - | - | - | - |
| Sales Revenue 2024 (US$ Billion) | 6.90 | 7.62 | 38.98 | 49.73 | 2.85 | 24.94 |
| EBITDA Margin (%) | 22.38% | - | - | - | 213.95% | - |
| ROE 2024 (%) | 27.21% | 20.52% | 10.24% | 14.67% | 16.34% | 11.19% |
| Net profit 2024 (US$ Billion) | 1.15 | 2.14 | 3.19 | 5.3 | 2.7 | 2.44 |

| Rank | 11 | 12 | 13 | 14 | 15 | 16 |
|---|---|---|---|---|---|---|
| Company | Vivo *Telefonica* | Eletrobras | Rede D'Or | Sabesp | BB Seguridade | B3 |
| Ticker | VIVT3 | ELET3 | RDOR3 | SBSP3 | BBSE3 | B3SA3 |
| Market value (US$ Billions) | 18.06 | 18.02 | 14.74 | 14.18 | 12.81 | 12.8 |
| Sector | Telecommunications | Public Utility | Health | Sanitation | Insurance and social security | Financial |
| Listing Date on B3 | 2000 | 1965 | 2020 | 1996 | 2013 | 2007 |
| Foundation | 1998 | 1962 | 1977 | 1973 | 2012 | 1890 |
| Exporter Status | - | - | - | - | - | - |
| Sales Revenue 2024 (US$ Billion) | 9,90 | 7.31 | 9.19 | 6.57 | - | 1,92 |
| EBITDA Margin (%) | 18,3% | 65.30% | 17.94% | 50.32% | - | 62.59% |
| ROE 2024 (%) | 10,5% | 8.51% | 15.57% | 25.94% | 89,77 | 24.91% |
| Net profit 2024 (US$ Billion) | 4,10 | 1.88 | 0,71 | 1.74 | 1.58 | 0.83 |

| Rank | 17 | 18 | 19 | 20 | 21 |
|---|---|---|---|---|---|
| Company | Suzano | Embraer | TIM | CPFL ENERGIA | Localiza |
| Ticker | SUZB3 | EMBR3 | TIMS3 | CPFE3 | RENT3 |
| Market value (US$ Billions) | 11.84 | 9.5 | 9.32 | 8.40 | 8.3 |
| Sector | Basic Materials | Airplane construction | Telecommunications | Public Utility | Cyclical Consumption |
| Listing Date on B3 | 1980 | 1989 | 1998 | 2000 | 2005 |
| Foundation | 1924 | 1969 | 1995 | 1998 | 1973 |
| Exporter Status | Yes | Yes | - | - | - |
| Sales Revenue 2024 (US$ Billion) | 8.62 | 6.44 | 4.63 | 7.75 | 6.76 |
| EBITDA Margin (%) | 52.56% | 14.41% | 49.25% | 30.62% | 31.97% |
| ROE 2024 (%) | -21,90% | 10.08% | 11.94% | 26.33 | 6.89% |
| Net profit 2024 (US$ Billion) | -1,28 | 0.35 | 0.57 | 1.05 | 0.33 |

| Rank | 22 | 23 | 24 | 25 | 26 |
|---|---|---|---|---|---|
| Company | Equatorial | Caixa Seguridade | Petro Rio S/A | Brasil Foods | Copel |
| Ticker | EQTL3 | BBSE3 | PRIO3 | BRFS3 | CPLE6 |
| Market value (US$ Billions) | 8.06 | 7.79 | 6.87 | 6.64 | 6.59 |
| Sector | Public Utility | Insurance and social security | Oil, gas and biofuels | Food | Public Utility |
| Listing Date on B3 | 2006 | 2020 | 2010 | 1997 | 1994 |
| Foundation | 1999 | 1967 | 2008 | 1934 | 1954 |
| Exporter Status | - | - | Yes | Yes | - |
| Sales Revenue 2024 (US$ Billion) | 8.25 | - | 2.61 | 11.16 | 4.12 |
| EBITDA Margin (%) | 24.80% | - | 65.73% | 16.89% | 24.41% |
| ROE 2024 (%) | 10.77% | 29.21 | 39.74% | 21.3% | 10.94% |
| Net profit 2024 (US$ Billion) | 0.68 | 0.68 | 1.96 | 0.67 | 0.51 |

| Rank | 27 | 28 | 29 | 30 | 31 | 32 |
|---|---|---|---|---|---|---|
| Company | Porto Seguro | JBS | Engie Brasil | RUMO S.A | Gerdau | Ultrapar |
| Ticker | PSSA3 | JBSS3 | EGIE3 | RAIL3 | GGBR4 | UGPA3 |
| Market value (US$ Billions) | 6.28 | 6.16 | 6.13 | 5.87 | 5.68 | 38,70 |
| Sector | Insurance | Food | Public Utility | Logistcal transport | Steel and Metallurgy | Conglomerate |
| Listing Date on B3 | 2004 | 2007 | 1998 | 1998 | 1947 | 1999 |
| Foundation | 1945 | 1953 | 1998 | 1997 | 1901 | 1937 |
| Exporter Status | - | Yes | - | - | Yes | - |
| Sales Revenue 2024 (US$ Billion) | 6.4 | 75.8 | 2.04 | 2.53 | 12.18 | 24,90 |
| EBITDA Margin (%) | 9.97% | 8.54% | 78.03% | 33.96% | 11.17% | 5,1% |
| ROE 2024 (%) | 18.82% | 21.47% | 37.98% | -9.78% | 7.88% | 15,1% |
| Net profit 2024 (US$ Billion) | 0.49 | 1.94 | 0.62 | -0,17 | 0.83 | 1,90 |

| Rank | 33 | 34 | 35 | 36 | 37 | 38 |
|---|---|---|---|---|---|---|
| Company | NEOENERGIA | AMBIPAR | MOTIVA | CSN Mineração | Naturgy | TOTVS |
| Ticker | NEOE3 | AMBP3 | MOTV3 | CMIN3 | CEGR3 | TOTS3 |
| Market value (US$ Billions) | 5.47 | 5.12 | 4.94 | 4.88 | 4.56 | 4.52 |
| Sector | Public Utility | Public Utility | Infrastructure | Mining | Public Utility (gas) | Information Technology |
| Listing Date on B3 | 2019 | 2020 | 2000 | 2021 | 1997 | 2006 |
| Foundation | 1996 | 1995 | 1998 | 1941 | 1969 | 1983 |
| Exporter Status | - | - | - | Yes | - | - |
| Sales Revenue 2024 (US$ Billion) | 8.9 | 1.16 | 3.96 | 3.46 | 1.39 | 0.95 |
| EBITDA Margin (%) | 25.72% | 27.99% | 32.16% | 32.56% | 12.64% | 22.9% |
| ROE 2024 (%) | 11.14% | -17.09% | 9.18,1% | 44.09% | 45.25% | 15.33% |
| Net profit 2024 (US$ Billion) | 0.67 | -0.03 | 0.24 | 0.82 | 0.13 | 0.13 |

| Rank | 39 | 40 | 41 | 42 | 43 | 44 |
|---|---|---|---|---|---|---|
| Company | RaiaDrogasil | Vibra Energia | Energisa | Klabin S/A | Eneva | Marfrig |
| Ticker | RADL3 | VBBR3 | ENGI11 | KLBN11 | ENEV3 | MRFG3 |
| Market value (US$ Billions) | 4.52 | 4.37 | 4.17 | 3.98 | 3.97 | 3.79 |
| Sector | Health | Oil, Gas and Biofuels | Public Utility | Basic materials (Paper) | Public Utility | Food |
| Listing Date on B3 | 1977 | 2017 | 1907 | 1997 | 2007 | 2007 |
| Foundation | 1935 | 1971 | 1905 | 1899 | 2001 | 2000 |
| Exporter Status | - | - | - | - | - | Yes |
| Sales Revenue 2024 (US$ Billion) | 7.06 | 31.32 | 6.13 | 3.57 | 2.07 | 27.06 |
| EBITDA Margin (%) | 11.15% | 5.41% | 23.64% | 33.68% | 34.26% | 5.93% |
| ROE 2024 (%) | 18.65% | 31.23% | 21.93% | 27.53% | 0.22% | 98.98% |
| Net profit 2024 (US$ Billion) | 0.22 | 1.16 | 0.84 | 0.37 | 0.1 | 0.70 |

| Rank | 45 | 46 | 47 | 48 | 49 |
|---|---|---|---|---|---|
| Company | Lojas RENNER | Ultrapar | HAPVIDA | Atacadão (Carrefour) | Hypera Pharma |
| Ticker | LREN3 | UGPA3 | HAPV3 | CRFB3 | HYPE3 |
| Market value (US$ Billions) | 3.64 | 3.52 | 3.49 | 3.25 | 3.18 |
| Sector | Cyclical consumption | Oil, Gas and Biofuels | Health | Food Retail | Health |
| Listing Date on B3 | 1977 | 1999 | 2018 | 2017 | 2008 |
| Foundation | 1965 | 1953 | 2001 | 1962 | 2008 |
| Exporter Status | - | Yes | - | - | - |
| Sales Revenue 2024 (US$ Billion) | 2.61 | 24.27 | 4.10 | 21.02 | 1.35 |
| EBITDA Margin (%) | 17.34% | 4.38% | 9.88% | 5.28% | 28.23% |
| ROE 2024 (%) | 11.11% | 15.59% | -1.30% | 8.42% | 11.09% |
| Net profit 2024 (US$ Billion) | 0.21 | 0.45 | -0.12 | 0.35 | 0.24 |

| Rank | 50 |
|---|---|
| Company | Grupo Mateus |
| Ticker | GMAT3 |
| Market value (US$ Billions) | |
| Sector | Cyclical consumption |
| Listing Date on B3 | 2020 |
| Foundation | 1986 |
| Exporter Status | - |
| Sales Revenue 2024 (US$ Billion) | 8.83 |
| EBITDA Margin (%) | 7.69% |
| ROE 2024 (%) | 13.38% |
| Net profit 2024 (US$ Billion) | 1.33 |

*Source: B3 and Companies' IR*

*Note: Values are for fiscal year 2024 and serve as a consolidated reference. Market value and ranking fluctuate daily with market conditions. Brazil is dynamic economy and market. Many companies change positions on ranking fluctuations.*

### 9.1.5. Financial Services: The Bedrock of the Brazilian Economy

The financial sector is by far the heaviest in the composition of the main B3 indices.

Its dominance is a direct reflection of Brazil's economic structure, characterized by a highly concentrated banking industry and a history of high interest rates.

Large banks generate massive profits through credit intermediation, charging significantly higher interest rates on loans than they pay on borrowings, a phenomenon amplified by a structurally high SELIC rate.

In addition, revenues from services, such as asset management, insurance and credit cards, form a diversified and resilient revenue base. The main challenge for incumbents is the rise of fintechs, which compete aggressively for customers with leaner cost structures and innovative digital solutions.

**Itaú Unibanco (ITUB4; ITUB3)**

- **Business Model:** Itaú Unibanco, the largest private bank in Latin America, generates cash through a diversified and robust business model. The main source of revenue is the financial margin with customers, or *Net Interest Income* (NII), from its vast credit portfolio for individuals and legal entities. The second most important line of revenue comes from service fees and commissions, which include fund management, brokerage, insurance (through the also listed company Porto Seguro (*ticker*: PSSA3), of which it holds a significant stake) and credit card operations. Its wholesale banking division, Itaú BBA, is a leader in investment banking and corporate banking, adding revenues from mergers and acquisitions (M&A), capital markets and treasury operations.
- **Performance Analysis:** With a market value of US$ 71.7 billion and a net profit of US$ 7.66 billion in 2024, Itaú stands out as one of the most profitable companies in the country. Its Return on Equity (ROE) of 20.8% is an indicator of extremely high profitability and efficient capital allocation. A deeper analysis reveals that this superior performance is not only a management feat, but a direct consequence of the Brazilian macroeconomic environment. High interest

rates allow the bank to operate with net interest margins (NIMs) that would be unimaginable in developed economies. This creates a formidable competitive moat against new entrants, but also exposes the bank to a risk of margin compression if Brazil enters a sustained cycle of low interest rates. This already happened in 2019, but this bank proved to be highly competitive, increasing revenues from services, including those from supporting the launch of new publicly traded companies. It is rock. The operating margin of 25.5% reinforces the image of a highly efficient and scalable operation.

- **Branding:** The strength of the Itaú brand is a crucial intangible asset. The core brand "Itaú" is ubiquitous in retail banking. For the high-income segment, the brand "Itaú Personnalité" offers exclusivity and differentiated services. In the corporate world, "Itaú BBA" is synonymous with sophistication in financial services.

- **History and Legacy:** Founded in 1924 and listed on the stock exchange in 1944, Itaú is an almost century-old institution, whose history is intertwined with the industrialization and development of the Brazilian financial system.

**Bradesco (BBDC4; BBDC3)**

- **Business Model:** Bradesco's model is similar to Itaú's, but with a fundamental strategic distinction: the deep and synergistic integration between banking and insurance operations. Bradesco Seguros is one of the largest insurance companies in the country and a massive and stable cash generator for the group. This duality allows Bradesco to diversify its revenues robustly, with the flow of insurance premiums complementing the bank's interest income. Cash generation therefore comes from credit intermediation, banking service fees and the results of the insurance operation, which includes life, health, automobiles and pensions. Bradesco, through its holding company, Bradespar (Ticker: BRAP4), has a significant stake in the mining company Vale. Bradespar holds approximately 3.83% of Vale's voting capital, in addition to seats on the mining company's Board of Directors, including the position of vice-chairman of the board.

- **Performance Analysis:** In 2024, Bradesco recorded a net profit of US$3.19 billion, with a market value of US$29.75 billion. Its ROE (Return on Equity) fell from 18.1% in 2023 to 10.24% in 2024, due to the increase in defaults, as it is a bank more focused on retail and domestic income. Its operating margin of 22.3%, robust, although slightly lower than that of its main competitor, Itaú, indicates fierce competition at the top of the sector. ROE in 2024 was around 10%. However, there are prospects for improvement for the bank due to reassessments it made, in early 2025, of credit quality, in order to neutralize the impacts of defaults on its results. The performance reflects the scale of its operations, but also the recent challenges in managing the credit portfolio, especially in the retail segment. Unlike Itaú, this bank operates more strongly in retail and with individuals. If the income of Brazilian citizens increases, this bank tends to profit more from services aimed at these people, whether in the line of direct credit to consumers, insurance, real estate and vehicle financing.

- **History and Legacy:** Founded in 1943 in Marília, in the interior of São Paulo, with a focus on small business owners and civil servants, Bradesco has a history of capillarity and financial inclusion. Its listing in 1946 positions it as another long-standing pillar of the Brazilian capital market.

**BTG Pactual (BPAC11)**

- **Business Model:** BTG Pactual operates a fundamentally different business model from large retail banks. It is the largest independent investment bank in Latin America, focusing on Investment Banking (M&A, ECM, DCM), Corporate Lending (credit for large companies), Asset Management (fund management) and Wealth Management (wealth management). Its cash generation is less dependent on interest margin and more tied to performance fees, advisory commissions and results from its trading desks. Its shares are traded on the stock exchange in the form of UNITs.
- **Performance Analysis:** BTG Pactual's figures reveal the profitability of its business model. With a profit of

US$ 2.4 billion on a market value of US$ 37.6 billion, the bank achieved an ROE of 20.5% and an impressive operating margin of 38.9%. A direct comparison of these indicators with those of retail banks is illuminating. The superior ROE and, especially, the much higher operating margin indicate that BTG's business model, based on high value-added services and intensive use of intellectual capital, is more profitable per unit of revenue. The explanation for this superior margin lies in the nature of its revenues: M&A advisory fees and management commissions are very high-margin activities, with less need for regulatory capital compared to mass lending. This suggests that, as the Brazilian capital market deepens, the growth potential for firms like BTG may surpass that of traditional banks.

- **History and Legacy:** Founded in 1983 as a brokerage firm (Pactual), the bank has undergone several transformations, including its sale to UBS and subsequent buyback, consolidating itself as a financial powerhouse. Its listing in 2012 is relatively recent, but its impact on the market is that of a consolidated player.

### 9.1.6. Commodities and Basic Materials: Moving Global and Domestic Markets

This sector is the backbone of Brazil's insertion into the global economy. The companies present here are world leaders in their respective markets and their performance has a direct and massive impact on the country's trade balance.

The business model is inherently cyclical, subject to the volatility of international commodity prices, which in turn are influenced by geopolitical factors, the health of the Chinese economy (the main consumer) and supply and demand shocks.

A fundamental characteristic of this sector is the dollarized revenue, which makes these companies a natural hedge against the devaluation of the Real.

**Vale (VALE3)**

- **Business Model:** Vale is the world's largest producer of iron ore and nickel. Its cash generation model is simple and powerful: extracting high-quality iron ore from its mines in Brazil, mainly in the Northern System (Carajás), and transporting it via railways and its own ports for export, mainly to China. The sales price is dictated by the international market, while a significant portion of its costs (labor, energy, local suppliers) are denominated in Reais. The company also has significant base metals operations (nickel and copper), which position it as a key player in the global energy transition.
- **Performance Analysis:** Vale is a true giant, with a market value of US$ 41.44 billion and a profit of US$ 5.53 billion in 2023. Revenue totaled US$ 37.45 billion, demonstrating its scale as an export powerhouse. Profitability metrics are world-class: ROE of 15.28% and operating margin of 34.94%. There is a direct causality between revenue in dollars and

operating margin. When the Real depreciates against the Dollar, each dollar of revenue converts into more Reais. Since costs in Reais do not rise at the same rate, the operating margin (Operating Profit in BRLs / Revenue in BRLs) expands. This mechanism makes Vale's shares a currency hedge for investors, but it also directly exposes it to the volatility of the price of iron ore.

- **History and Legacy:** Founded in 1942 as a state-owned company (Companhia Vale do Rio Doce), it was privatized in 1997. Its history is intrinsically linked to the industrial and infrastructure development of Brazil, having been listed on the stock exchange since 1943.

**Petrobras (PETR3 / PETR4)**

- **Business Model:** Petrobras is one of the largest integrated energy companies in the world. Its cash generation comes from three main segments: Exploration and Production (Upstream), where it extracts oil and natural gas, with emphasis on the ultra-productive pre-salt fields; Refining, Transportation and Marketing (Downstream), where it processes crude oil into derivatives such as gasoline, diesel and jet fuel for sale on the domestic market; and Gas and Energy. Most of its profits are generated in Upstream, where pre-salt extraction costs are among the lowest in the world.

- **Performance Analysis:** Petrobras is the most valuable company on the B3, with a market value of US$ 81.7 billion and an astronomical net profit of US$ 19.4 billion in 2024. Its revenue reached US$ 91.4 billion, and it is a major exporter of crude oil. Its ROE of 10% (affect by no exclusive events in last year - in anterior years was above of 18%) and EBITDA operating of 35.26% are exceptionally high and reflect the unique quality of its assets. However, this extraordinary profitability represents a double-edged sword. As a state-controlled company, Petrobras faces constant political pressure to subsidize fuel prices in the domestic market, especially when international oil prices rise. This pricing policy, when implemented, forces the company to sell its products below the import parity price, destroying part of the value for the shareholder. This political risk is a structural and permanent feature of the investment case for Petrobras, explaining why its valuation multiples are often discounted relative to those of its private global peers, despite its superior profitability.
- **History and Legacy:** Created in 1953 by the Getúlio Vargas government under the motto "Oil is ours", Petrobras symbolizes Brazil's quest for energy self-sufficiency. Listed since 1957, its trajectory is marked by technological achievements and political controversies.

**Suzano (SUZB3)**

- **Business Model:** Suzano is the world's largest producer of short-fiber market pulp, derived from eucalyptus. The company generates cash by planting eucalyptus in its vast forests, harvesting the wood, processing it into pulp in its high-tech mills and exporting the commodity to paper, packaging and tissue manufacturers around the world, mainly in Asia and Europe.
- **Performance Analysis:** With a loss for the fiscal year of US$ 1.28 billion, attributed mainly to the appreciation of the dollar against the real, this large exporting company has a market value of US$ 11.84 billion (this value has already been adjusted by the market due to the impacts on profits for the fiscal year 2024). According to the company's disclosure, the rise of the dollar against the real in 2024 negatively impacted Suzano's financial results, mainly due to the company's debt in foreign currency and foreign exchange hedging operations. Excluding this impact, Suzano presented impressive margin metrics in 2024. An EBITDA margin of 52.56%. These numbers are supported by a structural and almost insurmountable competitive advantage. Brazil's climate and soil allow Suzano's genetically modified eucalyptus to reach harvest point in about seven years, a cycle drastically shorter than the two to three decades required for pine in northern hemisphere climates. This results in a significantly lower cost of timber production per ton,

which translates directly into higher margins and superior returns on invested capital. It is a competitive advantage of biological and geographic origin that is difficult to replicate.

- **History and Legacy:** The company has its roots in 1924 and was listed on the stock exchange in 1980. Its transformation into a world leader was consolidated with the merger with Fibria in 2019.

### 9.1.7. Consumption and Retail: The Brands that Shape the Domestic Market

This sector is the thermometer of the Brazilian domestic economy. Its performance is directly linked to indicators such as the unemployment rate, household disposable income, consumer confidence and the availability of credit. Companies in this segment are in a constant battle for consumer preference, with competition intensifying between brick-and-mortar sales channels and the growing e-commerce ecosystem.

Margins tend to be tighter than in the financial and commodities sectors, and success depends on scale, logistical efficiency and brand strength.

**Ambev (ABEV3)**

- **Business Model:** Ambev, part of global conglomerate AB InBev, generates cash through the production, distribution and sale of beer and non-alcoholic beverages. Its business model is a classic consumer goods model: build strong brands, invest heavily in marketing and leverage a vast distribution network to reach millions of points of sale across Latin America. Massive scale enables cost efficiencies in production and logistics.

- **Performance Analysis:** With a market value of US$ 38.9 billion and a profit of US$ 2.7 billion in 2024, Ambev is a defensive company with stable cash generation. Its ROE of 14.64% and operating margin of 32.34% are healthy and reflect its dominant position in the market.
- **Branding:** Ambev has a portfolio of brands that are part of Brazilian culture. "Skol", "Brahma" and "Antarctica" are absolute leaders in the beer market. The company also sells major brands such as Budweiser, Stella Artois, and Spaten, among others. "Guaraná Antarctica" is an iconic brand in the soft drinks segment. Portfolio management is a core competency of the company.
- **History and Legacy:** Ambev was formed in 1999 by the merger of the two largest breweries in Brazil, Brahma and Antarctica. Listed in the same year, its creation gave rise to what would become the largest brewing group in the world.

### 9.1.8. Industrials, Energy and Utilities: The Diversified Core

This group includes companies from different sectors, but which share the characteristic of being the infrastructure and industrial base of the economy.

Utility companies (energy, sanitation) operate under concession models regulated by the government, which gives them predictable and long-term revenue streams, but also subjects them to regulatory risks.

Industrial companies, in turn, compete on the basis of technological differentiation, operational efficiency and, in many cases, the ability to export high value-added products.

**WEG (WEGE3)**

- **Business Model:** WEG is a global industrial powerhouse with a B2B (business-to-business) business model. The company generates cash by designing, manufacturing and selling a wide range of electronic equipment, with emphasis on electric motors (where it is one of the world leaders), generators, transformers and industrial automation solutions. It has recently become a relevant player in renewable energy, supplying wind turbines and solar energy systems.
- **Performance Analysis:** WEG is a remarkable case of industrial success. With a market value of US$ 31.69 billion and profit of US$ 1.15 billion, the company achieved a ROE of 27.21% in 2024. This return metric, comparable to that of a world-class mining company like Vale, is an anomaly for a Brazilian industrial company and deserves a deeper analysis. Industrial manufacturing is typically a medium-margin, capital-intensive business. WEG's exceptional performance does not derive from a natural resource, but rather

from a competitive advantage built over decades, based on three pillars: a deep verticalization strategy (WEG produces everything from copper wire to the insulating varnish for its motors, ensuring cost and quality control), continuous and disciplined investment in Research & Development (R&D) to create more efficient products, and a culture obsessed with operational excellence. It is a case study of how operational strategy, and not just market position, can generate extraordinary value for shareholders. The company is also a major exporter, with revenues of US$ 6.90 billion and factories on multiple continents.

- **History and Legacy:** Founded in 1961 in Jaraguá do Sul (SC) by three partners, WEG went public in 1971 and followed a consistent trajectory of growth and internationalization.

**Eletrobras (ELET3)**

- **Business Model:** Eletrobras is the largest electric power company in Latin America. Its cash generation comes mainly from the generation of electricity in its hydroelectric plants and from the transmission of energy through its vast network of high-voltage lines. The business model is typical of a utility: revenues are regulated and defined in long-term concession contracts with the government, which provides a highly predictable and stable cash flow.
- **Performance Analysis:** After its privatization in 2022, Eletrobras is undergoing a transformation process. In

2024, it recorded a profit of US$ 1.88 billion on a market value of US$ 18.02 billion. The ROE of 8.5% and the operating margin of 65.30% still reflect the structure of a former state-owned company in transition. The investment thesis in the company is based on the expectation that private management will be able to implement efficiency gains, reduce costs and optimize capital allocation, which should lead to a gradual improvement in these profitability indicators.

- **History and Legacy:** Created in 1962 as the federal government's arm for the electricity sector, Eletrobras was for decades the country's main instrument of energy policy. Its listing dates back to 1965, and its recent privatization marks a turning point in its long history.

**Embraer (EMBR3)**

- **Business Model:** Embraer is a global leader in the aerospace and defense sector, operating with a B2B (business-to-business) and B2G (business-to-government) business model. The company generates cash through the design, manufacture and sale of aircraft and systems in three main segments: Commercial Aviation, focused on regional jets with up to 150 seats, where it is the world leader; Executive Aviation, with a portfolio ranging from light to ultra-large jets; and Defense & Security, which produces military transport aircraft such as the C-390 Millennium and light attack aircraft such as the A-29

Super Tucano, as well as radar and monitoring systems. A growing and crucial source of revenue is the Services & Support business, which provides maintenance, parts and training for its global fleet of aircraft.

- **Performance Analysis:** Embraer represents a unique case of technological success in Brazil. With a market value of US$ 9.5 billion and a profit of US$ 350 million in 2024, the company achieved a ROE of 11.94%. This return, more modest than that of commodity giants or WEG, reflects the nature of its sector: a business with extremely high technological intensity, long development cycles and massive capital. Embraer's value does not derive from natural resources or extreme verticalization, but rather from a competitive advantage built on intellectual capital, innovation and cutting-edge engineering. Its ability to identify and dominate market niches, such as regional aviation, where the major powers Airbus and Boeing do not compete directly, was fundamental to its success. The company stands out for its excellence in engineering and design, creating highly efficient and reliable products that position it as a brand of global prestige. Embraer is, by definition, an exporter, with revenues of US$ 4.63 billion and a supply chain and customers spread across the globe. Its performance is a case study in how technological specialization and the conquest of global niches can generate significant value in one of the most competitive industries on the planet.

- **History and Legacy:** Founded in 1969 in São José dos Campos (SP) as a state-owned company initiated by the Brazilian government to develop a national aeronautics industry, Embraer was born from a strategic technological development project. After decades of operating under state control, the company was privatized in 1994, a milestone that boosted its competitiveness and global expansion. The company went public on the stock exchange in 2000, and since then has followed a path of innovation, launching families of commercial and executive jets that have become sales successes and consolidated its position as the third largest manufacturer of commercial jets in the world. Its legacy is proof that Brazil can compete and lead in high-tech sectors, transforming a state-owned project into a global icon of engineering and innovation.

### 9.1.9. Synthesis and Strategic Perspective

The detailed analysis of the profiles of the 50 companies above reveals macro patterns and dynamics that define the Brazilian corporate elite. This final section synthesizes these observations to offer a holistic view of the current scenario and the trends that may reshape the list of the largest companies on B3 in the future.

#### *9.1.9.1. The Great Divide: A Comparative Analysis of Profitability Models*

Financial data from the 50 largest companies on the B3 clearly demonstrates that there is no single path to profitability. Instead, Brazil's corporate elite is divided into distinct camps with fundamentally different business models.

On one side, there are the **"Global Cyclicals"**, which comprise the Mining, Oil & Gas and Pulp & Paper sectors. Companies such as Vale, Petrobras and Suzano exhibit very high operating margins (often above 30-40%) and high ROEs. Their profitability, however, is highly volatile and directly linked to commodity prices in international markets and the exchange rate. They represent a bet on the global economy.

On the other side, there are the **"Domestic Champions,"** led by the financial sector. Banks such as Itaú and Bradesco have consistently high ROE (around 20%), but with more moderate operating margins. Their high return on equity is driven by the use of leverage and a robust interest spread, both dependent on the interest rate environment and the health of the credit cycle in Brazil. They represent a bet on the domestic economy.

A third group, **"Consumption and Retail,"** presents a large company like Ambev, which operates in an environment with low margins and more modest ROEs. In this sector, valuation generally depends more on growth prospects and market share gains than on current profitability. In this book, we will limit ourselves to talking a little about Ambev, as it is a beverage giant and is listed among the fifty largest companies on the Brazilian stock exchange. However, there are companies that were once among the 50, with very high market value, such as Magalu, but which today, due to the dynamics of the Brazilian domestic market, have lost market value. The attentive investor can evaluate companies in this sector, which present seasonality and circumstances more closely linked to the country's macroeconomy. Factors such as taxes, interest rates and income significantly affect the various companies that operate in this sector, especially in Brazil..

Finally, anomalies like WEG show that it is possible to achieve world-class profitability in the industrial sector through operational and technological excellence, a model that is distinct from both global cyclicals and domestic champions.

It is worth noting that there are possibly companies like WEG in the next quadrant of the more than 400 companies listed on the B3. It is up to the investor to rank and study this.

*9.1.9.2. The Export Engine: Quantifying Brazil's Corporate Global Reach*

An analysis of dollar revenues reveals the crucial role of exports for the Brazilian economy, but also a strong concentration. When aggregating the foreign currency revenues of companies identified as exporters, it becomes clear that a small number of companies account for a disproportionate share of the total.

Vale (US$ 37.45 billion) and Petrobras (US$ 91.4 billion, including exports and sales linked to international prices) are by far the largest generators of foreign exchange.

Along with players such as Suzano, Gerdau (steel) and Klabin (cellulose and paper), the commodities sector is the main source of export revenue for the B3 elite.

This creates a systemic vulnerability: the aggregate international performance of the Ibovespa is highly sensitive to a drop in iron ore or oil prices.

Although industrial companies such as WEG are successful exporters, their aggregate impact on the trade balance of the 50 largest is significantly smaller.

Here lies the interesting point from the point of view of the foreign or global investor: you cannot rely on the Brazilian stock market index for your investment strategies in the financial market, since the index tends to reflect much more the performance of these commodity companies. Never forget: there are more than 400 companies.

It often happens that the herd effect of foreign capital, in the face of shocks or hiccups, causes indexes to fall, with some repercussions in other sectors, which are not entirely justifiable. Foreign investors need to understand that in this scenario, the dollar rises, with the real depreciating, and withdrawing capital from the country can cancel out the gains. In the best case scenario, in this case, the most sensible alternative seems to be to invest in interest, in the purchase of government bonds.

#### *9.1.9.1.3. Corporate Dynasties: The Enduring Legacy of Brazil's Old Guard*

An analysis of the founding and listing dates on the B3 reveals a striking characteristic of the Brazilian corporate elite: it is dominated by mature institutions, often centuries old.

The average age of a company at the top of the B3 is significantly high. Institutions such as Banco do Brasil (founded in 1808), Gerdau (1901), Klabin (1899), Itaú (1924) and Vale (1942) are not exceptions, but the rule.

This fact suggests a business environment with high barriers to entry, where capital, scale and historical legacy create competitive moats that are difficult to overcome. In contrast to developed market indices, such as the S&P 500 in the US, which feature a strong presence of technology companies founded in the last two or three decades, the B3 has a relative dearth of "new economy" companies at its top echelon.

This indicates that the Brazilian economy, at its highest level, is still structured around legacy industries. The rise of companies like BTG Pactual, XP and Magazine Luiza shows that change is possible, but the incumbents still maintain an overwhelming dominance.

## 9.2. Future Outlook and Emerging Risks

Looking ahead to the next decade, several trends have the potential to reshape this list:

- **The ESG (Environmental, Social and Governance) Mandate:** The growing pressure for decarbonization and sustainability represents both a risk and an opportunity. For Petrobras and Vale, emissions management and environmental impact will be increasingly scrutinized by investors. For companies like Suzano, with its planted forests, and WEG, with its renewable energy solutions and electric motor development, the ESG trend could be a powerful tailwind.

- **Digital Disruption:** The battle between incumbent banks and fintechs is far from over. The ability of companies like XP, Nubank (currently listed on the NYSE, but a dominant player originating in Brazil) and BTG Pactual to continue to innovate and steal market share from the big banks will be one of the main stories to watch. In retail, the consolidation of e-commerce will continue to put pressure on traditional business models. Companies like RENNER are struggling, but are reinventing themselves to compete with companies like SHEIN. AMAZON has been operating in the country for a long time and should coexist without major risks with retail companies. The risk lies with the Chinese. New entrants have also posed risks that can squeeze margins, such as the entry of Shopee and other similar companies.

- **The Question of Reindustrialization:** WEG's global success raises the question of whether Brazil can replicate this model and develop other high-tech industrial champions, or whether the economy will continue to rely predominantly on finance and commodity exports. There are, however, midcap and smallcap companies that seem to be on this path. Time will tell and they need to be discovered and monitored more closely.

- **Political and Regulatory Risk:** This continues to be an omnipresent factor in Brazil. The risk of government intervention in prices (Petrobras), regulatory changes (Eletrobras, banks) and changes in fiscal policy affects the predictability of cash flows and remains a structural discount to the valuation of many of Brazil's leading companies. These risks also embed an additional tax on the economy's basic interest rate, where money can also be made at low risk.

# Final word: Brazil as a strategic player

We have reached the end of our journey. If you started reading this book as a skeptical investor, wary of the headlines and the complexity of Latin America, I hope you now have a new perspective.

The goal was never to erase your fears, but rather to replace them with a structured understanding. Brazil is not, and probably never will be, a smooth investment. Volatility is inherent in its DNA. However, what once seemed like unpredictable chaos can now be seen as a system of paradoxes with an internal logic: inequality that creates opportunities for innovation; bureaucracy that is combated by a vibrant civil society; political instability that forges resilient companies.

Socially impactful startups, inclusive fintechs, and technology-centric business models have emerged precisely from attempts to overcome these challenges. Investors who see only the risk in the headlines miss the opportunity that lies hidden in solving these problems.

In a world where developed markets are increasingly correlated, Brazil offers something valuable: diversification. Its economic cycles do not always align with those of the US or Europe. Adding a small, thoughtful allocation to Brazil can, paradoxically, reduce the overall risk of a global portfolio.

This book has given you the map, the compass, and the field guide. The decision to embark on the expedition, and the path to follow, are now yours. For those willing to understand it, Brazil ceases to be a risk to be feared and becomes what it really is: a challenging and rewarding value frontier.

The journey starts now.

If you still don't feel confident about investing in the country, we recommend that you visit the country if you are interested and curious.

We think it's worth visiting Brasília, as it is the country's capital, and you will be surprised by how different (and so much better) it is than Rio de Janeiro or the Amazon. Don't forget to visit São Paulo, a financial center and a large metropolis. Visit the northeast, where there are wonderful beaches. Santa Catarina is an excellent place to get to know the southern region. Look for cities in Rio Grande do Sul and the interior of Paraná. In Minas Gerais, there are opportunities to travel to historical sites, such as Ouro Preto, Mariana, and Tiradentes. Also visit the so-called South of Minas and the Triângulo Mineiro. It is a large state.

Want to learn about the power of agriculture? Visit Mato Grosso and Goiás.

But if you still feel insecure about all this, be sure to look for financial agents in your own country who invest through funds in Brazil. It could be an opportunity to get to know them little by little, as long as you, in addition to putting your money to work with them, always seek contact with the financial consultants in charge of these investments, always seeking information about where the resources are being invested, and about their views on these investments and Brazil.

Brazil is a giant that is still asleep. Don't wait until the giant awakens to seize the opportunity!

Disclaimer:

Every investor's situation is unique and you should consider your investment objectives, risk tolerance and time horizon before making any investment in any country.

Investing involves risk and you may incur profits or losses regardless of the strategy you select.

The contents of this book do not constitute a recommendation to buy or sell any individual asset or any combination of assets.

All information provided in this book does not constitute a complete summary or statement of all available data needed to make an investment decision and does not constitute a recommendation.

International investment options, whether stocks, real estate funds, treasury bills or any others mentioned may not be suitable for all investors.

All types of investments, including funds, involve risk. Risk refers to the possibility that you may lose money (both principal and any gains) or not make a profit on an investment. Changes in market conditions can create fluctuations in the value of an investment in funds, bonds or stocks. In addition, there are fees and expenses associated with investing.

Global investors also need to be aware of changes in the legislation of the country invested in and their own country, as there are interferences in the legal and tax fields, as well as exchange rates and insurance for some investments, among others.

As a final word, I would like to thank you for dedicating yourself to reading this book. I sincerely thank you for this and I hope it has been useful to you, adding some knowledge.

Otherwise, be happy! We only live once! Do what is good! Share knowledge, even if others don't believe it. And remember: there is only one humanity. The separation between countries is, above all, a human creation.

www.ingramcontent.com/pod-product-compliance
Lightning Source LLC
Chambersburg PA
CBHW071348230926
51846CB00002B/477

# Private International Law in Spain

**Diego P. Fernández Arroyo**
**Miguel Checa Martínez**
**&**
**Pilar Maestre Casas**

This book was originally published as a monograph in the International Encyclopaedia of Laws/Private International Law.

General Editors: Roger Blanpain, Frank Hendrickx
Volume Editor: Bea Verschraegen

Wolters Kluwer

*Published by:*
Kluwer Law International B.V.
PO Box 316
2400 AH Alphen aan den Rijn
The Netherlands
Website: www.wklawbusiness.com

*Sold and distributed in North, Central and South America by:*
Wolters Kluwer Legal & Regulatory U.S.
7201 McKinney Circle
Frederick, MD 21704
United States of America
Email: customer.service@wolterskluwer.com

*Sold and distributed in all other countries by:*
Turpin Distribution Services Ltd.
Stratton Business Park
Pegasus Drive, Biggleswade
Bedfordshire SG18 8TQ
United Kingdom
Email: kluwerlaw@turpin-distribution.com



ISBN 978-90-411-8269-2

e-Book: ISBN 978-90-411-8298-2
web-PDF: ISBN 978-90-411-8314-9

This title is available on www.kluwerlawonline.com

# Private International Law in Spain

# The Authors

Professor Diego P. Fernández Arroyo, born in La Plata (Argentina), is currently a professor and co-director of the Global Governance Programme at Sciences Po Law School, Paris. He teaches international dispute resolution, arbitration and private international law. Former President of the American Association of Private International Law, he was distinguished as Honorary Professor by the National University of Cordoba and the University of Buenos Aires (Argentina). He is a member of the Curatorium of The Hague Academy of International Law and the Secretary-General of the International Academy of Comparative Law. He is part of the Argentinean Delegations before UNCITRAL (Working Group on Arbitration) and CIDIP (Organization of American States). As a visiting professor, he has been teaching and conducting research in universities and research institutions of Australia, Brazil, Canada, Cuba, France, Germany, Japan, Mexico, the Netherlands, Paraguay, Philippines, Spain, Switzerland, Uruguay, USA and Venezuela. Professor Fernández Arroyo is actively involved in the practice of international arbitration as an arbitrator and an expert.

Professor Miguel Checa Martínez is a professor of Private International Law at Cadiz University since 1997. He has been Vice-Dean at the Law School (2004–2012), and formerly Secretary-General of the same University (1999–2002). Born in 1965, he was awarded a Bachelor's Degree in Law in July 1988 at Cadiz University and a Doctorate Degree in Law in November 1992 at Complutense University in Madrid. His teaching and research experience has been mainly focused on the Law of International Trade, Private International Law and Comparative law. He is also Of Counsel since 2005 to the international law firm Martinez-Echevarria Abogados, whose head office is located in Marbella, Spain, and his areas of practice include international contracts and international litigation for corporate clients and international family law and succession for private clients, both expatriates and non-residents with interests in Spain.

**The Authors**

Professor Pilar Maestre Casas, born in Burgos, is a professor at Salamanca University since 1998. She was awarded a Bachelor's Degree in Law in 1986 at Valladolid University and her Doctorate Degree in Law at Complutense University in Madrid in October 1994. She has concentrated on international issues of Banking Law, in particular those related to restrictions of competition, and International Family Law. She has been Vice-Dean of the Salamanca University School of Law.

# Table of Contents

# List of Abbreviations

| | |
|---|---|
| ADC | Anuario de Derecho Civil |
| AEDIPr | Anuario Español de Derecho Internacional Privado |
| AP | Audiencia Provincial (Provincial Court) |
| BIMJ | Boletín Informativo del Ministerio de Justicia |
| BOE | Boletín Oficial del Estado |
| CC | Código Civil (Civil Code) |
| CCJC | Cuadernos Cívitas de Jurisprudencia Civil |
| CCom | Código de Comercio (Commercial Code) |
| CDT | Cuadernos de Derecho Transnacional |
| DGRN | Dirección General de los Registros y del Notariado (General Direction of the Registry and Notary) |
| DO | Diario Oficial de la Unión Europea |
| EC | European Community |
| ECJ | Court of Justice of the European Union |
| EU | European Union |
| La Ley | Revista Jurídica Española La Ley |
| LCD | Ley de competencia desleal (Unfair Competition Act) |
| LDC | Ley de defensa de la competencia (Competition Defence Act) |
| LEC | Ley de Enjuiciamiento Civil (Civil Procedure Act) |
| LME | Ley de Modificaciones Estructurales de las Sociedades Mercantiles (Structural Changes in Commercial Companies Act) |
| LOPJ | Ley Orgánica del Poder Judicial (Judicial Power Act) |
| LRC | Ley del Registro civil (Civil Registry Act) |
| LSC | Ley de Sociedades de Capital (Companies Act) |
| OJ | Official Journal |
| R des C | Recueil des Cours |

| | |
|---|---|
| RCDI | Revista Crítica de Derecho Inmobiliario |
| RDM | Revista de Derecho Mercantil |
| RDN | Revista de Derecho Notarial |
| RDP | Revista de Derecho Privado |
| REDI | Revista Española de Derecho Internacional |
| REEI | Revista Electrónica de Estudios Internacionales |
| RGD | Revista General de Derecho |
| RJC | Revista Jurídica de Cataluña |
| RN | Reglamento Notarial (Notary Regulation) |
| RRC | Reglamento del Registro Civil (Civil Registry Regulation) |
| RRM | Reglamento del Registro Mercantil (Commercial Registry Regulation) |
| TC | Tribunal Constitucional (Constitutional Court) |
| TEDH | Tribunal Europeo de Derechos Humanos (European Court of Human Rights) |
| TS | Tribunal Supremo (Supreme Court) |
| TSJ | Tribunal Superior de Justicia (Superior Court of Justice of a Spanish Autonomous Community) |

# General Introduction

## §1. Historical Development and General Data

*1.* Comparative law scholars unanimously agree that the Spanish legal system belongs to the Roman-Germanic legal family.[1] This assertion implies, first, that the Spanish legal system is based on Roman Law, although some Germanic customs should also be taken into consideration, and, second, that civil law is codified and the principle of certainty of the law (Article 9.3 Spanish Constitution) governs all judicial activity, without the judge having the capacity to create the law as it happens in common law countries. Of course, there are also some discrepancies regarding the existence of some legal sub-families in continental Europe, where the Spanish legal system would be situated into a so-called purely Roman group,[2] with France, Belgium and Luxembourg.

One of the most relevant factors in the historical formation of what is now known as Spain could be the Arabian presence in Spanish territory for over eight centuries. In spite of the importance of the cultural legacy of *Al-Andalus*, the legal influence of that presence is non-existent. After the conquest of the Muslim Kingdom of Granada by the Catholic Kings in 1492, the remains of the legal tradition of *Al-Andalus* were absolutely eliminated. Therefore, it is the medieval history of the different Christian Kingdoms which the territory of Spain is made of that is the basis of the legal historical tradition of Spain. The Kingdom of Castile is the most significant and constant historical factor, although the legal traditions of the former Kingdoms of the Crown of Aragon (Aragon, Catalonia and Valencia) and the Kingdom of Navarre must be taken into consideration when dealing with the civil laws of these territories.

*2.* The same year (1492) another event, the discovery of the Americas, had an enormous impact and historical relevance throughout the world and especially in Spain since, in a few decades, Spain seized control over the greatest part of the American territory, establishing a series of governmental royal delegations known as *Virreinatos*. Through these delegations of the royal power, Spain developed its

1. K. Zweigert & H. Kötz, *An Introduction to Comparative Law*, 63–73 (3d ed., Clarendon Press 1998); L.-J. Constantinesco, *Traité de droit comparé*, t. III, 84–85 (Picon & Durand-Auzias, 1983).
2. See the classification of O. Remien, *Illusion und Realität eines europäischen Privatrechts*, Juristen Zeitung, No. 6 (1992), 278.

political and economic control over its American colonies[3] and at the same time, imposed its culture, language and religion (Catholicism). From a legal standpoint, the conquest of the Americas facilitated the expansion of the Roman-Germanic family of law throughout this vast territory.[4] In spite of the process of independence from Spain in the nineteenth century, Latin-American countries continued to have a strong relationship with the former colonial power, and this is also noticeable in the legal history of each of the different Latin-American countries. Also, during most of the twentieth century, many Spaniards who were fleeing from poverty, the Civil War (1936–1939) or the dictatorship (1939–1975) established themselves in the former colonies in a massive exodus of millions of people. In the last years, Spain, or more precisely Spanish companies, has become the major investor in the Latin-American region, especially because of the implementation of a general policy of privatization of the public sector in these countries. Currently, Spanish enterprises have control over most part of the strategic economic sectors of the economies of Latin-American countries, especially in banking, energy and telecommunications.

*3.* Today, this country of 504,752 square kilometres has a population of 47 million people. Its fertility rate is very low (1.39 children per woman), although it is higher than few years ago (1.16 in the second half of 1990) due to the growth of immigration. Fertility rate sharply contrasts with a very high life expectancy rate (84.56 years for women and 78.55 years for men). For these reasons, sociologists have predicted the progressive aging of the Spanish population. The national economy relies heavily on tourism. Spain has the second highest level of unemployment in the EU (20.8%), only second to Greece. Immigrants still play a key role in the Spanish economy and most of them are generally employed in the agricultural, construction or service sectors. A different group of immigrants are the retirees from other EU countries who generally settle down in the Mediterranean coast (mainly from the United Kingdom). The total number of immigrants in just the ten years increased from less than 2% to 12% (6 million people) of the total Spanish population. This immigration has come mainly from other EU countries (2.3 million), among which Romania is the first country of origin (870.258) followed by the United Kingdom (385,000). The second most important area of origin is Latin America (1.4 million), mostly from Ecuador, Colombia, Bolivia, Peru, Dominican Republic, Brazil, Argentina and Paraguay. The third area of origin is Northern Africa, particularly from Morocco (792.158). On the other hand, numbers from Asia are relatively small (378.000), mainly from China (181.701) and Pakistan (81.365). Foreign population in Spain has actually decreased in the period 2011–2015 by almost 500,000 persons, falling to 10.1% of the total population, as a consequence of the burst of the real estate bubble and the ensuing financial and economic crisis suffered by Spain after 2009. Also during the economic crisis (2009–2013), emigration from Spain has increased, although it is difficult to arrive at reliable data. At

3. The current territories of Argentina, Uruguay, Paraguay, Chile, Bolivia, Peru, Ecuador, Colombia, Venezuela, Panama, Costa Rica, Honduras, EL Salvador, Nicaragua, Guatemala, Mexico, Dominican Republic, Cuba, Puerto Rico and a significant part of the US.
4. See J.M. Castán Vázquez, *El sistema de Derecho privado iberoamericano*, in *Estudios de Derecho civil en honor del profesor Castán Tobeñas*, 155–188 (Pamplona 1969).

present, the total official number of Spanish nationals residing in foreign countries is 2.31 million : 1.4 million in the American Continent (mainly in Argentina, Venezuela, Cuba, Brazil, USA, Mexico, etc.) and 0.7 million in Europe (mainly in France, Germany, Switzerland, UK, Belgium, etc.).

## §2. General Principles

*4.* Beyond these historical and general facts, it is important to consider the basic characteristics of the Spanish legal system. One of them is the existence of a written Constitution, approved in 1978, which constitutes an essential element of the political consensus in favour of the establishment of a social and democratic State, after decades of the ominous dictatorship that followed the end of the Spanish Civil War (1936–1939) and continuous violations of human rights. The Constitution has primacy over the rest of the Spanish legal order according to Article 9.1 CE.

*5.* The fundamental rights recognized by the Spanish Constitution have a strong influence over the field of private law.[5] Obviously, Private International Law (PIL) is not an exception.[6] With respect to this sector of the Spanish legal system, there is a principle of openness to other legal systems, which derives from the Preamble, Articles 16.3 and 93–95 of the Spanish Constitution.[7] This principle implies that in the Spanish legal system it is perfectly admissible for a case connected with Spain to be decided by another jurisdiction and that foreign judgments (with some exceptions) should be recognized. It also implies that there must be co-operation between Spanish and foreign authorities in international civil procedures. Similarly, the principle of openness justifies the fact that the system of PIL is mainly composed of multilateral conflict of laws rules, which opens the way for the application of foreign laws by the national courts. In addition, this principle prevents nationalistic interpretations that might blatantly favour the jurisdiction of national courts over that of foreign courts and the application of Spanish law over foreign law.[8]

*6.* Article 9.3 of the Spanish Constitution states:

> The Constitution guarantees the principle of legality, the normative hierarchy of legal provisions, the publicity of rules of law [and] … the [principle of] legal certainty. …

5. The relevant jurisprudence of the Constitutional Court related to Private Law and its comments may be consulted in the review *Derecho privado y Constitución*, published by the *Centro de Estudios Políticos y Constitucionales.*
6. See judgments of Spanish Constitutional Court 156/1993 and 39/2002.
7. J.D. González Campos held that this principle is essential to the Spanish PIL. *El sistema español de Derecho internacional privado. Formación histórica y fuentes*, in *Derecho internacional privado*, vol. 1, 54–55 (3rd ed., E. Pérez Vera (ed.), Madrid: UNED, 2001).
8. *Ibid.*, criticizing the judgment of the Provincial Court of Castellón, 2nd section, civil, 18 Jul. 1997, which preferred the Spanish jurisdiction, instead of a foreign one, and purely on the basis of the defendant's convenience and economy.

*7.* The last topic deserves special mention. The principle of legal certainty, without impairing the legislator's freedom to establish whichever PIL laws are considered appropriate in each case (rigid or flexible, simple or complex connecting factors), requires the legislator to take into account all the necessary elements so that certainty as to the content of these laws can be determined. Thus, the existence of special rules that deal with certain application problems of the conflict of laws rules (Article 12 of the Spanish Civil Code on characterization, renvoi, *ordre public*, etc.) does not compromise the principle of legal certainty, even though the application of these rules may result in the application of different laws than those established by the conflict of laws rules.[9]

*8.* The principle of equality (Article 14) is also relevant to PIL. The legislator (generally) cannot enact laws that provide for a different treatment in identical situations,[10] nor can introduce connecting factors that establish unreasonable distinctions.[11] In addition, the principle of equality plays a fundamental role in the configuration of Spanish public policy, especially as a ground for denying the application of a foreign law or for rejecting the recognition of a foreign judgment because of its contradiction with the principle of equality.

## §3. Nature and Scope

*9.* Spain is a parliamentary monarchy. The Spanish Kingdom has a decentralized political system, which consists of seventeen political regions defined as *Comunidades Autónomas* (Autonomous Communities). Nevertheless, this decentralization is not homogeneous because some *Comunidades Autónomas*, those considered to be 'historical', were granted more autonomy than others. Even though the Constitution entered into force in 1978, the political and legal process of decentralization is still unfinished. Since 1978, there have been many conflicting issues regarding the distribution of power between the central Government and the *Comunidades Autónomas*. The Constitutional Court has jurisdiction to solve such constitutional conflicts. Nevertheless, these conflicts have increasingly become political rather than strictly constitutional issues, thus surpassing the legal powers of the Constitutional Court, which is also being increasingly questioned because of the openly known political affiliation of some of its members and the allegedly political hidden motivations of its decisions.

*10.* It must also be emphasized that Spain has been immersed for decades in an international process of a very distinct nature: European integration. In 1985, Spain – along with Portugal – entered the European Community (EC); the entry became effective from 1 January 1986. The thirty years following the entry have resulted in a profound transformation of Spain. There has been an impressive social, industrial

9. *Ibid.*, 52.
10. Judgments TC 62/1987, 158/1993 and 69/2007.
11. Judgment TC 39/2002.

and commercial modernization and a no less spectacular development of infrastructure. Obviously, the content and functions of Spanish law have been adapted to the demands of EU Law.

## §4. Special Characteristics of National Private International Law (PIL)

*11.* The Spanish Civil Code of 1889 (*Gaceta de Madrid*, 25 July 1889) did not contain many provisions on PIL. Therefore, the system of PIL initially consisted mainly of case law and general legal doctrine. It was not until 1974 that a more developed set of choice-of-law rules was adopted by the introduction of a new Preliminary Title to the Civil Code by Decree 1846/1976 (*BOE*, 9 July 1974). As for rules on international jurisdiction, the first systematic regulation was provided by Articles 21 et seq. of the Judicial Power Organic Act 1985 (*Ley Orgánica del Poder Judicial*, *BOE*, 2 July 1985) and, prior to that date, only scarce authority and case law were available. The rules governing recognition and enforcement of foreign judgments were adopted in Articles 951 et seq. of the Civil Procedure Act 1881 (*Ley de Enjuiciamiento Civil*, *Gaceta de Madrid*, 5–22 February 1881) and have been derogated only very recently by the introduction a new Act on International Judicial Cooperation for Civil Matters (Ley 29/2015) which entered into force on August 2015. It is important to emphasize that most Spanish legal scholars agree on the content of PIL; for most of them it consists of three sectors: conflict of laws (*Derecho aplicable*), jurisdiction (*competencia judicial internacional*) and recognition and enforcement of foreign acts and judicial decisions (*reconocimiento y ejecución*).

*12.* Spain is one of the very few examples in Europe of a State with a multiple legal system, since in addition to the Spanish Civil Code there are other civil laws, mainly dealing with family and succession law in some Autonomous Communities, those with constitutional competence on civil law matters: Aragon, Catalonia, Balearic Islands, Galicia, Basque Country, Navarre and Valencia. The coexistence of different civil law regulations may result in interregional conflicts of laws,[12] which are governed by the Preliminary Title of the Civil Code (Articles 13–16). It must be said that only the State, and not the *Comunidades Autónomas*, has the power to legislate on matters referring to PIL, and that, more precisely, according to Article 149.1.8 of the Spanish Constitution, the State has exclusive powers to elaborate both international and internal (interregional) conflict of laws rules.[13]

---

12. In general: A. Borrás Rodríguez, *Les ordres plurilégislatifs dans le droit international privé actuel*, R. des C., 1994, 145; M.E. Zabalo Escudero, *Pluralidad legislativa y conflictos de leyes internos en el ordenamiento español, Cursos de Derecho internacional de Vitoria-Gasteiz*, 1994, 257; J.J. Álvarez Rubio, *Las normas de Derecho interregional de la Ley 3/1992, de 1 de julio, Derecho foral civil del País Vasco* (Oñati, Instituto Vasco de Administración Pública, 1995); E.M. Rodríguez Gayán, *Heterogeneidad y sistema en las relaciones entre Derecho internacional privado y Derecho interregional*, RGD, 1996, 8069.
13. Judgments TC 88/1993, 156/1993, 31/2010.

# Part I. General Principles (Choice-of-Law Technique)

## Chapter 1. Sources of Private International Law (PIL)

### §1. NATIONAL LAW

*13.* The Spanish statutory rules on conflict of laws can be primarily found in the Preliminary Title of the Civil Code (Articles 8–16) enacted by Decree 1836/1974, 31 May 1974 (BOE, 9 July 1974). However, many of its provisions have been modified, particularly, with regard to choice-of-law rules on the effects of marriage (Article 9.2), matrimonial property agreements (Article 9.3) and rights of the surviving spouse (Article 9.8) by means of the Reform of the Civil Code to Avoid Sex Discrimination Act 1990 (BOE, 18 October 1990). More recently, the laws applicable to filiation (Article 9.4), protection of minors (Article 9.6) and maintenance obligations (Article 9.7) have been modified by the Law on the Protection of Infants and Adolescents (Ley 26/2015). Not all of Spanish conflicts of laws rules are included in the Preliminary Title to the Civil Code. Other rules can be found in other sections of the Civil Code (e.g., Articles 49–51 on the law applicable to marriage celebration, Article 107 on the law applicable to matrimonial nullity, separation and divorce: profoundly modified first in 2003, and now again in 2015 to take into account the entry into force of Regulation Rome III on the law applicable to separation and divorce) or in other statutory sources. Therefore, the Spanish system of PIL is not codified in a single body of law, but is fragmented or dispersed in different statutory sources. This dispersion has been increasing through the years, since several special acts have included its own choice-of-law rules.

*14.* Interregional conflicts of laws are governed by Article 16 of the Civil Code. Article 16 establishes the application of the rules that govern international conflict of laws to interregional conflict of laws. The general connecting factor, which in international conflict of laws is based on nationality, is substituted by civil vicinity or *vecindad civil* (Article 16.1.1). Defined in detail by Articles 14 and 15 of the Civil Code, *vecindad civil* is a specific personal connecting factor for interregional conflict of laws.[14] Other exceptions for interregional conflict of laws are the exclusion

14. The proof of *vecindad civil* can be made relying on evidence supported by the Civil Registry of the place of birth or the place of domicile, because the legal criteria set out in Arts 14 and 15 of the Civil Code also include the possibility of declaring the will of the interested party to maintain,

of the Spanish Civil Code rules on characterization, renvoi and public policy exception (*ordre public*) (Article 16.1.2). The exclusion of the rule on characterization (Article 12.1 Civil Code) is doubtful, since there are no unitary or common classification criteria for the different civil legal systems that coexist in Spain, which may result in difficult situations when trying to discern the applicable conflict of laws rule. On the contrary, the exclusion of renvoi is only logical since the Autonomous Communities cannot enact conflict of laws rules of their own. The exclusion of the public policy exception is also understandable, since there is only one Constitution in the Spanish legal system.

*15.* The solution contained in Article 16 Civil Code can also be applicable to all those cases in which a foreign or conventional conflict of laws rule designates the Spanish law as applicable. In the absence of a specific rule on remissions to a multiple legal system in the foreign PIL legal system or conflict of laws international convention, the designation of Spanish law must be understood as a general remission. Therefore, the identification of the specifically applicable civil law system should be the result of the application of the Spanish interregional conflict of laws rules, which are essentially those also applicable to international conflicts of laws.[15]

## §2. Multilateral and Bilateral Treaties

*16.* Due to the existence of a non-democratic political system in Spain at the end of the Civil War in 1939 which was aligned to the Axis during the Second World War, Spain was absolutely isolated from the international community from 1939 until 1953 when the United States saw in Spain a close ally in the cold war. Even after 1953 Spain would still be isolated for most PIL purposes. At the end of the dictatorship in 1975, a political transition process began, that implied a gradual recovery of democratic institutions and liberties. This new situation also affected Spain's international relations, provoking stronger bonds with other countries and international organizations. With respect to international codification, Spain began to participate in numerous international conventions in the final years of the dictatorship and many of those conventions were relate to PIL issues. Thus, from the start of the 1970s to the end of the 1980s, the Spanish PIL system had changed into a treaty-based system and today the number of PIL rules derived from treaties is truly remarkable.

---

acquire or choose a certain *vecindad civil*, see Arts 1–7, 46, 63–65 of the Civil Registry Act, 8 Jun. 1957 and Arts 225–237 of the Civil Registry Regulation, 14 Nov. 1958, for inscription of *vecindad civil*. For a general description on the legal regime of *vecindad civil*, see R. Bercovitz Rodríguez-Cano, *La regulación de la vecindad civil derivada de la Ley 11/1990, de 15 de octubre, sobre reforma del Código Civil, en aplicación del principio de no discriminación por razón de sexo, y de la Ley 18/1990, de 17 de diciembre, sobre reforma del Código Civil en materia de nacionalidad*, Revista Jurídica de Castilla-La Mancha, 1991, 169.

15. S. Sánchez Lorenzo, *La aplicación de los Convenios de la Conferencia de La Haya de Derecho internacional privado a los conflictos de leyes internos: perspectiva española*, REDI, 1993, 131.

*17.* The number of international conventions in force in Spain affects all PIL sectors. This is an important factor for several reasons. First, international conventions have resulted in a notable modernization of Spanish PIL. Second, it is necessary to emphasize that, according to the Spanish Constitution (Article 96.1), treaty rules have superior hierarchy. This means that in the Spanish PIL system, rules elaborated by the Spanish legislator only are to be applied where there is no applicable conventional rule in force in Spain.

*18.* There are many international conventions in force in Spain relating to choice of law and international civil procedure. The following deserve special mention:[16]

**Multilateral**

*United Nations*

- 1948 Universal Declaration on Human Rights (Article 10.2 Spanish Constitution).
- 1956 New York Convention on Getting Maintenance Abroad (BOE, 24 November 1966).
- 1958 New York Convention on the Recognition and Enforcement of Foreign Arbitral Awards (BOE, 11 July 1977).
- 1961 Geneva European Convention on International Commercial Arbitration (BOE, 4 October 1975).
- 1962 New York Convention on Consent to Marriage, Minimum Age for Marriage and Registration of Marriages (BOE, 29 May 1969).
- 1980 Vienna Convention on Contracts for the International Sale of Goods (BOE, 30 January 1991).
- 1989 New York Convention on the Rights of the Child (BOE, 31 December 1990).

*European Union (EU)*

- 1968 Brussels Convention on Jurisdiction and the Enforcement of Judgments in Civil and Commercial Matters (BOE, 28 January 1991; correction, BOE, 30 April 1991). This convention was replaced by the European Regulation No. 44/2001 (Brussels I), now replaced by Regulation 1215/2012 (Brussels I bis) on 10 January 2015.
- 1980 Rome Convention on the Law Applicable to Contractual Obligations (BOE, 19 July 1993). This convention was replaced by the European Regulation 593/2008 of the European Parliament and of the Council on the law applicable to contractual obligations (Rome I).

16. In parentheses, the official publication date in Spain.

*European Union and European Free Trade Association*

– 1988 Lugano Convention on Jurisdiction and the Enforcement of Judgments in Civil and Commercial Matters (BOE, 20 October 1994; correction, BOE, 10 January 1995), replaced by 2007 Lugano bis Convention on jurisdiction and the recognition and enforcement of judgments in civil and commercial matters (OJ, L 339 21 December 2007).

*Hague Conference on Private International Law*

– 1954 Convention related to Civil Procedure (BOE, 13 December 1961).
– 1956 Convention on the law applicable to maintenance obligations towards children (BOE, 12 December 1973).
– 1958 Convention concerning the recognition and enforcement of decisions relating to maintenance obligations towards children (BOE, 6 May 1974).
– 1961 Convention abolishing the Requirement of Legalisation for Foreign Public Documents (BOE, 25 September 1978).
– 1961 Convention concerning the Power of Authorities and the Law Applicable in respect of the Protection of Minors (BOE, 20 August 1987).
– 1961 Convention on the Conflicts of Laws relating to the Form of Testamentary Dispositions (BOE, 17 August 1988).
– 1965 Convention on the Service Abroad of Judicial and Extrajudicial Documents in Civil or Commercial Matters (BOE, 25 August 1987).
– 1970 Convention on the Taking of Evidence Abroad in Civil or Commercial Matters (BOE, 25 August 1987).
– 1971 Convention on the Law Applicable to Traffic Accidents (BOE, 4 November 1987).
– 1973 Convention on the Law Applicable to Products Liability (BOE, 25 January 1989).
– 1973 Convention on the Law Applicable to Maintenance Obligations (BOE, 16 September 1986).
– 1973 Convention on the Recognition and Enforcement of Decisions relating to Maintenance Obligations (BOE, 12 August 1987; correction, BOE, 25 November 1987).
– 1980 Convention on International Access to Justice (BOE, 30 March 1988; correction, BOE, 11 April 1989).
– 1980 Convention on the Civil Aspects of International Child Abduction (BOE, 24 August 1987; correction, BOE, 30 June 1989).
– 1993 Convention on Protection of Children and Co-operation in respect of Intercountry Adoption (BOE, 1 August 1995).
– 1996 Convention on Jurisdiction, Applicable Law, Recognition, Enforcement and Co-operation in Respect of Parental Responsibility and Measures for the Protection of Children (BOE, 2 December 2010).

- 2005 Convention on Choice of Court Agreements (OJ, L 133 22 May 2009 and L 353, 10 December 2014).[17]
- 2007 Protocol on the Law Applicable to Maintenance Obligations (OJ, L 331, 16 December 2009).
- 2007 Convention on the International Recovery of Child Support and Other Forms of Family Maintenance (OJ, L 192, 22 July 2011).

*Council of Europe*

- 1950 Convention for the Protection of Human Rights and Fundamental Freedoms (BOE, 10 October 1979).
- 1968 London European Convention on Information on Foreign Law (BOE, 7 October 1974); 1978 Protocol (BOE, 24 June 1982).
- 1977 Strasbourg European Agreement on the Transmission of Applications for Legal Aid (BOE, 21 December 1985).
- 1980 Luxembourg European Convention on Recognition and Enforcement of Decisions concerning Custody of Children and on Restoration of Custody of Children (BOE, 1 September 1984).
- 2008 Strasbourg European Convention on the Adoption of Children – revised – (BOE, 13 July 2011).

*International Commission on Civil Status*

- 1958 Istanbul Convention on the International Exchange of Information relating Civil Status (BOE, 21 July 1994).
- 1958 Istanbul Convention on Changes of Surnames and Forenames (BOE, 18 January 1987).
- 1961 Rome Convention extending the Competence of Authorities Empowered to Receive Declarations acknowledging Natural Children (BOE, 12 August 1987).
- 1962 Brussels Convention on the Establishment of Maternal Descent of Natural Children (BOE, 18 April 1984).
- 1964 Paris Convention to facilitate the Celebration of Marriages Abroad (BOE, 19 January 1977).
- 1977 Athens Convention on the Exemption from Legalisation of Certain Records and Documents (BOE, 11 May 1981; corrections, BOE, 18 June and 16 July 1981).

17. The Hague Choice of Court Agreement Convention is only applicable by EU member States in relation to Mexico, and only with regard to choice of courts agreements made after its entry into force on 1 Oct. 2015. More ratifications of this Convention are not exactly in the horizon, and therefore the practical relevance of this Convention is quite doubtful, especially if we take into account the long drafting process of the Convention and the long period of time that has been needed for its entry into force, adding up more than two decades. Now it is applicable only because of its ratification by the EU where the Convention will be applied only in relation to the other Contracting State, which is Mexico.

- 1980 Munich Convention on the Law Applicable to Surnames and Forenames (BOE, 19 December 1989).
- 1980 Munich Convention on the Issue of a Certificate of Legal Capacity to Marry (BOE, 16 May 1988).
- 1982 Hague Convention on the Issue of a Certificate of Differing Surnames (BOE, 10 June 1988).
- 1990 Madrid Convention on the Recognition and Updating of Civil Status Booklets (BOE, 27 May 1992).
- 1998 Paris Convention on the Issue of a Life Certificate (BOE, 12 August 2004).
- 1999 Lisbon Convention on the Issue of a Certificate of Nationality (BOE, 9 November 2010).
- 2000 Vienna Convention on the Recognition of Decisions recording a Sex Reassignment (BOE, 11 February 2011).

*Inter-American Specialized Conference on Private International Law (Organization of American States)*

- 1975 Panama Inter-American Convention on Letters Rogatory (BOE, 15 August 1987).
- 1979 Montevideo Convention on Proof and Information of Foreign Law (BOE, 13 January 1988).

**Bilateral**

- 1896 Convention with Switzerland (judgments enforcement in civil and commercial matters) (*Gaceta de Madrid*, 9 July 1898).
- 1908 Convention with Colombia (civil judgments enforcement) (*Gaceta de Madrid*, 18 April 1909).
- 1929 with the United Kingdom (legal co-operation in civil and commercial matters) (*Gaceta de Madrid*, 10 April 1930).
- 1969 Convention with France (judgments recognition in civil and commercial matters) (BOE, 14 March 1970).
- 1973 Convention with Italy (legal co-operation and judgments recognition in civil and commercial matters) (BOE, 15 November 1977).
- 1983 Convention with Germany (recognition and enforcement of judgments in civil and commercial matters) (BOE, 16 February 1988).
- 1984 Convention with Austria (recognition and enforcement of judgments in civil and commercial matters) (BOE, 29 August 1985).
- 1987 Convention with Czechoslovakia, now Czech Republic and Slovak Republic (legal co-operation, and recognition and enforcement of judgments in civil and commercial matters) (BOE, 3 December 1988; correction, BOE, 26 January 1989).
- 1987 Convention with Uruguay (law applicable, jurisdiction, and recognition and enforcement of judgments of maintenance obligations) (BOE, 5 February 1992).

- 1987 Convention with Uruguay (legal co-operation, and recognition and enforcement of judgments in civil and commercial matters) (BOE, 30 April 1998).
- 1989 Convention with Mexico (recognition and enforcement of judgments in civil and commercial matters) (BOE, 9 April 1991; corrections, BOE, 6 May and 20 September 1991).
- 1989 Convention with Israel (recognition and enforcement of judgments in civil and commercial matters) (BOE, 3 January 1991; correction, 23 January 1991).
- 1989 Convention with Brazil (legal co-operation, and recognition and enforcement of judgments in civil, commercial, labour, and administrative matters) (BOE, 10 July 1991; correction, BOE, 13 August 1991).
- 1990 Convention with the USSR, now with Russia (legal co-operation, and recognition and enforcement of judgments in civil and commercial matters) (BOE, 25 June 1997).
- 1992 Convention with China (legal co-operation, and recognition and enforcement of judgments in civil and commercial matters) (BOE, 31 January 1994; correction, BOE, 11 March 1994).
- 1993 Convention with Bulgaria (legal co-operation, and recognition and enforcement of judgments in civil and commercial matters) (BOE, 30 June 1994).
- 1997 Convention with Morocco (legal co-operation, and recognition and enforcement of judgments in civil, commercial, and administrative matters) (BOE, 25 June 1997).
- 1997 Convention with Morocco (legal co-operation, and recognition and enforcement in matters relatives to minors) (BOE, 24 June 1997).
- 1997 Convention with Rumania (jurisdiction, and recognition and enforcement in civil and commercial matters) (BOE, 5 June 1999).
- 1997 Convention with Portugal (legal co-operation in criminal and civil matters) (BOE, 21 January 1999).
- 1998 Convention with Thailand (legal co-operation in civil and commercial matters) (BOE, 7 May 1999).
- 2000 Convention with El Salvador (jurisdiction, and recognition and enforcement in civil and commercial matters) (BOE, 25 October 2001).
- 2001 Convention with Tunisia (legal co-operation, and recognition and enforcement in civil and commercial matters) (BOE, 1 March 2003).
- 2003 Convention with Dominican Republic (legal co-operation in civil and commercial matters) (BOE, 23 October 2003).
- 2005 Convention with Algeria (legal co-operation in civil and commercial matters) (BOE, 1 May 2005).
- 2006 Convention with Mauritania (legal co-operation in civil and commercial matters) (BOE, 8 November 2006).

## §3. EU Law

*19.* Even more important than international conventions is the great influence that EU Law has on the Spanish PIL system. It is a well-known principle that EU Law Regulations have supremacy over the legal sources of the Member States and must be given direct effect.[18] This supremacy affects both international and national rules in force in every EU Member State. This means that where EU Law Regulations are to be applied, neither treaties nor statutory rules can be applied. Originally, there were not too many EU rules on PIL, apart from some isolated rules in EU Directives, especially in consumer, insurance, travel and multi-property matters. Common problems were mostly related with the necessary coordination between the latter rules and the PIL conventions in force in the EU Member States (1968 Brussels and 1980 Rome Conventions).[19] This situation totally changed when Article 65 of the EC Treaty was enacted by the Amsterdam Treaty of 2 October 1997 (it entered into force on 1 May 1999), later replaced with minor alterations by Article 81 of the Treaty on the Functioning of the EU as a result of the Lisbon Treaty. Since then, the EU has had the power to elaborate both PIL and international civil procedure rules. Upon this new basis, the EU has already approved several Regulations.[20]

Most of them are in force in all EU Member States, except Denmark.[21] However, the Successions Regulation 650/2012 does not apply, in addition to Denmark, to

18. ECJ 15 Jul. 1964 (Case 6/64: *Costa v. ENEL*).
19. E. Jayme & Ch. Kohler, *L'interaction des règles de conflit contenues dans le droit derivé de la Communauté européenne et des conventions de Bruxelles et de Rome*, Rev.crit.dr.int.pr., 1995, 1.
20. Council Regulations:

- 1346/2000 on insolvency proceedings; to be replaced in 2017 by Regulation 848/2015.
- 1393/2007 on the service in the Member States of judicial and extrajudicial documents in civil or commercial matters (service of documents), repealing Regulation (EC) No 1348/2000.
- 44/2001 on jurisdiction and the recognition and enforcement of judgments in civil and commercial matters (Brussels I); now replaced by Regulation 1215/2012 (Brussels I bis).
- 1206/2001 on co-operation between the courts of the Member States in the taking of evidence in civil or commercial matters
- 2201/2003 concerning jurisdiction and the recognition and enforcement of judgments in matrimonial matters and the matters of parental responsibility (Brussels II), repealing Regulation (EC) No 1347/2000.
- 805/2004 creating a European Enforcement Order for uncontested claims.
- 1896/2006 creating a European order for payment procedure.
- 861/2007 establishing a European Small Claims Procedure.
- 864/2007 on the law applicable to non-contractual obligations (Rome II).
- 593/2008 on the law applicable to contractual obligations (Rome I).
- 4/2009 on Jurisdiction, Applicable Law and Recognition and Enforcement of Foreign Judgments on Maintenance Obligations (Brussels III).
- 1259/2010 on the law applicable to divorce and judicial separation (Rome III).
- 650/2012 on Jurisdiction, Applicable Law and Recognition and Enforcement of decisions and acceptance and enforcement of authentic instruments in matters of succession and on the creation of a European Certificate of Succession.
- 1215/2012 on Jurisdiction and the recognition and enforcement of judgments in civil and commercial matters (recast).
- 655/2014 establishing a European Account Preservation Order procedure (in force in January 2017).

21. Nevertheless, Denmark has concluded two agreements with the EC on 19 Oct. 2005 (entered in force on 1 Jul. 2007) in order to apply Regulations 44/2001 and 1348/2000 (on recognition and enforcement of judgments in civil, and commercial matters and service of judicial and extrajudicial documents in civil or commercial matters).

Ireland and the United Kingdom, and Regulation 1259/2010 (Rome III) only applies to the States that participate in that specific enhanced co-operation mechanism.[22]

*20.* The legal force of an increasingly comprehensive substantive EU Law does not eliminate the need for the development of a common body of PIL laws that traditionally came from treaties but are now channelled through EU secondary legislation by means of Article 81 of the TFEU. These EU PIL rules have a strong influence on national PIL law.[23] It could be argued that, as harmonization of the substantive law of the EC legislation advances, there will be less need for a legal discipline that takes the existence of different legislations as its most basic presumption. However, since the end of such legal substantial diversity is not yet envisioned, it is not yet the time to say that conflict of laws rules are irrelevant. Quite on the contrary, the EU is advancing rapidly towards an EU PIL system.[24] Among the signals of this process, the most conclusive are:

(1) The always increasing number of PIL regulations which eliminate the possibility of application of national PIL rules; and
(2) Some clear, though controversial, ECJ decisions expanding the scope of application of EU PIL rules.[25]

## §4. Case Law

*21.* Spain's incorporation into the international community cannot only be evidenced by the number of international conventions to which it is now a contracting State, but also by the growing number of PIL cases that have been decided by Spanish courts. It can be said that, even if the Spanish legal system (as is general in all civil law systems) prefers legislation, instead of case law, jurisprudence on PIL issues has reached an important role. Particularly, this is the case of the decisions of the highest courts: the Supreme Court (*Tribunal Supremo*) and the Constitutional Court (*Tribunal Constitucional*).[26] It should be taken into consideration that decisions by lower courts going against the doctrine established by the Supreme Court can be annulled by appeal courts and eventually (*recurso de casación*) by the Supreme Court itself. Insofar as the European Court of Justice is competent to interpret EU Law, its jurisprudence must be taken into account when EU PIL rules are to be applied.

22. Until now, they are: Belgium, Bulgaria, Germany, Spain, France, Greece, Italy, Latvia, Lithuania, Luxembourg, Hungary, Malta, Austria, Portugal, Romania and Slovenia.
23. See, ad ex., Art. 2 1980 Rome Convention, and Arts. 6 and 7 Regulation 2201/2003.
24. H. Gaudemet-Tallon, *Quel droit international privé pour l'Union Européenne?*, in *International Conflict of Laws for the Third Millennium. Essays in Honor of Friedrich K. Juenger* (Ardsley, Transnational Publishers, 2001), 317, 329–338.
25. See ECJ, 1 Mar. 2005, aff. 281/02 *Owusu*, and EJC, 7 Feb. 2006, avis 1/03, *Competence of the Community to Conclude the New Lugano Convention*. See also M. Wilderspin & A.-M. Rouchaud-Joët, *La compétence externe de la Communauté européenne en droit international privé*, Rev.crit.dr.int.pr., 2004, 1.
26. The Spanish jurisprudence on PIL, well systematized, is easily available at REDI (published twice a year) and, since 2000, also at AEDIPr (published once a year).

## §5. Public International Law

*22.* Public International Law has a strong influence on PIL issues. The number of international conventions in force in Spain requires an effective application of the rules and techniques of Public International Law, especially those in relation to the law of treaties. Moreover, international conventions on Human Rights are extremely important in the elaboration and application of PIL rules.[27] Article 10 Spanish Constitution clearly determines that:

> The rules related to the fundamental rights and freedoms recognised by the Constitution will be interpreted in accordance with the Universal Declaration of Human Rights and the international treaties and agreements on the same matters ratified by Spain.[28]

*23.* Another relevant issue is the sovereign immunity of States. Particularly immunity plays a role as a limitation to the exercise of jurisdiction. Article 21.2 of the Judicial Power Act LOPJ, 1985 (as redrafted by Law 16/2015) establishes, as an exception to the extension of the Spanish jurisdiction, 'the issues on immunity of jurisdiction and enforcement established under Spanish legislation and by Public International Law rules'. Consequently, in order to determine whether immunity exists or not, Spanish judges must apply conventional rules in force (if they exist), Spanish legislation or international custom. With regard to Spanish legislation, only very recently has the matter been codified by the enactment of a new Act, Law 16/2015, 27 October, on Privileges and Immunities of Foreign States, International Organizations and Conferences (BOE 28 October 2015) which entered into force on 17 November 2015, following principles of relative immunity of jurisdiction and enforcement. The Constitutional Court has consistently held that a relative immunity from jurisdiction and enforcement[29] is a legitimate limitation to the constitutional right of access to justice (Article 24.1 of the Spanish Constitution), as long as it conforms to these principles: sovereign equality of States, international pacific co-operation and reciprocity.[30]

---

27. See, in general, A. Sáiz Arnaiz, *La apertura constitucional al Derecho internacional y europeo de los derechos humanos. El artículo 10.2 de la Constitución Española* (Madrid: Consejo General del Poder Judicial, 1999); J.L. Requejo Pagés, *Sistemas normativos, Constitución y ordenamiento* (McGraw-Hill 1995).
28. Among these, the most important is the 1950 European Convention for the Protection of Human Rights and Fundamental Freedoms (BOE, 10 Oct. 1979). According to the Spanish Constitutional Court, the jurisprudence elaborated by the European Court of Human Rights is an essential interpretative parameter to the Spanish Constitution (Judgment 114/1984).
29. Judgments of TC 140/1995 (jurisdiction immunity), and 107/1992 and 292/1994 (enforcement immunity). The relative immunity rule, i.e., only with regard to acts *iure imperii* and not in relation to acts performed according to private law rules can be seen in Judgments by the Supreme Court, 25 Jun 2012, TSJ Madrid 5 May 2008, and TSJ Cataluña 25 Jun. 2014.
30. See J.D. González Campos, *Competencia Judicial Internacional. Aspectos Generales*, in E. Pérez Vera (ed.), *Derecho internacional privado*, 298–302 (3rd ed., UNED 2001).

§6. DOCTRINE

*24.* During the period in which Spain was practically isolated from the international community (the isolation was almost total from 1945 to 1959, with the exception of military co-operation with the US which started in 1953, but was gradually softened from 1959 to 1975 during the years of the 'Spanish economic miracle' which also meant some degree of economic openness), there were very few PIL cases decided by Spanish courts and the most important legislative enactment occurred only in 1974 (new Preliminary Title to the Civil Code containing Private international law rules in Articles 8–16 CC) All this time, Spanish PIL remained predominantly doctrinal. That is, PIL was a matter treated more in books of a scholarly nature and written mainly for academic or purely theoretical purposes. Moreover, PIL did not achieve an important development because it was considered, until the end of the 1970s, as part (and a small part) of Public International Law Departments in all Spanish Universities. However, in the last three decades, the number of university professors and even lawyers dedicated exclusively to PIL has risen spectacularly and Spanish publications on PIL are as numerous as they are varied, following academic standards similar to those in France, Italy, UK or Germany, the EU countries with which Spanish academia is more acquainted. The main PIL printed journals in Spain are *Revista Española de Derecho Internacional* (REDI) and *Anuario español de Derecho internacional privado español* (AEDIPR), while the main online journals are *Cuadernos de Derecho Transnacional* (www.uc3m.es/cdt) y la *Revista electrónica de Estudios internacionales* (www.reei.org).

# Chapter 2. Connection

## §1. Choice-of-Law Rules

### I. Multilateral/Unilateral Conflict Rules

*25.* Codified conflict of laws rules are the basis of Spanish PIL. Most of them are multilateral. This is clearly visible in the rules at Articles 9, 10 and 11 CC. As it is well known, the multilateral conflict of laws rules do not give a direct or material solution to the PIL issue but just an indication as to which (national, in principle) legal order must be applied. The result of this mechanism is that the legal system designated by the connecting factor (*lex causae*) can be, in principle, any legal system in the world. In contrast, unilateral conflict of laws rules do not treat all legal systems equally, because their only concern is the determination of the circumstances under which the *lex fori* is to be applied.

*26.* Within the Spanish PIL system, one may also find examples of laws that follow the 'direct' approach, rather than an 'indirect' or choice-of-law method. Scholars have distinguished between imperative substantive rules and special substantive rules. Imperative substantive rules affect matters considered of the utmost importance and are characterized as public policy of the State legislator (political, economic, social and cultural matters); therefore, these rules must be applied whatever the circumstances of the specific case (Article 8.1 CC).

*27.* Special substantive rules contain specific material solutions for PIL law cases. These rules can be truly international (not only according to its purpose, but also to its source) if they are contained in a treaty (as in the 1980 Vienna Convention on Contracts for the International Sale of Goods), but they also may appear as national legislation. In the Spanish legal system, we can take, as an example, the second paragraph of Article 135 of the Bills of Exchange and Cheques Act 1985 (*Ley cambiaria y del cheque*), which establishes a period of presentation for foreign cheques to be paid in Spain (twenty days for those drawn in Europe and sixty days for those drawn outside Europe).

### II. Elements of a Rule

*28.* As it happens in any other legal rule, typical multilateral conflicts rules are made up of two parts: a legal category and a legal consequence. The nexus between these parts is carried out by the connecting factor. Better said, the applicable law (legal consequence) for the PIL situation (legal category) will be the law of the country where the connecting factor is located. The following example, taken from the Spanish PIL system, may give us an explanation:

> Article 9.8 CC: Succession to the estate of deceased persons is governed by the national law of the deceased …

*29.* In this multilateral conflict of laws rule, we can identify the legal category (succession to the estate), the connecting factor (nationality of the deceased) and the applicable law (*lex causae*) as indicated by the connecting factor (law of the country of the decedent's nationality).

## III. Legal Consequences

*30. Conflict of laws rules may lead to the application of a foreign legal order as lex causae.* Indeed, it is widely known that a unique characteristic of the multilateral conflicts rule is that, in principle, it treats all legal systems equally: principle of equality between *lex fori* and the foreign *lex causae*. Nevertheless, the way in which foreign law can be applied in Spain has always been, and continues to be, troublesome.

*31.* The main problem here is a kind of indecision on the part of the Spanish legislator about whether or not the applicable foreign law determined by the Spanish conflicts rules must be applied by the court of its own motion. As it is provided in Article 12.6 CC: 'The courts and authorities will apply of their own motion the conflicts rules of the Spanish law.'

*32.* This statement clearly establishes the imperative character of the Spanish conflict of laws rules. However, when a foreign law, instead of the lex fori, must be applied, this clearness suddenly vanishes, because Spanish procedural rules require the parties' allegation and proof of the content of such foreign law. Thus, although it may seem contradictory, the conflicts of law rules are imperative but Spanish courts cannot apply the foreign applicable law of their own motion. In fact, the Spanish Civil Procedure Act (LEC) of 2000 expressly requires proof of the foreign law by the parties, in Article 281.2:

> The foreign law shall be proved with respect to its contents and operation and the court may use as many means of verification as it deems necessary for its application.[31]

*33.* Article 282 LEC sets forth that:

> All evidence shall be presented by the parties. Nevertheless, the court may of its own motion permit that certain evidence be presented or that certain documents be obtained, as may also other opinions or means of proof, when the law permits.

---

31. This rule replaces the second paragraph of Art. 12.6 CC, which also required the invocation and proof of the foreign law. On the former situation, see F.J. Garcimartín Alférez, *Sobre la norma de conflicto y su aplicación procesal* (Tecnos 1994).

*34.* Spanish courts have generally required the parties to invoke and prove foreign law. The contents of Articles 281.2 and 282 of the LEC do not allow us to predict a fundamental change in this attitude, especially because it is not clear in what cases the court may apply foreign law of its own motion.[32] The new 2015 Act on International judicial co-operation in civil matters includes in Article 33 a restatement of what up to this moment has been the practice of the Spanish Courts under LEC 2000 and therefore the new Act has been a lost opportunity, since no significant change has been introduced.

*34.1.* The Spanish Constitutional Court has not acted decisively on this issue, since it has just stated that Spanish judges and courts cannot validly reject a claim in cases where the parties have not effectively proven the applicable foreign law, *lex fori* being applicable in that case as a last resort solution.[33] Until now, the Constitutional Court has affirmed that the parties' invocation and proof of foreign law is just an ordinary legal question without any constitutional relevance.[34] Nonetheless, if a litigant tries to prove the applicable foreign law without success, the court may act concurringly in order to arrive ex officio at a complete proof of the foreign applicable law; otherwise, the non-intervention of the court would infringe the litigant's right to an effective access to justice.[35] In addition, the Constitutional Court is less demanding than the Supreme Court when dealing with the requirements of proof of foreign law by the parties, admitting just a sufficient proof, instead of the rigorous evidence standards that the Supreme Court often imposes.[36]

*34.2.* Indeed, the Spanish Supreme Court has been traditionally reluctant to apply foreign law as true law even if it is so established by Spanish conflict rules.[37] Habitually, the Supreme Court has applied Spanish law whenever the parties do not invoke nor prove the applicable foreign law according to the Spanish conflicts rules.[38]

---

32. See A.L. Calvo Caravaca & J. Carrascosa González, *Aplicación del Derecho extranjero en España y la nueva Ley de enjuiciamiento civil*, 1155 (Tribunales de Justicia, Nov. 2000); A.L. Calvo Caravaca & J. Carrascosa González, *The Proof of Foreign Law in the New Spanish Civil Procedure Code 1/2000*, 170 (IPrax 2005–2); A.L. Calvo Caravaca & J. Carrascosa González, *El Tribunal Constitucional y el Tribunal Supremo ante la falta de alegación y prueba del Derecho extranjero (en torno a la STS, Social, de 4 de noviembre de 2004)*, La Ley, No. 6238, 2005, 1; S. Álvarez González, *La aplicación judicial del Derecho extranjero bajo la lupa constitucional*, 205–223 (REDI 2002); S. Álvarez González, *Aplicación judicial del Derecho extranjero: la desconcertante práctica judicial, los estériles esfuerzos doctrinales y la necesaria reforma legislativa*, La Ley, No. 6287, 2005.
33. Judgments of TC 10/2000 and 33/2002.
34. Judgment of TC 29/2004.
35. Judgment of TC 10/2000.
36. Judgment of TC 172/2004.
37. Some exceptions may be found in some Judgments of TS (civil chamber): 23 Mar. 2010 and 24 Jun. 2010.
38. See Judgments of TS (civil chamber) of 4 Jul. 2007, 27 Dec. 2006, or 30 Apr. 2008.

§2. CONNECTING FACTOR

## I. Nationality

*35.* The main personal connecting factors used by the Spanish system of conflict of laws are nationality and residence, while domicile is only relevant for rules on international jurisdiction.[39]

*36.* With respect to nationality as a connecting factor, situations of double nationality are governed by Article 9.9 CC (positive conflicts of nationality) stating the preference for the law of the nationality that coincides with the law of the last habitual residence, and in absence of that, the law of the last nationality is to be applied. However, that rule only applies to situations of double nationality that arise under bilateral conventions in force in Spain or that are contemplated by Spanish law in Article 24 CC, which refer to Spaniards who acquire the nationality of Iberian-American countries, Andorra, The Philippines, Portugal or Equatorial Guinea, and vice versa.[40] If the double nationality is not recognized under those rules and one of them is Spanish, Spanish nationality will always prevail as the connecting factor.[41] If the situation of double nationality involves two foreign nationalities none of which is the Spanish nationality, the law of habitual residence will be applied. In situations of lack of nationality or impossibility to determine nationality (negative conflicts), the law of the place of habitual residence will be applied (Article 9.10 CC).[42]

## II. Habitual Residence

*37.* Residence or habitual residence are factual situations of presence or regular presence in a certain country, and are not governed by any specific provision in Spanish law. On the contrary, domicile of natural persons is a legal concept defined in Article 40 CC, which establishes a concept equal to that of habitual residence, but case law adds the requirement of a second element: permanence based on an intention to stay indefinitely (*animus manendi*); other specific additional criteria for determination of domicile for procedural issues are regulated in Articles 50–52 LEC.

39. See P. Maestre Casas, *Doble nacionalidad y forum patriae en divorcios internacionales*, CDT, Vol. 2, nº 2, 2010, 290-304. http://www.uc3m.es/cdt.

40. For a case on double nationality (Venezuelan and Spanish) and the determination of the applicable law in matters of succession, see Judgment of SAP of Pontevedra 27/2013, 15 Jan 2013.

41. M. Virgós Soriano, *Nationality and Double Nationality: Principles in the Spanish Private International Law System*, in *Nation und Staat im internationalem Privatrecht*, 237 (E. Jayme & H.P. Mansel eds, Müller 1990); P. Rodríguez Mateos, *La doble nacionalidad en la sistemática del Derecho internacional privado*, 463 (REDI 1990); E. Cano Bazaga, *El sistema español de doble nacionalidad*, in *El Derecho español y europeo, Derecho civil a 200 años del Código de Napoleón*, 641 (J.L. Collantes González & F. Serrano Migallón eds, Porrua/UNAM 2005).

42. For a case of non-determined nationality, see Judgment of SAP of Granada 723/2004, 15 Dec. 2004.

*38.* Even if it is commonly said that the Spanish conflict of laws system is based on the nationality principle and that this has been so because of the influence of the Italian Civil Codes of 1865 and 1942, the successive reforms of the Preliminary Title of the CC have combined this dominating principle with numerous references to habitual residence or have changed the main connecting factor from nationality to habitual residence (Article 9.4 and 9.6 CC as the result of the Law 26/2015 on the Protection of Infancy and Adolescence). It must also be taken into consideration that international treaties dealing with choice-of-law rules in force in Spain normally use habitual residence as a connecting factor, and that the existing and future EU PIL Regulations also use predominantly habitual residence, what will diminish the importance of nationality as a connecting factor to a very small number of cases.[43]

## III. *Lex Rei Sitae*

*39.* In the Spanish PIL system, *lex rei sitae* applies to conflicts issues related to both immovable and movable property (Article 10.1 CC). With respect to immovable property, this solution allows the Spanish court with exclusive jurisdiction over immovable property located in Spain (Article 24 Regulation 1215/2012) to apply its own law.

## IV. *Lex Loci Actus*

*40.* *Lex loci actus* is just one of the connecting factors regarding formal validity of legal acts such as contracts, marriages, wills, etc. Article 11.1 CC establishes a series of alternative connecting factors, accepting, besides the application of the formal validity requirements of the *lex loci actus*, those required by the law applicable to the merits of the case (*lex causae*), or by the parties' personal law(s), and even those required by the *lex rei sitae* when dealing with real property. As an exception to the application of the different alternative connecting factors, Article 11.2 CC sets out that if the law applicable to the merits of the case requires a solemn form or public instrument this requirement must be satisfied.[44] It is important to take into

43. See A. Rodríguez Benot, *El criterio de conexión para determinar la ley personal: un renovado debate en Derecho internacional privado,* CDT, Vol. 2, nº 1, 2010, 186–202. http://www.uc3m.es/cdt. A.L. Calvo Caravaca, *El Derecho internacional privado multicultural y el revival de la ley personal,* Diario La Ley, No. 7847, 22 Apr. 2012.

44. Judgment AP of Santa Cruz de Tenerife, No. 391/2006, 22 November, overruling Resolution of the DGRN 7 Feb. 2005, has admitted the registration of a public instrument made abroad by a German notary with regard to the sale of property in Spain. Judgment TS 19 Jun. 2012, and Resolutions DGRN 22 Nov 2013 and 23 Feb. 2015, have reaffirmed the the validity of foreign public instruments in Spain in accordance with PIL rules, provided that the foreign public instrument is functionally equivalent to a Spanish public instrument. The solution has now been embodied in Art. 60 Law 29/2015 on International Judicial Cooperation in Civil Matters, which governs access to Spanish Registries of foreign public instruments. See B. Añoveros Terradas, *Effects in Spain of a Deed of Sale and Purchase of a Property, Located in Spain, Authorised by a German Notary Public*, vol. 7, 277–282 (Yearbook of Private International Law, 2005); S. Sánchez Lorenzo, *La eficacia registral*

consideration that there are international conventions in force in Spain which include rules as to the law applicable to formal validity: the 1961 Convention on the Conflicts of Laws relating to the Form of Testamentary Dispositions, and Regulation Rome I on the law applicable to contractual obligations both of which have a universal scope of application.

### V. Intention of the Parties

*41.* An essential principle of EU PIL is party autonomy. With regard to contracts, the 1980 Rome Convention allowed the selection of the law applicable by the parties in broad terms (Article 3) and so continues to do Rome I Regulation (Article 3). The 1968 Brussels and 1988 Lugano Conventions (Article 17), and Regulation (EC) 44/2001 (Article 23), now Regulation 1215/2012 (Article 25), have allowed parties to agree that a court or the courts of a Member State (or a contracting State in the case of the Lugano Convention) are to have jurisdiction to settle any disputes which may arise in connection with a particular legal relationship.[45] Brussels and Lugano Conventions (Article 18) and Regulation Brussels I (Article 24), now Regulation 1215/2012 (Article 26), have also established jurisdiction of the court before which a defendant enters an appearance,[46] except when appearance was entered to contest the jurisdiction, or when another court has exclusive jurisdiction.

*42.* Before the incorporation of Spain into the EC (effective 1 January 1986), the Spanish PIL system already had provisions on party autonomy. As to contracts, Article 10.5 CC allowed the selection of the law by the parties to contract, provided the choice was clearly connected with the transaction. More recently, some reforms have given greater opportunities for party autonomy. In family law, the spouses may choose the applicable law to the effects of marriage in an authentic instrument prior to the celebration of marriage (Article 9.2 CC), or choose the applicable law in a matrimonial property agreement (*capitulaciones*) after marriage by reference to the law applicable to the effects of marriage, or to the law of the nationality or residence of any of the spouses at the time of the agreement (Article 9.3 CC).[47]

## §3. Changes in the Connecting Factors; Changes in the *Lex Causae*

*43.* For most legal scholars, the problem posed by the existence of consecutive choice-of-law rules is solved in Spanish PIL with resort to the principle of

---

*de las escrituras públicas de compraventa de inmuebles otorgadas ante notario extranjero a la luz de la doctrina reciente de la DGRN*, La Ley, No. 6425, 2006, 1–14. P. Blanco-Morales, *Del cándido europeísmo al turismo documental: reflexiones a propósito de la inscripción en el registro de la propiedad de una escritura autorizada por notario alemán. Comentario a la sentencia del Pleno de la Sala de lo Civil del Tribunal Supremo de 19 de junio de 2012*, Diario La Ley, nº 7940, 9 Oct. 2012.

45. For insurance, consumer, and employment contracts, party autonomy is also allowed but with restrictions.

46. See also Regulation (EC) No. 2201/2003 on jurisdiction and the recognition and enforcement of judgments in matrimonial matters and parental responsibility (Art. 12).

47. See Arts 9.2 and 9.3 CC (*infra* Ch. 6.2.IV.D).

prohibition of retroactivity (as stated in the first transitory disposition of the Civil Code). Thus, new conflict of laws rules cannot affect the validity or effects of acts or relationships already in existence under the previously applicable choice-of-law rule.[48]

*44.* Another transitory problem is the effect that may be given to a change in the *lex causae*. In order to solve this issue the principle of the integral remission to the *lex causae* may give some guidance, since the reference to the *lex causae* should be understood as a reference to a legal order in its entirety, including any changes that may have occurred in that law after the event or issue to be decided took place,[49] though that reference is of course also extended to the transitory rules of the *lex causae*. Transitory rules of the *lex materialis fori* would only be applicable if the rules of the foreign *lex causae* cannot be ascertained or violate the forum's public policy.[50]

## §4. Combination of Connecting Factors

*45.* Some Spanish conflict of laws rules combine several connecting factors. In some cases, this combination is in a relation of subsidiarity. An example is Article 9.2 CC, which governs the legal effects of marriage. Connecting factors in this rule (common personal law, party autonomy, habitual common residence,and place of the celebration of marriage) apply in a hierarchical order. That means that a connecting factor applies only in cases where the preceding one or preceding ones are non-existent.

*46.* In Article 11.1 CC, however, connecting factors are combined alternatively. Thus, any of the laws mentioned in this general rule may be applied in order to recognize formal validity to a legal act. In other words, the legal act is considered formally valid if it satisfies the requirements of any of those laws. This conflicts rule is inspired by the principle of *favor negotii*, so that the formal validity may be ascertained by reference to any of the laws designated in that article. Article 11.1 CC reads as follows:

---

48. Thus, Judgment TC 39/2002, 14 Feb. 2002, declares that the connecting factor in Art. 9.2 CC prior to its reform in 1990 (which ordered the application of the husband's national law) is against the Spanish Constitution. However, Judgment AP Balearic Island No. 542/2002, 10 Sep. 2002, applies later this connection, in order to determine the matrimonial property regime of a marriage celebrated before the entry into force of the Constitution: '*following strictly the non-retroactivity principle*'. See also Judgments of TS, 11 Feb. 2005, which applies the husband's civil vicinity law, and AP Barcelona 24 Mar. 2009, which applies the husband's Bolivian law to a marriage celebrated before the Constitution entering in force.
49. Judgment AP Girona, 254/2000, does not admit a 'separation by mutual agreement' of two Swiss spouses because this form of separation was not allowed in Switzerland at the time of the spouses' petition, even if they had proved that Swiss law had changed.
50. In Resolution of the DGRN, 10 Mar. 1978, it was held that the transitory rules of Rumanian law, common nationality of the spouses at the time of marriage, were inapplicable because both spouses had been deprived of their nationality before the entry into force of a Rumanian reform of family law that might have been otherwise applicable.

Forms and solemnities of contracts, wills and other acts shall be governed by the law of the state in which they may be granted. Nevertheless, also shall be valid those celebrated according to the forms and solemnities required by the law applicable to its content, as well as those celebrated in conformity with the personal law of the grantor or the common law of the parties. Also valid shall be the acts and contracts relating to immovable property celebrated according to the forms and solemnities of the place where property is situated.

# Chapter 3. Basic Terms

## §1. CHARACTERIZATION

*47.* The Spanish system of conflict of laws adheres to the *lex fori* theory regarding issues of characterization, as expressly stated at Article 12.1 CC: characterization to determine the applicable choice-of-law rule shall be done according to Spanish law.

*48.* Most commentators agree that this solution is only partial. There can be no doubt that Article 12.1 CC deals only with the classification of facts and legal concepts and categories necessary to find and select the appropriate choice-of-law rule applicable to the issue at hand, but once the choice-of-law rule has designated the applicable law to govern the issue, the problem of characterization reappears when trying to identify the material laws of the *lex causae* that may be applied to the case. Therefore, a second rule of classification according to the *lex causae* would be necessary at this stage of the application of the choice-of-law rule.[51]

*49.* Since Spanish courts characterize the issues before them according to their own legal notions, another problem that may be encountered when dealing with issues of characterization is that of legal institutions unknown to the forum. In that case, Article 12.1 CC offers no useful guidance and we should proceed according to functional criteria for the selection of the equivalent institution from a comparative perspective.[52]

## §2. PRELIMINARY QUESTION

*50.* The Spanish system of PIL has no specific rule on this subject. Most scholars agree that the Spanish courts are bound to apply conflicts rules specifically applicable to each preliminary issue, and not the conflicts rules of the *lex causae* or the *lex materialis causae*. This solution conforms to the imperative character of conflict of laws rules in the Spanish PIL system (Article 12.6 CC). However, reported cases of Spanish courts are scarce and not conclusive.[53]

51. See Judgment AP Las Palmas de Gran Canaria, 15 Jan 2013, with regard to a characterization issue in a case involving a gift of immovable property located in Spain as intended advanced devolution of the hereditary estate, and comment by A. Font i Segura, REDI, 2014, 287–292.

52. The *kafala*, for instance, is an Islamic institution which plays a role similar to the Spanish *acogimiento familiar*. Thus, the conflict rule determining the applicable law to the *acogimiento familiar* shall also apply to the *kafala*. See Resolution (*Resolución-circular*) DGRN on recognition and registry of international adoptions on the Spanish Civil Register, of 15 Jul. 2006. RDGRN of 21 Mar. 2006, Judgment of TS, 10 Feb. 2009; Judgment AP Barcelona, 28 Mar. 2006; Judgment AP Cádiz, 11 Dec. 2008; Judgment AP Barcelona, 26 Jul. 2011.

53. See Judgments of TS of: 15 Mar. 1955, 10 Oct. 1960; 29 Sep. 1961; 27 Feb. 1964; and 4 Apr. 1991. AP Tarragona, 23 Jun. 2008.

§3. RENVOI

*51.* Renvoi is admitted only if the result of its application is a remission back to Spanish law (first degree renvoi); therefore, it is to be excluded if it leads to the application of the law of a third State (second degree renvoi). This rule is clearly stated at Article 12.2 CC:

> Remission to a foreign law shall be understood as to its substantial law, without consideration to the renvoi that its choice-of-law rules can make to any other law that is not the Spanish law.

*52.* While most Spanish legal writers oppose renvoi on theoretical and practical considerations, as it is most commonly held in other countries, there is considerable case law applying renvoi, especially in the area of succession and family law. However, renvoi is not automatically admitted by courts and other criteria, such as the respect for the will of the testator or the unity and universality of the succession, may result in the rejection of renvoi, as can be understood from decisions on the law applicable to testamentary succession by the Spanish Supreme Court from 15 November 1996 and 21 May 1999. In the most relevant Spanish Supreme Court decision on the issue, dated 23 September 2002, renvoi has been admitted and consequently led to the annulation of a last will and testament made by an Englishman in Spain following English law. In order to accept renvoi from English PIL rules, according to the Supreme Court, two conditions must be met, first, the deceased should have had his last habitual residence in Spain and, second, all his immovable property must be located in Spain. The rationale of the rule is that only in this way, Spanish law is applicable to the whole estate of the deceased, including all movable and immovable property and wherever located.

*53.* Another area to illustrate the practical relevance of renvoi is that of matrimonial property. It has been observed that Article 12.2 CC generically admits first-degree renvoi, that is, a renvoi that eventually might lead to the application of Spanish law. Case law shows the application of renvoi in cases of marriages of foreign nationals with residence in Spain. This is the case in the decision rendered by the Provincial Court of Malaga (*Audiencia Provincial*), 7 February 1994, that considered an English marriage, subject in principle to an absolute separation of property under English law (which was the law applicable as common personal law of the spouses under Article 9.2 CC), to be governed by the community of property regime of the Spanish Civil Code by way of renvoi, since the spouses had not entered into a matrimonial property agreement and their domicile of choice was Spain; being the intended matrimonial domicile at the time of marriage the connecting factor employed by the English choice-of-law rules on matrimonial property.[54]

*54.* However, the admission of renvoi should not be an automatic consequence of the rule set out in Article 12.2 CC. On the contrary, and far from a merely formal approach to renvoi, the application of renvoi should be sufficiently founded on

54. For a critical commentary on that decision see A. Pérez Voituriez, *REDI*, 1995, 233.

reasons of substantial justice to the parties. In fact, the admission of renvoi results in more inconveniences than benefits to the parties directly concerned. Let us think of the increasing number of married couples from northern Europe that because of tourism purposes or their retirement, choose to relocate in the warmer climate of southern Europe taking up residence in Spain, Portugal or Greece. In such cases, spouses would not be aware that relocation may affect the legal regime applicable to their matrimonial property and it should indeed not be so, especially if this goes against the expectations of the parties. Admission of renvoi can also be contested from the notary public perspective, since renvoi creates uncertainty as to the legal regime under which a Spanish notary may authorize a matrimonial property agreement (*capitulaciones*) concluded in Spain.

*54.1.* More recently, Spanish courts have accepted some kind of a 'functional' or 'substantially oriented' renvoi. This means that the remission made by the foreign choice-of-law rule is accepted by the Spanish legal order where the remission allows a good outcome from a material justice and constitutional law perspective. Thus, for example, in matters of matrimonial capacity, it should be accepted if the Spanish law favours the *ius connubii*.[55]

*55.* There are also two special provisions (exceptions to the general rule of Article 12.2 CC) concerning renvoi in commercial matters: Articles 98 and 162 of the Bills of Exchange and Cheques Act (Act 19/1985, 16 July; BOE, 19 July 1985). According to these conflicts rules on the law applicable to legal capacity to conclude an obligation by means of a bill of exchange or a cheque, renvoi to a third legal system (second degree renvoi) is accepted.

### §4. *Ordre Public* (Public Policy)

*56.* The exclusion of the applicable law in cases where its content is against what may be characterized as public policy in the Spanish legal order is also expressly stated at Article 12.3 CC: 'In no case shall the foreign law be applied if it is contrary to public policy.'

*57.* The determination of those rules and principles of the Spanish law that may be considered as pertaining to public policy and therefore might be used as grounds for a rejection of the foreign applicable law is a difficult question. It is commonly agreed that fundamental rights, values or interests of constitutional relevance according to the Spanish Constitution of 1978 are the core of the public policy exception, but it is a matter of debate and case law development the determination of what other rules may be included within the public policy exception.[56]

---

55. See Resolution (*Resolución-Circular*) of the DGRN on same-sex marriages of 29 Jul. 2005, and Resolution of the DGRN 6/2006, of 1 Jun. 2006.
56. See, as an example, Judgment AP Murcia 166/2003, 12 May 2003 (separation of Moroccan spouses both resident in Spain), and comment by J. Carrascosa González, REDI, 2004, 245–249. See Judgments AP Barcelona, 28 Oct. 2008; AP Madrid, 23 Mar. 2006; AP Guadalajara, 23 Mar. 2996.

*58.* In general, there are not many Spanish court decisions grounded on *ordre public*. Only with regard to family or succession issues where the applicable law is that of a Muslim country we can find significant case law applying the *ordre public* exception (rejection of polygamous marriages or repudiations), but even on these matters Spanish *ordre public* is not very demanding (some polygamous marriages or repudiations that have taken place in a Muslim country can be recognized in Spain if the substantial effect sought is favourable to the woman: enjoyment of public pensions, welfare benefits, damages awards for more than one spouse, recognition of foreign repudiations as a means to facilitate the woman's recovery of matrimonial capacity when her desire is to celebrate a new marriage in Spain, etc.).[57] In patrimonial matters, *ordre public* has been used to avoid the application of foreign laws considered incompatible with a market economy.[58]

## §5. Evasion of the Law

*59.* The relevant rule for evasion of the choice-of-law rule or fraud to the applicable law is included in Article 12.4 CC: 'It shall be considered as fraud to the law the employment of a choice-of-law rule in order to evade an imperative Spanish law.'

*60.* Nevertheless, there are certain issues with regard to evasion of law that are not well regulated by Article 12.4 CC: (a) most importantly, the determination of the consequences of a conduct that can be categorized as evasion of the law under Article 12.4; (b) the evasion of foreign imperative rules, since Article 12.4 CC is only concerned with the evasion of Spanish imperative rules. Article 6 Spanish Civil Code applies to these issues not specifically covered by Article 12.4 CC.

*61.* The foregoing rules should be put into question after proper consideration is given to the existing Spanish case law, since, in most cases, the public policy exception has attracted all cases where the fraud exception would have been applicable, and therefore it can be said that there is scarce authority as to what type of cases

57. See Resolutions of DGRN 11 May 1994, 14 Sep. 1994, 8 Mar. 1995, 5 Nov. 1996, 3 Dec. 1996, 20 Feb. 1997, 14 May 2001, and 30 Sep. 2009. During the last years, some Spanish courts have started to apply, when dealing with the so-called collateral effects of polygamy, a softer notion of *ordre public* in matters such as social security widow's pension, accident damages awards, and succession, making it possible that a number of female spouses might benefit from a right that in principle should only be recognized to the first wife. See Judgments TSJ Galicia 2 Apr. 2002, and TSJ Madrid 456/2002, 29 Jul. 2002 and M. Checa Martínez. *Reconocimiento de la poligamia y del repudio islamicos en perspectiva comparada: a proposito de la mudawwana marroquí*, 245–287 (J.V. Gavidia Sánchez (dir.), Marcial Pons 2011), Nevertheless, other decisions following this soft doctrine (Judgments of the Social Court No. 6 of Barcelona, of 10 Oct. 2001, and Social Court No. 5 of Alicante, of 14 Jan. 2005) were reversed by the Judgments of the TSJ Catalonia 5255/2003, of 30 Jul. 2003, and TSJ Comunidad Valenciana 1821/2005, of 6 Jun. 2005, respectively; both TSJ Catalonia and TSJ Comunidad Valenciana applied the traditional (hard) doctrine of the *ordre public*. Other examples of the application of hard doctrine are Judgments TS of 26 Feb. 2010 and 19 Dec. 2011 (rejecting nationality by polygamy).
58. Judgments of AP Madrid, 27 Jan. 1990; TS, 25 Sep. 1992.

would fall under the scope of Article 12.4 CC.[59] Only quite recently, the Supreme Court (Decisions 5 April 1994, and 14 September 2009) has resorted to the fraud exception in cases of interregional conflict of laws where testators have taken civil vicinity in another *Comunidad Autonoma* with the sole purpose of avoiding the forced heirship provisions of the law of a former civil vicinity.

## §6. Remission to a Multiple Legal Order

*62.* In the event that a Spanish choice-of-law rule designates the law of a State where there are different territories with their own legal system for civil matters (e.g., United Kingdom, Canada, United States of America, Australia, etc.), the application of the choice-of-law rule needs additional criteria to single out a concrete applicable law. To that effect, Article 12.5 CC reads as follows:

> Where a choice-of-law rule designates the law of a state in which different legal system coexist, the determination of the applicable law among them shall be made according to the law of that state.

*63.* This rule adopts the criterion of indirect remission: the connecting factors employed by the Spanish choice-of-law rules cannot be directly applied to the different legal orders that coexist in a State with multiple legal orders. Instead, the remission to a complex legal system raises a second choice-of-law process that must be solved according to the conflict of laws rules of that State which are applicable to interstate or interregional conflicts of laws. This indirect solution, although theoretically correct, can be severely criticized since, in most cases, in those States with multiple legal orders there are no common, federal or unitary interstate or interregional choice-of-law rules (this is the case in the USA or the UK), which renders the solution included in Article 12.5 CC useless. Therefore, Spanish case law has tried to solve the issue by the direct application of the Spanish conflict of laws rules whenever it is possible to do so. The direct application of the connecting factor based on nationality poses additional difficulties, because in this case no direct application is possible to the law of a particular state and consequently nationality should be replaced by the state of the person's last domicile or habitual residence.

59. J.C. Fernández Rozas & S. Sánchez Lorenzo, *Derecho internacional privado*, 139–141 (8th ed., Thomson-Civitas 2015).

# Part II. Rules of Choice of Law

## Chapter 1. Persons

### §1. Natural Persons

#### I. Legal Capacity

*64.* Legal capacity is one of the institutions included in the so-called matters of personal status, which include those legal institutions that establish the legal condition of an individual. The Spanish legal system offers a wide concept of personal status, as it includes issues related to capacity of individuals, birth, extinction of personality, and legal rights inherent to personality. This also includes family rights, obligations and succession by death. It should be noted that the protection of personality rights (right to life, personal and family honour, physical integrity, personal intimacy) is also recognized beyond the conflicts method, since those are fundamental rights with international and constitutional protection.

*65.* According to Article 9.1 CC:

> The personal law which corresponds to natural persons is determined by their nationality. This law governs capacity and civil status, family rights and obligations and succession by death.

*66.* Capacity is governed by the personal law of natural persons, which in Spanish law is determined by nationality. This solution refers to capacity in a generic way, which makes it difficult to determine whether within its scope we can include not only the general capacity of a person but also special capacity requirements for the performance of certain legal acts. The majority opinion is that the law of nationality governs all capacities. The law of nationality determines legal capacity (entitlement to rights and obligations), as well as capacity to act (to execute legal acts). Therefore, the Spanish legal system does not follow the common law rule which states that special capacity requirements for the execution of certain acts are governed by the *lex causae*. In Spanish PIL, the national law of a natural person is always the law applicable to issues of capacity to execute legal acts and not the *lex rectori acto*.[60]

*67.* For instance, the consequences of marriage upon the name of the spouses or their contractual capacity or, in more general terms, upon their legal capacity to act, are issues outside the scope of the law applicable to the matrimonial regime. Such issues will be solved according to the personal law determined by Article 9.1 CC and therefore to the law of the nationality of the spouse whose name or legal capacity to act may be subject to change as a result of marriage. Nevertheless, if the wife's contractual capacity is denied or diminished as a consequence of this rule, resort to the public policy exception may imply the exclusion of any foreign law that introduces unjustified sex discriminations from the Spanish constitutional perspective.

*68.* There are other exceptions to the application of the personal law determined by nationality. One of them is the exception of national interest that allows applying the *lex loci actus* instead of the law of nationality of the parties to the contract (Article 10.8 CC),[61] a rule that has been replaced for most cases by the similar Article 13 of the Rome I Regulation on the law applicable to contractual obligations. Article 10.8 CC lays down that:

> According to the Spanish legal system an onerous contract celebrated in Spain by a foreigner, who is considered incapable pursuant to his national law, shall be valid if the cause of incapacity is not recognised by the Spanish legislation. This rule will not be applied to contracts relating to property situated in a foreign country.

*69.* Another exception has to do with the fact that the Spanish PIL system does not allow the application of foreign laws that are against Spanish public policy (Article 12.3 CC). For instance, laws establishing civil death or laws going against the principle of non-discrimination, as it is the case of the laws that establish the incapacity of a married woman, as outlined above.

*70.* The third exception has to do with the doctrine of renvoi. In cases where the *lex causae* uses the domicile as a connecting factor, there could be renvoi if such domicile is situated in Spain (Article 12.2 CC allows a single or first-degree renvoi).

*71.* Another important exception to the law of nationality is to be taken into consideration when dealing with interregional conflict of laws within the Spanish legal order. In such cases nationality is always replaced by civil vicinity or *vecindad civil*, (Article 16.1 CC).

60. See Resolution DGRN, 27 May 1994, about capacity to join in matrimony that recognizes the capacity of a 15-year-old Moroccan woman to marry a man according to her national law; Resolution DGRN, 16 Mar. 2007, about capacity to join in matrimony; Resolution DGRN, 27 Mar. 2007.

61. See A.L. Calvo Caravaca, *La doctrina del interés nacional y su ámbito espacial de aplicación*, ADC, 1991, 85.

*72.* The same connection, i.e., the law of the person's nationality, governs special situations of incapacity of natural persons. Limitations on capacity are a matter reserved for statutory law. Declarations of absence or death are also under the national law rule. Incapacitation of adults has also been governed by the person's national law, which is sociologically of some importance in Spain because elderly people from other European countries take residential homes as retirees and their eventual incapacitation would be governed not by Spanish law but by their personal law. Unfortunately, Spain has not ratified the Hague Convention on the protection of adults. However, the result of the recent amendment to Article 9.6 CC (Act on the system of protection of infancy and adolescence 2015) has been the inclusion of a new paragraph dealing the protection of adult people which refers the issue to the application of the law of habitual residence.

Second paragraph in Article 9.1 CC governs the effects of a change of nationality when this mobile conflict might have as a result the loss of the legal capacity acquired under another personal law: 'The change of personal law will not affect the full legal age acquired in conformity with a previous personal law.'

## II. Name

*73.* 'Name' is to be included under the category of personal status, but it is the only right of personality specifically submitted to special conflicts solutions.[62] Of course, PIL issues regarding the law applicable to names and surnames arise in connection with their registration, i.e., at birth or registration of other legal acts such as adoption, marriage or nationality. Civil Register Regulation sets out the rule that 'the name and the surname of a foreign person are governed by his personal law' (Article 219 RRC).

*74.* But, sources on the law applicable to the name of a person are are conventional: 1980 Munich Convention, 5 September, on the Law Applicable to Surnames and Forenames. It is true that Spanish case law traditionally connected name regulation with the individual's national law and systematically ignored the existing conventional law.[63] However, the most recent Spanish case law seems to be more sympathetic to the Munich Convention, giving application to the Convention as a means to make sure that a person only has one name. This does not represent a major change for practical purposes since the main connecting factor in the Munich Convention is also nationality.[64] The Istanbul 1958 convention on change of names and surnames is also applicable in Spain but only with regard to a very limited number of States: Germany, Austria, France, Italy, Luxembourg, Netherlands, Portugal and Turkey.

62. See J.J. Forner Delaygua, *Nombres y apellidos. Normativa interna e internacional* (Bosch 1994); A. Lara Aguado, *El nombre en el Derecho internacional privado* (Comares 1998).
63. Resolutions DGRN, 20 Jan. 1997; 1 Feb. 2006.
64. Resolutions DGRN: (3rd), 7 Dec. 1999; (1st), 5 Apr. 2000; (7th), 16 Sep. 2002.

When a foreign individual acquires Spanish nationality, there is a procedure to adapt the name to the Spanish law, as the 'new personal law',[65] but a voluntary declaration in order to maintain the original surnames in conformity with the previous applicable national law is permitted (Articles 199 and 213 RRC, and Article 56 LRC 2011).[66]

*75.* Therefore, the general rule is the nationalization of the person's name. In order to implement the above-said exception in favour of former personal law, the interested party must expressly request so, and the declaration must be made within a certain period, excluding the possibility of extension. In spite of this possibility, the requirement of two surnames has been compulsory, because according to DGRN compliance with this principle is considered a matter of public policy that every Spanish citizen must respect.[67] This two surnames rule does not necessarily imply that the first surname belongs to the father and the second one to the mother, because parents may decide the order of surnames and the individual may file a petition to alter the order of surnames once attained the age of majority. Foreigners who acquire the Spanish nationality and want to keep their surnames of origin according to their former national law can do it,[68] Provided that limitations imposed by Article 54 LRC are observed, foreigners also can keep their names in a foreign language.[69]

*76.* In cases of married women, the rule to be applied is also the personal law, but the Spanish legislation requires additionally the specification at the Civil Registry of the woman's maiden name (Article 137.2 RRC). In addition, birth registration requires the statement of the foreign name in a feminine or masculine gender (Article 200 RRC).[70]

*77.* Sometimes, when an stateless individual acquires the Spanish nationality, the DGRN allows him/her to keep the surnames that he/she 'in fact' had,[71] but in other cases the DGRN has not permitted that, affirming that an stateless individual 'lacks any previous personal law'.[72]

---

65. Resolutions DGRN, 5 Mar. 1997; (3rd) 26 Sep. 2002; (1st), 3 Dec. 2002; (4th), 18 Dec. 2002; (2nd), 10 Sep. 2003; (1st), 11 Feb. 2004; (5th), 20 Jan. 2004; (2nd), 4 Feb. 2005. Nevertheless, although it is imposed to have a name following Spanish law rules, the foreign spelling of the names is respected: Resolution DGRN (1st), 3 Jun. 2003, and 30 Jan. 2009.
66. Resolution DGRN (2nd), 28 Feb. 2005. LRC 2011 shall enter into force on 21 Jul. 2014. See C.L. García Pérez, 'Art. 56: Apellidos con elemento extranjero', *Comentarios a la Ley del Registro Civil* (J.A. Cobacho Gómez and A. Leciñena Ibarra, dirs.), 833–845 (Thomson-Reuters 2012).
67. Resolutions DGRN: 12 Sep. 1996; (2nd), 28 Jul. 2003; (1st), 7 Oct. 2003; (2nd), 11 May 2004; (2nd), 12 May 2004.
68. Resolutions DGRN: (2nd), 3 Jan. 2003; (2nd), 23 Dec. 2002; (2nd), 19 Sep. 2003; (1st), 31 Oct. 2003; (3rd), 16 Jun. 2004; 24 Sep. 2004.
69. Resolutions DGRN: (1st), 21 Apr. 2003; (1st), 14 May 2003; (7th), 27 May 2003.
70. Resolutions DGRN: (1st), 15 Oct. 1998; (3rd), 23 Dec. 2002.
71. Resolution DGRN: (6th), 27 May 2003.
72. Resolutions DGRN: (4th), 28 May 2003; (2nd), 27 Sep. 2003; (3rd), 19 Nov. 2004; (1st), 3 Mar. 2005.

*78.* Case law in the EU (Decisions ECJ 2 October 2003, *Carlos García Avelló*, C-148/2002; 14 October 2008, *Stefan Grunkin*, C-353/06) requires mutual recognition of names and surnames acquired under the law of another Member State of the EU (for reasons of double nationality, birth or residence in another country of the EU). Even if the name or surname of the individual does not comply with local laws, the authorities of the Member State whose rules have not been complied with cannot impose the modification or alteration of a person's name or surname already acquired under the laws of another Member State of the EU, and double nationals may choose between the different personal laws.[73]

## III. Nationality

*79.* Nationality as a connecting factor may require the solution of problems posed by the existence of stateless persons and persons with multiple nationalities.

*80.* In cases of more than one nationality, Article 9.9 CC gives a solution distinguishing between double nationality situations foreseen by Spanish laws and those situations of double nationally that are not regulated by the Spanish laws. Article 9.9 states that:

> To the effects of this chapter, double nationality situations foreseen by Spanish laws will be governed by international treaties, if nothing is established, the nationality that corresponds with the last habitual residence shall be preferred, and in its defect, the last one acquired.
> The Spanish nationality shall prevail over other nationalities that are not foreseen in our laws or in international treaties.

*81.* The rule is only applicable to positive conflicts of nationality, but not for determining a person's nationality (this confusion can be seen in the case that gave rise to the Decision of the European Court of Justice, 7 July 1992, *Micheletti v. the Government Delegation of Cantabria, Spain*).

*82.* Double nationality situations foreseen by Spanish laws are a consequence of the existence of double nationality treaties with Iberian-American countries or with other countries that have had a particular historical connection with Spain (Article 11.3 Spanish Constitution). But it is also a consequence of the rule of automatic double nationality for Spanish individuals who naturalize in such countries (Iberian-American countries, Andorra, The Philippines, Equatorial Guinea, and Portugal),

73. Instructions DGRN 23 May 2007 and 24 Feb. 2010. See M. Gardeñes Santiago, *Ciudadanía europea, doble nacionalidad y aplicación de la ley nacional de la persona*, 19–26 (Gaceta Jurídica de la Unión Europea 2004); A. Quiñones Escámez, *Ciudadanía europea, doble nacionalidad y cambio de los apellidos de los hijos: autonomía de la voluntad y conflicto positivo entre las nacionalidades de dos Estados miembros*, 851–874 (RJC 2004); A. Lara Aguado, *El impulso de la ciudadanía de la Unión Europea al reconocimiento intracomunitario de los actos de estado civil*, Diario La Ley, n. 7104, 2009, 1-10; N. Magallón Elósegui, *La DGRN ante la jurisprudencia europea en materia de nombres y apellidos,* REDI, Vol. LXII, nº 2, 2010, 149–164.

since they do not lose the Spanish nationality of origin (Article 11.3 Spanish Constitution). Another hypothesis of double nationality foreseen by Spanish laws regards the case of a Spanish national that keeps Spanish nationality by express declaration made within a three-year period after having acquired a foreign nationality. The solution to the first case, i.e., double nationality situations foreseen in a treaty, depends on the content of the international treaty. In double nationality treaties signed by Spain with Iberian-American Countries, only one nationality is active, while the other one stays latent until the former nationality is reactivated. The active nationality determines the personal law for conflict of laws issues. This active nationality will be, according to the terms of the different treaties, that of the person's habitual residence (as it is the case in treaties with Chile, Peru, Guatemala, Nicaragua, Bolivia and Honduras) or the most recent nationality (as it is foreseen in treaties with Argentina, Paraguay, Colombia, Ecuador, Costa Rica and Dominican Republic). Apart from treaties on double nationality, Article 9.9 CC sets out the rule for double nationalities situations foreseen by Spanish laws that the prevailing nationality shall be that of the last habitual residence or, in absence of a habitual residence, the last acquired nationality.

*83.* Double nationality situations not foreseen in Spanish laws are also frequent because of the effect of different legislations on the attribution and acquisition of nationality. Here the distinction to be made is whether one of the nationalities is Spanish or whether all of them are foreign nationalities. In the first case, Spanish nationality always prevails.[74] If the person possesses several foreign nationalities, the law of the habitual residence will be applied (Article 9.9, paragraph 2 in fine).

*84.* Article 9.10 CC governs situations such as statelessness or indeterminacy of nationality, substituting nationality with habitual residence as connecting factor (in Spanish system domicile is equal to habitual residence according to Article 40 CC).

## IV. Change of Sex (Trans-sexuality)

*85.* In the Spanish PIL system we cannot find a rule about change of sex, but it is reasonable to consider that this question is included within matters of personal status and, therefore, the issue is subject to the law of the person's nationality.

*86.* Although there is no PIL rule, it is necessary take into consideration Act 3/2007 of 15 March 2007, dealing with the rectification of the mention about the individual sex on the registry.[75] This act establishes the requirements to modify the registered sex, contemplating also the corresponding change of name. According to the Preamble of this Act, Spain seeks to join other European countries that have introduced specific legislation giving legal certainty for trans-sexual persons with a

---

74. Resolutions DGRN, 14 Jun. 2001; 3 Feb. 2009.
75. BOE No. 65, 16 Mar. 2007. Judgments AP Cordoba, 27 Mar. 2007, and TS 465/2009, 22 Jun. 2009.

medical diagnostic.[76] Spanish Supreme Court has also followed this comparative approach.[77] According to Article 1 of the Act 3/2007 only Spanish nationals, adults and with full capacity, are enabled to demand this change from the Civil Registry, but not foreigners that should go through a judicial procedure to obtain the same result. The request must be presented before the Civil Registry of the domicile of the petitioner (Article 3). This statutory regulation also includes the necessary elements to construe the *ordre public* notion in the matter. Even before the enactment of this Act, Spanish case law has protected trans-sexuality as an expression of the right to the free development of personality (Article 10.1 of the Spanish Constitution). Thus, the DGRN decided in 2005 that the law of Costa Rica, which did not authorize a change of sex by a Costa Rican national in Spain, was contrary to the Spanish international *ordre public*.[78]

## §2. LEGAL PERSONS

*87.* The general choice-of-law rule applicable to legal persons is Article 9.11 CC that sets out the following: 'The personal law in relation to legal persons is the one determined by its nationality, and it will govern questions related to capacity, incorporation, representation, operation, transmission, dissolution, and extinction.'

*88.* This rule uses a wide concept of legal persons which includes all 'organizational forms' that develop a function which is similar to those developed by 'legal persons' admitted in civil and commercial law: associations, foundations, private limited companies, public limited companies and so on. Therefore, the rule is applicable irrespective of the legal form taken by the legal person and without consideration given to whether such legal form exists under Spanish law.[79]

*89.* The employment of nationality as the connecting factor for legal persons encounters some difficulties. Article 9.11 CC does not precise the criteria to determine the nationality of a legal person, neither Spanish nor foreign. Therefore, there is a need to resort to other complementary rules for each legal person category. With regard to capital companies, such as public limited companies (*sociedades anónimas*) and limited liability companies (*sociedades de responsabilidad limitada*), Article 8 LSC (Act on Capital Companies 2010)[80] follows the real or effective seat

76. Article 4.2 of this Act provides that proof of a chirurgical change of sex is not necessary for the registry whenever there are reasons either of health or of age, and these reasons are certified by a doctor.
77. See Judgment TS, civil chamber, 17 Sep. 2007, which makes a comparative analysis of the legislation of the European countries, as well as the case law of the ECHR on this matter.
78. Resolution DGRN (3rd), 24 Jan. 2005. See R. Arenas García, *Transexualidad y matrimonio en el Derecho internacional privado*, in *Matrimonio homosexual y adopción: perspectiva nacional e internacional*, 191 (S. Navas Navarro (ed.), Reus 2006).
79. Resolution DGRN, 29 Feb. 1992.
80. Royal Legislative Decree 1/2010 of 2 July, approving the Consolidated Text of the Corporate Enterprises Act (BOE, 3 Jul. 2010; correction BOE 30 August). Later by Act 25/2011 of 1 August (BOE 2 August 2011), which integrate into the Spanish body of law the Directive 2007/36/EC of the European Parliament and of the Council of 11 Jul. 2007 on the exercise of certain rights of shareholders

theory, laying down the rule that capital companies that have their domicile in Spanish territory will be considered Spanish and will be governed by the Spanish law. Additionally, capital companies which have their principal establishment or exploitation in Spanish territory must have their domicile in Spain (Article 9.2 LSC).[81] Nevertheless, case law by the ECJ requires that companies validly incorporated or constituted under the laws of another Member State of the EU must be recognized in Spain under the principles of mutual recognition of companies and free establishment of legal persons (Decisions ECJ, *Centros*, 9 March 1999, C-212/97; *Überseering*, 5 November 2002, C-208/00; *Inspire Art*, 30 September 2003, C-167/01), even though the company in question might have its principal establishment or place of exploitation in Spain.

*90.* The determination of Spanish nationality of other legal persons, such as associations or foundations, must be made in accordance with Article 28.1 CC:

> Those corporations, foundations and associations, recognized by the law and domiciled in Spain, will be of Spanish nationality, provided that they are considered legal persons according to the provisions of the present Code.

Nevertheless, regarding associations, account should be taken of Article 9 of the Organic Act 1/2002, 22 March 2002, on the right to association;[82] in the case of foundations, Article 6 of the Act 50/2002, of 26 December 2002 applies.[83]

*91.* Special rules govern specific conflict of laws situations relevant for capital companies such as the transfer of domicile, which may bring about a change of the *lex societatis*. This issue is governed by Articles 92–103 LME (Act on the Structural Modifications of Commercial Companies 2009),[84] which under certain requirements establishes the procedure to be followed in order to validly transfer the

in listed companies, is added the Art. 11 *bis* relating to Company website, subsequently amended by Act 1/2012 of 22 June (BOE, 23 Jun. 2012) which integrate into the Spanish body of law the Directive 2009/109/EC of the European Parliament and of the Council of 16 Sep. 2009 amending Council Directives 77/91/EEC, 78/855/EEC and 82/891/EEC, and Directive 2005/56/EC as regards reporting and documentation requirements in the case of mergers and divisions, and which added the Arts 11*ter* and 11*quater* relating to Information published on the website.

81. See F.J. Garcimartín Alférez, *Derecho internacional privado*, 336–340 (3rd ed., Thomson-Reuters 2016); P. Maestre Casas, *Nacionalidad y domicilio de las personas jurídicas en la nueva Ley de Sociedades de Capital*, in *Algunos retos que plantea la realidad social, económica y jurídica actual en los ámbitos societario y laboral,* 51–67 (M. Sabido Rodríguez (dir.), Aranzadi 2012).
82. BOE, 22 Mar. 2002.
83. BOE, 27 Dec. 2002; correction BOE, 17 Apr. 2003. See M. Gardeñes Santiago, *El Derecho internacional privado de fundaciones a la luz de la nueva Ley 50/2002, de 26 de diciembre*, 251–271 (REDI 2004).
84. Act 3/2009 of 3 April on Structural Changes in Commercial Companies (BOE, 4 Apr. 2009) which integrate into the Spanish body of law: Directive 2005/56/EC of European Parliament and of the Council of 26 October on Cross-Border Mergers of Limited Liability Companies into the Spanish body of law; and Directive 2007/63/EC of European Parliament and of the Council of 13 Nov. 2007, Amending Council Directives 78/855/EEC and 82/891/EEC as Regards the Requirement of an Independent Expert's Report on the Occasion of Merger or Division of Public Limited Liability Companies. It was subsequently amended by Act 1/2012 of 22 Jun. (BOE, 23 Jun. 2012). See F.J.

company's seat or domicile to another country (Articles 95–103 LME) and conditions that must be satisfied in order to transfer the seat or domicile into Spain by a foreign company (Article 94 LME). Another special situation is the merger of two companies of different nationality, a possibility already envisaged by Article 9.11 Spanish Civil Code requiring the distributive application of all laws concerned, but governed by Directive 2005/56/EC on Cross-border Mergers of Limited Liability Companies and implemented by Articles 54–67 LME in Spanish Law.

Although the legal person's national law governs the internal questions such as incorporation, representation, operation, dissolution and extinction, etc., some formation issues are outside the scope of that rule, and would be governed by other conflict of laws rules as a result of the process characterization, such as the founding partners capacity (the personal law of each founding member is to be applied),[85] or the legal form to be given to the memorandum of association or the articles of incorporation (subject to the general conflicts rules on formal validity of legal acts in Article 11 CC).

---

Garcimartín Alférez, *El cambio de lex societatis: una forma especial de transformación societaria. Comentario a la Sentencia del TJUE Vale Epitési*, Diario La Ley, n. 7992, 28 Dec. 2012; F. Esteban de la Rosa, *El nuevo régimen de transferencia internacional de la sede social en el sistema español de Derecho internacional privado*, Cuadernos de Derecho y comercio, n. 54, 2010, 73–106; P. Rodas Paredes, *El nuevo régimen jurídico del traslado internacional del domicilio social*, Noticias UE, n. 309, 2010, 71–83.

85. Resolution DGRN, 4 Mar. 1981.

# Chapter 2. Obligations

## §1. Law of Contract

### I. Rome Convention on the Law Applicable to Contractual Obligations and Regulation 593/2008 (Roma I)

*92.* The Rome Convention on the law applicable to contractual obligations, 19 June 1980, entered into force in Spain on 1 September 1993.[86] All contracts made after that date were under the scope of the Rome Convention (Article 17), provided that the case was also within its material scope of application (Article 1). It should be added that the Rome Convention has a universal scope of application and therefore the national statutory choice-of-law rules on contracts were almost entirely displaced (Article 2). Given the fact that Article 1 of the Convention designs a wide scope of application covering all contractual obligations involving a choice between the laws of different countries, the applicability of Spanish statutory choice-of-law rules for contracts has been eliminated; their application could only be possible in the limited number of contractual questions expressly excluded from the Rome Convention. Article 1.2 Rome Convention excludes contractual obligations relating to wills and succession, rights in property arising out of a matrimonial relationship, rights and duties arising out of a family relationship, parentage, marriage or affinity, including maintenance obligations. The Rome Convention was replaced by Regulation 595/2008, 17 June 2008, for contracts concluded after 17 December 2009, date of entry into force of Rome I Regulation.[87]

### II. Statutory Choice-of-Law Rules

*93.* Even if Spanish statutory rules on choice of law for contracts are displaced as a consequence of the universal scope of application of the Rome I Regulation on the law applicable to contractual obligations, the choice of law rules which are set out at Article 10.5 CC are here included:

> To contractual obligations shall be applied the law to which the parties have expressly submitted, provided that it is somehow connected with the transaction. In absence of parties' choice of law, the law of the common nationality of the parties; in its defect, the law of the common habitual residence and, lastly, the law of the place of conclusion of the contract.

---

86. BOE, 19 Jul. 1993. Spain also accepted the unilateral extension of the application of the Convention to the territory of Gibraltar made by the United Kingdom (Resolution of the Spanish Ministry of Foreign Affairs, 29 Jun. 1995, BOE, 8 Jul. 1995). See A. Calvo Caravaca & J. Carrascosa González (dirs.), *Estudios sobre contratación internacional* (Colex 2006).

87. In general, see M.ª D. Ortíz Vidal, Ley aplicable a los contratos internacionales y eficiencia conflictual (Comares 2014); J. Carrascosa González, *Ley aplicable a los contratos internacionales: el Reglamento Roma I* (Colex 2009); F.J. Garcimartín Alférez, *El Reglamento 'Roma I' sobre ley aplicable a las obligaciones contractuales: ¿Cuánto ha cambiado el Convenio de Roma de 1980?*, Diario La Ley, nº 6957 de 30 mayo 2008.

*94.* The connecting factors used by Article 10.5 CC are mostly of a personal nature (common nationality, common habitual residence) and therefore not suitable to govern contractual obligations. The closing connecting factor based on the place of conclusion of the contract (*lex loci celebrationis*) is indeed rigid and may lead to the application of a law only vaguely connected with the contract. The locus celebrationis rule requires the application of Article 1262 CC in cases of distance contracts, as a legal presumption to the effect that the contract has been made in the place of the offer. Spanish legal scholars have criticized the shortcomings and defects of Article 10.5 CC and welcome the entry into force of the Rome Convention in Spain.[88]

*95.* After the Rome Convention (now Rome I Regulation) entered into force, Article 10.5 CC now covers only three situations:

(a) Matters of a contractual nature expressly excluded from the scope of application of the Rome Convention by virtue of Article 1.2.
(b) Contracts made prior to the entry into force in Spain of the Rome Convention (1 September 1993).
(c) Interregional conflicts of laws concerning contractual obligations (excluded from the Convention by Article 19.2, where it is said that States with multiple legal systems are not bound to apply the Convention to conflicts between the laws of the different territorial units of such a State).

*96.* Other statutory conflict of laws rules displaced by the Rome Convention are the following:

- Article 10.6 CC and Article 1.4 ET on employment contracts, which will be referred to later;
- Article 10.7 CC on donations (since the Rome Convention is also applicable to gifts not characterized as pertaining to Family or Succession Law under the exclusion rule in Article 1.2);
- Article 10.8 CC on contractual capacity (exception to the law of nationality based on the national interest rule); and
- Article 10.10 CC determining the scope of application of the *lex contractus*.

## §2. Particular Contracts

### I. Employment Contracts

*97.* The entry into force of the Rome Convention and its special choice-of-law rule on employment contracts in Article 6 (now Article 8 Regulation 593/2008, Rome I) also displaced Article 10.6 CC, a Spanish statutory choice-of-law rule on employment contracts, that can no longer be applied, and Article 1.4 of the Workers

88. For all see M. Virgós Soriano, *Article 10.5*, in Comentarios al Código Civil y Compilaciones forales, *supra*, 623–625.

Statute, a unilateral rule determining the scope of application of Spanish Labour Law to employment contracts.[89] It should be added that, following the EU Directive on the issue (Directive 96/71EC), in cases of displacement of workers there are special conflict rules in Articles 2 and 3, Displacement of Workers Act, 29 November 1999.[90]

## II. Insurance Contracts

*98.* The Rome Convention 1980 was applicable to contracts of insurance that covered risks situated outside the territories of the Member States of the EU (Article 1.3). However, the Rome Convention was not applicable to contracts of insurance covering risks located in the EU, except in cases of re-insurance. The law applicable to insurance contracts covering risks in the EU was harmonized by European Directives and, as a result of the adaptation of those Directives, the Spanish statutory rules on choice of law for insurance contracts were embodied in Articles 107–109, Insurance Contract Act, 8 October 1980.[91] This situation has significantly changed after the entry into force of Regulation Rome I 593/2008, which is applicable independently of the place where risk is situated, therefore including both insurance contracts covering risks located in or outside the EU. With regard to re-insurance contracts and insurance contracts whose risk is located outside the EU, the general conflict of laws rules in Articles 3 and 4 Rome I Regulation are applicable. However, with regard to insurance contracts for great risks and insurance contracts covering risks located in the EU, special rules in Article 7 Rome I Regulation are applicable.[92]

## III. Consumer Contracts

*99.* Article 6 Rome I Regulation covers choice-of-law issues for consumer contracts, but it has a narrow scope of application, first, because certain categories of consumer contracts are excluded (transportation –except holiday packages-, contracts concerning real estate –except timesharing-, etc.) and, second, because it is only applicable to passive consumers, i.e., consumers who are targeted in the market of their own place of residence. This narrow scope gives rise to a number of questions that could be addressed by other rules, even imperative rules in the sense

89. Royal Legislative Decree 1/1995, 24 Mar. 1995. See L.F. Carrillo Pozo, *La ley aplicable al contrato de trabajo en el Reglamento Roma I,* Revista Española de Derecho del Trabajo, vol. 152, 2011, pp. 1023–1068; M. Gardeñes Santiago, *La regulación conflictual del contrato de trabajo en el Reglamento Roma I: una oportunidad perdida,* AEDIPr, t. VIII, 2008, pp. 387–424; P. Maestre Casas, *El contrato de trabajo de marinos a bordo de buque*, in CDT, vol. 4, no. 2, 2012. http://www.uc3m.es/cdt.

90. BOE, 30 Nov. 1999. See Judgment TSJ (Sala Social) Oviedo 230/2013, 1 Feb. 2013, and comment by L. Carballo Piñeiro, REDI, 2013, 326–330.

91. BOE, 17 Oct. 1980.

92. C. Caamiña Domínguez, *Los litigios en materia de seguros en la UE* (Comares 2014).

of Article 9 Rome I Regulation.[93] In addition, there is a growing tendency in EU harmonization legislation to rule on specific consumer contracts and even afford a different level of protection from that already established by the Rome Convention 1980 and Rome I Regulation (Directives on timesharing, distance contracts, contracts negotiated outside business premises, etc.). As a result, some Directives have led to specific adaptation statutes in Spanish law that also deal with the issue of conflict of laws in certain categories of consumer contracts.[94] More generally, the European Directive on Unfair Terms in Consumer Contracts, 5 April 1993, was adapted in Spanish Law by means of the General Conditions Act 1998, 13 April, and the scope of application of this Act, according to Article 3, included also cases in which a foreign law had been chosen as the applicable law, provided that the adherent was resident in Spain and the submission of his contractual declaration had also taken place in Spain.[95] This scope of application was considered a wrong adaptation –for being too restrictive- of the Directive by Decision of ECJ 9 September 2004 (C-70/03, Commission/Spain). The applicable rule now is contained in the General Act on Defence of Consumers 2007 (BOE 30 November 2007) where Article 67.1 sets out the spatial criteria that determine the existence of a close relationship with Spanish law or the law of any other country of the European Economic Area, and therefore make applicable Spanish consumer protection laws even if the parties have chosen the law of a third country as applicable to the contract; in this regard, choice of law

93. See E. Castellanos Ruiz, *Régimen jurídico de los consumidores: competencia judicial internacional y ley aplicable* (Comares 2010); A.L. Calvo Caravaca, *El Reglamento Roma I sobre la ley aplicable a las obligaciones contractuales: cuestiones escogidas*, CDT, vol. 1, n. 2 2009, 52–133, in http://www.uc3m.es/cdt; A. López-Tarruella Martínez, 'Contratos internacionales celebrados por consumidores: las aportaciones del nuevo Art. 6 Reglamento Roma I', AEDPIr, 2008, 511–529; M. Requejo Isidro, 'Contratos de consumo y Roma I: ¿un poco más de lo mismo?', AEDIPr, 2008, 493–510.

94. E.g., the Directive 2008/122/EC of the European Parliament and of the Council of 14 Jan. 2009 on the protection of consumers in respect of certain aspects of timeshare, long-term holiday product, resale and exchange contracts, is adapted by the Spanish Act 4/2012, 6 Jul. (BOE, 7 Jul. 2012). According to Art. 17, 'consumer may invoke the legal protection of this Act against choice of law clauses in the following cases: a) if any of the immovable properties concerned is situated within the territory of a Member State of the European Economic Area; b) if the contract it is not related to immovable property, but it is related with the activities the trader pursues within a Member State or those activities have a projection within a Member State. See E. Torralba Mendiola, *El aprovechamiento por turno de bienes inmuebles y otros productos afines ante la prueba del Derecho internacional privado*, Revista CESCO de Derecho de Consumo, no. 3, 2012, http //www.revista.uclm.es/index.php/cesco.

95. BOE, 14 Apr. 1998. See B. Añoveros Terradas, *Los contratos de consumo intracomunitarios (cuestiones de Derecho aplicable)*, 313–335 (Colex 2006); P. De Miguel Asensio, 'La tutela de los consumidores en el mercado global: evolución del marco normativo', Estudios sobre Consumo, n. 85, 2008, 23–44; F. Esteban de la Rosa, 'Régimen de la contratación electrónica de consumo en el sistema español de Derecho internacional privado', Aranzadi Civil, n. 2, 2009, 15–45; K. Fach Gómez, 'La inadecuación del sistema español de Derecho internacional privado de las cláusulas abusivas al Derecho comunitario: claves para una nueva transposición y propuesta legislativa', La Ley, n. 6242, 2005, 1–7; A. Quiñones Escámez, *Concepto de vínculo estrecho en las Directivas de consumo: repercusiones de la STJCE (As. 70/03, Comisión c. España) en las leyes nacionales y en la propuesta de Reglamento Roma I (2005)*, in A. Calvo Caravaca & J. Carrascosa González (dirs.), *Estudios sobre contratación internacional, supra*, 465–479.

and choice of jurisdiction clauses against the interest of the consumer are considered typical unfair terms by Article 90 of the Act.[96]

## IV. Contracts of Carriage

*100.* Spain has ratified most of the uniform law conventions existing in the field of international contracts for the carriage of goods.[97] The uniform law solutions embodied in those conventions prevail over choice-of-law rules, even over those in Article 5 Rome I Regulation, provided that the issue falls under the uniform law convention's scope of application. As to carriage of goods by road, Spain has ratified the 1956 Convention on the Contract for the International Carriage of Goods by Road (CMR), applicable where Spain is the place of loading or the destination (Article 1).[98] Spain has also ratified the 1980 Berne Convention concerning International Carriage by Rail (COTIF).[99] Maritime transportation of goods is also under a strong trend towards uniform law international codification. Maritime carriage of goods in Spain is subject to the 1924 Bill of Lading Convention, including the amending protocols of 1968 and 1979 (the Hague-Visby Rules). The Hague-Visby rules are to be applied in cases where Spain is the place of the port of shipment, the bill of lading has been issued in Spain or there is a submission in the bill of lading to the Convention or to the laws of Spain.[100] Spain has also shared the widely common opposition with regard to the 1978 Hamburg Rules concerning bills of lading, although it has recently ratified the Rotterdam Rules (not yet in force). Charterparties and multimodal transport of goods are currently under no uniform law international convention in force; Spanish law does not specifically address such transport contracts in any statutory choice-of-law rule, but Article 5 Rome I Regulation is applicable. International carriage of goods by air is subject to the Warsaw Convention of 1929, as amended in 1955 and 1975;[101] however, the Warsaw Convention and the amending Protocols have been displaced between State parties by the new Montreal Convention of 28 May 1999 concerning the unification of certain rules for International Carriage by Air, which entered into force in Spain on 28 June 2004.[102]

96. On the nullity of jurisdictional and applicable law clauses contained in general conditions see see JudgmentCommercial Judge (*Juzgado Mercantil*) n. 5 Madrid, 30 Sep. 2013,Case *Ryanair*, and comment by C.I. Cordero Álvarez, REDI, 2014, 281–284.

97. See C. Llorente Gómez de Segura, *La ley aplicable al contrato de transporte internacional según el Reglamento Roma I*, CDT, vol. 1, n. 2, 2009, 160–178, http://www.uc3m.es/cdt.

98. BOE, 7 May 1974, the 1978 amending protocol has also been ratified by Spain (BOE, 18 Dec. 1982).

99. BOE 18 Jan. 1986. Amended by 1990 Protocol (BOE, 23 Sep. 1996).

100. The Convention was adapted into Spanish Law by the 1949 Act on Unification of Rules for Bills of Lading (BOE, 24 Dec. 1949). For reference to the amending Protocols see BOE, 11 Nov. 1984.

101. *Gaceta*, 21 Aug. 1931. As to the amending Protocols of The Hague (1955) and Montreal (1975) see BOE, 4 Jun. 1973 and 9 Feb. 1999.

102. BOE, 20 May 2004. See A. Hernández Rodríguez, *El contrato de transporte aéreo de pasajeros: algunas consideraciones sobre competencia judicial internacional y derecho aplicable*, CDT,

## V. Leasing/Factoring/Franchising

*101.* Spain has not ratified the 1988 Ottawa UNIDROIT Conventions on international leasing and international factoring.[103] There is no special conflict of laws rule in Spanish law in this regard and the question must be solved according to the general rules in Rome I Regulation.[104]

## VI. Negotiable Instruments

*102.* Choice-of-law rules for bills of exchange and cheques are well-developed in Spanish conflict of laws. The question is outside the scope of application of the Rome Convention or the Rome I Regulation (Article 1.2.c. excludes obligations arising under bills of exchange, cheques and promissory notes and other negotiable instruments). Statutory choice-of-law rules are embodied in the Bills of Exchange and Cheques Act 1985.[105]

*103.* Questions of capacity are dealt with at Articles 98 and 162 Bills of Exchange and Cheques Act. Capacity to be held validly obligated by means of a bill of exchange or cheque is subject, generally, to the law of nationality. *Renvoi* is admitted even if it is a further remission or second grade *renvoi*. This is a special solution different from the general rule on *renvoi* in Article 12.2 CC, which only accepts first grade *renvoi*, that is, renvoi to the Spanish Law. The rule of nationality finds an exception in favour of the *lex loci actus*, so that the incapable can enter into a valid commitment under a negotiable instrument in a country whose legislation would consider him capable of such an act.

*104.* Formal validity is governed by the law of the place of emission of the bill of exchange or cheque (Articles 99 and 164). With respect to cheques, compliance with the requirements of the law of the place of payment can also be sufficient (Article 164.1). The place of emission also governs the dates for the exercise of actions arising out of the bill of exchange or cheque (Articles 101 and 166).

*105.* The obligations or effects for the acceptor arising out of the bill of exchange are governed by the law of the place of payment. Effects for other parties such as drawer, endorser, etc., are subject to the law of the place where those parties

---

vol. 3, n. 1, 2011, 179–194, http://www.uc3m.es/cdt; See P. Maestre Casas, *El pasajero aéreo desprotegido: obstáculos a la tutela judicial en litigios transfronterizos por incumplimiento de las compañías aéreas (a propósito de la STJUE de 9 julio 2009, Rehder, As C-204/08)*, CDT, vol. 3, n. 2, 2011, 282–303.

103. International Institute for the Unification of Private Law, *UNIDROIT Convention on International Financial Leasing*, Ottawa, 28 May 1988.

104. See P. Rodríguez Mateos, *El contrato de leasing mobiliario internacional* (Eurolex 1997); Y. Dutrey Guantes, *El contrato de factoring internacional* (Universidad Complutense de Madrid 2001).

105. BOE, 19 Jul. 1985. In general, see S. Sánchez Lorenzo, *Derecho aplicable al cheque en el comercio internacional* (Eurolex 1996).

submitted their declarations in writing (Article 100). The latter rule is also applicable to all effects derived from cheques (Article 165).

*106.* The duties of the holder with respect to protest or any other act necessary to exercise or preserve his rights under the bill of exchange or promissory note are governed by the law of the country where the protest or equivalent act are to be made (Article 104). With respect to cheques, the same question is subject to the law of the place of payment (Article 167).

## §3. Non-contractual Obligations

### I. Law of Tort (Delict): *Lex Loci Delicti*

*107.* In the Spanish legal system, non-contractual obligations cover all obligations that come into existence out of a cause that is different from contract. This generic category includes legal obligations, quasi-contracts and illicit acts or torts, irrespective of their civil or criminal characterization. This wide concept allows one single rule to include all kinds of responsibilities that arise from a non-contractual obligation, and not only liability for torts.

*108.* With regard to the law applicable to responsibility for illicit acts, Article 10.9, paragraph 1 CC states that 'non-contractual obligations shall be governed by the law of the place where the fact from which they derive occurred'. This has been the general conflict of laws rule for torts in Spanish PIL until the entry into force of Regulation 864/2007, Rome II Regulation, on the law applicable to non-contractual obligations, 11 July 2007, and which has been applicable from 11 January 2009.[106] The universal scope of application of Rome II Regulation means that, to a large extent, Article 10.9 CC has been replaced by the EC Regulation. One possible area of application of Article 10.9 CC are matters expressly excluded from the scope of application of Regulation 864/2007, such as violations of privacy and rights relating to personality, including defamation (Article 1.2 g Regulation 864/2007).[107]

*109.* It is well known that civil responsibility rules govern a wide variety of possible tortious acts and this situation explains the demand for specific solutions to the different illicit international cases. In the Spanish system, specialization has only reached some areas. Some of those special rules are uniform material law conventions (environmental damages, damages derived from the use of transports, etc.) or

106. See A. Calvo Caravaca & J. Carrascosa González, *Las obligaciones extracontractuales en Derecho internacional privado. El Reglamento Roma II* (Comares 2008).

107. See J.J. Alvarez Rubio, *Jurisdicción competente y ley aplicable en materia de difamación y protección de los derechos de la personalidad*, AEDIPr, 2011, 89–118; M. Amores Conradi & E. Torralba Mendiola, *Difamación y Roma II*, 251–265 (AEDIPr 2007); C.I. Cordero Alvarez, *La ley aplicable a la difamación y a los atentados a los derechos de la personalidad en Europa: la reforma del Reglamento Roma II*, La Ley (Unión Europea), n.1, 2013, 21–38; E. Torralba Mendiola, *La difamación en la era de las comunicaciones: Nuevas perspectivas de Derecho internacional privado europeo?*, InDret, 2012.

conflicts of laws conventions. In this regard, it should be noted that the Hague Conference choice-of-law Conventions prevail over Regulation 864/2007 (as it is so established in the compatibility rule in Article 28.1 Regulation 864/2007, with regard to international conventions already in force between Member States and third states), and since Spain has ratified the 1971 Hague Convention on the Law Applicable to Road Accidents and the 1973 Hague Convention on the Law Applicable to Manufacturer's Responsibility for His Products, these Conventions are still be applicable after the entry into force of Regulation 864/2007.[108]

*110.* Case law has emphasized that the rigid connection in Article 10.9.1 CC may in some cases lead to illogical and unexpected results, selecting as the applicable law a legal order not closely related to the situation.[109] It does not contemplate the distinction between the place of actual damage and the place where the tortious act was committed. Therefore, the precision of the *locus delicti* must be done case by case, and some flexibility should be possible, due to the large variety of situations under this terminology, in order to select the law most closely related to the situation, the expectations of the parties, and the protection of material interests.[110] Therefore, the entry into force of Rome II Regulation with a general rule based on the *lex loci damni* (Article 4.1), but modified by the eventual application of the common habitual residence of the parties in Article 4.2, the exceptional application of an escape clause in Article 4.3 (in favour of the proper law of the tort the place most closely connected with the circumstances), and the existence of many special rules for different types of tortious acts (Articles 5–12), seems to satisfy the shortcomings of pre-existing Spanish conflict of laws rules on these issues.

*111.* The entry into force of Article 6 Rome II Regulation has provoked that the unilateral rules of Spanish statutory law governing unfair competition are no longer applicable. This is specially the case of Articles 1, 2 and 4 of the LDC (Competition Defence Act of 3 July 2007).[111] A similar consideration can be me made with regard to the impact of Rome II Regulation on Article 4 of Unfair Competition Act of 10 January 1991,[112] but this rule has been repealed by the Act 29/2009 of 30

108. A. Espiniella Menéndez, *Las reclamaciones derivadas de accidentes de circulación por carretera transfronterizos* (Fundación Mapfre 2012); L. Garau Juaneda, *La conveniencia de una denuncia por parte de España del Convenio de La Haya de 1971sobre responsabilidad civil derivada de accidentes de circulación*, 497–504 (AEDIPr 2007); P. Jiménez Blanco, *Acción directa y protección del perjudicado en el Reglamento Roma II*, 727–740 (Revista española de seguros, 2009).

109. Judgment AP of Madrid, 4 Jan. 1994 (litigation between Spanish citizens for non-contractual responsibility derived from a traffic accident which took place in a foreign country). See also Judgments AP Girona, 5 Mar. 2007; AP Girona, 8 Oct. 2008; AP Barcelona, 30 Sep. 2009.

110. See I. Martínez García, *La sentencia de la Talidomida en España, o de cómo es justo y conforme a derecho –y por tanto necesario– dictar un fallo extraordinario al ser juzgado un daño también extraordinario. A propósito de la sentencia del Juzgado de Primera Instancia núm. 90 de Madrid de 19 de noviembre de 2013*, Diario La Ley, n. 8219, 27 Dec. 2013.

111. BOE, 4 Jul. 2007. See L. Carballo Piñeiro, *Derecho de la competencia, intereses colectivos y su proyección procesal*, 465–495 (AEDIPr 2007); E. Rodríguez Pineau, *Ley aplicable a la responsabilidad derivada de actos contrarios a la libre competencia*, 447–463 (AEDIPr 2007).

112. BOE, 11 Jan. 1991.

December[113] that modified the Spanish regime of unfair competition and advertising.

## II. Negotiorum Gestio[114]

*112.* Article 10.9, paragraph 2 CC sets out that: 'Conducting someone else's affairs shall be governed by the law of the place where the promoter carries out the principal activity.' This rule should now be considered replaced by Article 11 Regulation 864/2007, Rome II.

## III. Unjustified Enrichment

*113.* Article 10.9, paragraph 3, CC sets out the rule that the applicable law to unjustified enrichment shall be the law which caused the transfer of patrimonial value in favour of the enriched person. This rule is now replaced by Article 10 Regulation 864/2007, Rome II.

113. BOE, 31 Dec. 2009. See J.I. Paredes Pérez, *Sobre la conveniencia de una norma de conflicto bilateral sobre competencia desleal*, 427–440 (AEDIPr 2006).

114. Conducting someone else's affairs without the authority to do so.

# Chapter 3. Law of Property

## §1. General Rules

### I. *Lex Rei Sitae*

*114.* The general conflicts rule on property rights and interests is found in Article 10.1 CC, which states that:

> Possession, property, and other rights over immovable goods, as well as publicity, shall be governed by the law of the place where they are situated. The same law will be applicable to movable goods.

*115.* Therefore, the rule *lex rei sitae* is applied without distinguishing between movable or immovable goods. This rule is considered the general rule for the protection of rights over corporeal or material goods. The protection of rights and interests over intangible goods has a specific regime, and it is also the case with regard to cultural property pertaining to the Spanish cultural or patrimonial heritage.

*116.* The scope of the *lex rei sitae* rule includes the following issues: the system of constitution of rights in rem, conditions of modification, transmission, loss and extinction of rights in rem; content of a right in rem (rights and obligations of the holder of such right); effects of rights in rem in relation to third parties; publicity of the acts of constitution, transmission, and extinction of rights in rem constituted over movable and immovable goods.[115] Nevertheless, the *lex rei sitae* rule does not govern the issue of capacity to acquire rights in rem, which is under the nationality rule in Article 9.1 CC. It does not govern either formal validity issues of the legal acts necessary for the acquisition or transmission of property rights, which are generally submitted to the rule of Article 11 CC, or to Article 11 Regulation 593/2008, Rome I, in the case of contracts for the acquisition of property. Neither does the *lex rei sitae* rule govern issues of substantial validity of the title by virtue of which a real right is acquired or transmitted, such as a sale purchase contract, which is subject to Rome I Regulation with regard to the determination of the applicable law to the validity of the contract.

*117.* Article 10.2 CC establishes a particular rule for ships, aircrafts, and means of transport by railroad, giving preference to the law of the flag:

> Ships, aircrafts and means of transport by railroad, as well as all the rights constituted upon them, will be submitted to the law of the place of the flag, matriculation or registration of the respective country.

---

115. These aspects have been pointed out in the Judgment of TS, 9 May 1998. See also Resolution DGRN, 20 Jan. 2011. In general, see I. Heredia Cervantes, 'Algunos apuntes sobre la regulación conflictual de los derechos reales', *Pacis Artis. Obra Homenaje al profesor Julio D. González Campos*, 1645–1661 (Eurolex 2005).

Immediately after, the *lex rei sitae* rule is applicable to means of transport by road:

> Automobiles and other means of transport by road will be submitted to the law of the place where they are situated.

The distinction between the different means of transportation obeys to the number of transactions, far greater in relation to the means of transport by road, which may explain the interest of the State of the place of location to govern the issue.

## II. Movable and Immovable Property

*118.* The Spanish legislator has not considered specific problems of precision of the *lex rei sitae* rule, such as property situated in two States or those situated in extraterritorial spaces. Neither has the legislator contemplated the fact that movable goods can be changed of location, thus ignoring the problem of 'mobile conflict' (*conflicto móvil*). The *lex rei sitae* rule lacks any temporal concretization in Spanish PIL. Article 10.1 CC submits movable property to the law of the country of location, avoiding any mention to the problem of mobile conflict, although there are special rules for goods in transit.

*119.* A distinction is made if property is integrated in an estate. In succession matters, the hereditary rights over goods pertaining to the decedent's estate are governed by the rule of Article 9.8 CC and not by the rule contained in Article 10.1 CC, as some judgments of the Spanish Supreme Court have pointed out.[116]

*120.* If property does not form part of an estate, but is instead contemplated in an isolated way, as an independent patrimonial unit, in this case the applicable rule is Article 10.1 CC.[117]

## III. Transfer of Property

*121.* *Lex rei sitae* governs modes of acquisition of rights in rem, the moment of transfer of ownership in a sale contract, or registration requirements of authentic documents in cases of mortgage contracts. In Spain, the transfer of ownership requires a title, generally a contract and an act of transmission (*traditio*), causally connected with the former.

*122.* The rule determining the applicable law to rights in rem does not govern the title of acquisition, which in most cases will be a contract. The regime of contractual obligations is determined by Rome I Regulation or, exceptionally, by

116. Such as TS, 15 Nov. 1996, and 19 Jul. 1989.
117. Judgment TS, 15 Mar. 1984.

Article 10.5 CC.[118] Transfer of property effects of contracts is not governed by Rome I Regulation. Transfer, modification, or constitution of property rights are governed by the *lex rei sitae* (Articles 10.1 and 10.2 CC). The law of the place where property is located at the time of entering into the contract determines if the latter produces a direct transfer of property or only personal obligations, as is the case in Spanish law.

## §2. Special Rules

### I. Goods in Transit

*123.* Article 10.1, paragraph 3 CC determines a fictional place of situation. According to this rule, goods in transit will be considered located in the place of expedition, unless the parties have agreed, tacit or expressly, that they should be considered located in the place of destination.

*124.* We are dealing here with a useful presumption for cases in which the goods are to be sold when still in the process of transportation. The rule is that the goods will be considered as located in the place of expedition, but if the parties have agreed so the property can be considered as located in the place of destination, which can also bring certainty as to the law applicable to the constitution and transfer of property rights upon goods in transit.

*125.* This special rule exclusively deals with the validity and content of rights in rem between contracting parties and cannot be opposed to *bona fide* third parties. The effects of property rights in relation to third parties will be determined, again, by the general *lex rei sitae* rule.

*126.* It can be submitted that the same rule is applicable to goods bound for exportation. Certainly in this case it seems more convenient for the parties to agree on the application of the law of the place of destination in order to anticipate the application of the laws of the market where property is to be located after expedition.[119]

### II. Other Special Rules

*127.* The *lex rei sitae* is applied to possession, property, and other rights or interests in rem over movable and immovable goods, such as usufruct, as well as security interests (retention of title, pledge, mortgage, chattel mortgage).

118. See *supra*, paras 96 and 97. See also D.P. Fernández Arroyo, *El arrendamiento de inmuebles en la Unión Europea* (Civitas 1998).
119. See M. Virgós Soriano, *Las cosas y los derechos reales*, in *Derecho Internacional privado. Parte especial*, 241–285 (6th ed., J.D. González Campos et al., Madrid: Eurolex, 1995).

*128.* In Spanish law, it is usually said that there is a *numerus clausus* system of property rights, and therefore it would be difficult to admit the validity of some property interests like the English floating charge.[120] Even though the parties can create atypical rights between them, in their relations with third parties, only typified rights in rem are recognized. This raises the problem of the validity of property rights unknown to the applicable *lex causae*.

*129.* There is a lack of a specific PIL rules for security interests. Obviously, the problem refers to movable goods that may change their place of location. If the legal systems involved require different conditions as to the constitution and the effects of security interests, there is a problem of mobile conflict. The most commonly proposed solution is to apply the same rule applicable to goods in transit. In this way, the security interest will be governed by the law of the place of the goods location at the time of constitution of the security interest. If the movable good changes its location to a different country, the content and effects of the security interest against third parties and in insolvency situations are governed by the law of the place of the new location of the good, but its validity and effects *inter partes* is to be ascertained by the law of the place of the original location. This means that if the law of the place of the new location is more restrictive than the previous one, because it requires, not only an agreement between the parties, but also, as is the case in Spanish law, a public registration of the security interest in order to exercise the right and oppose it to third parties, it would be necessary to proceed to the completion of the requirements of the law of the place of the new location.[121]

*130.* As a clear example of a security interest, the retention of title enables the seller to retain title of ownership of the sold goods until the deferred payments of the sale price have completely been made. In this manner, in case of non-performance of the payment obligation, the seller may claim the goods back exercising his ownership rights against the buyer or even against a third party. Retention of title must be governed by the property rights conflicts rule (Article 10.1 CC), and not by the law of the contract. The constitution of this security interest is to be governed by the law of the place of the location of the goods at the time of entering into the sale purchase contract that includes a clause of retention of title. This law will be applicable to the formal and substantial validity requirements and effects of the security interest, such as the existence of a right of seizure over the goods or their liquidation value. If the movable goods change of country of location, the content and effects of the security interest against third parties or in situations of insolvency will be governed by the law of the new place of location of the goods.[122]

120. See J.C. Fernández Rozas & S. Sánchez Lorenzo, *supra*, 661–672.

121. See N. Bouza Vidal, *Las garantias mobiliarias en el comercio internacional* (Marcial Pons 1991); D.P. Fernández Arroyo, *Garantías reales en el comercio internacional de nuestros días*, Revista Mexicana de Derecho Internacional Privado, No. 10, 2001, 11–58.

122. See S. Sánchez Lorenzo, *Garantías reales en el comercio internacional* (Civitas 1993).

# Chapter 4. Intangible Property Rights

## §1. Rights of Personality

*131.* As a first approach, we could characterize rights of personality as part of the personal status and therefore subject to the law of the nationality. However, the protection of personality rights (right to life, physical integrity, personal and familiar honour) is beyond the conflict-of-laws method, since international conventions on human rights are also applicable.

Nonetheless, from a conflict-of-laws perspective, the violation of such rights results in civil liability cases to which the non-contractual responsibility choice-of-law rules are to be applied. This matter is expressly excluded from the scope of Regulation 846/2007, on the law applicable to non-contractual obligations (Article 1.2.g). The solution would be to apply the rule of Article 10.9.I CC: '*non-contractual obligations shall be governed by the law of the place where the event from which they result took place*', in other words, *lex loci delicti commissi*. This may encounter two difficulties:

(a) In multi-located damages, the determination of the place of damage may be difficult. It seems that Spanish case law, in relation to damages caused by an illegitimate infringement of private life, opts for the application of the law of the place of the domicile of the company which publishes or distributes the newspaper or magazine, because starting from that moment what was only of private knowledge by the publishing house becomes public knowledge for everyone.[123]
(b) In cases where there are multiple locations of damages potentially giving way to a distributive application of laws, the solution would be to retain a single applicable law which would be that of the residence of the victim.[124]

*132.* Therefore, Article 10.9 CC is applicable to all issues which are not governed by any international convention or EU instrument and particularly, is applicable in cases of damages as result of a violation of the rights of personality (right to privacy and personal image, honour, all of them rights of protection of the person's private life).

The rule in Article 10.9 Cc creates a difficulty of interpretation between the law of the place of the illicit act or event (*lex loci delicti commissi*) and the place where the damage actually occurs (*lex loci damni*); however, in line with the solution given in Regulation Rome II, the place of actual damage should be taken into account, which means the application of the laws of the different places in which the information has been made public (through internet, televisión, radio or press) damaging or threatening to damage the person's reputation or rights of personality, provided that the victim is known in these places; this means the application of different

123. Decision of AP Madrid, 1 Mar. 1993.
124. See M. Eslava, *El locus delicti commissi en los ilícitos contra la vida privada cometidos a través de Internet*, Informática y Derecho, no 34, 2004, 15–38; A.L. Calvo Caravaca & J. Carrascosa González et al., *Derecho internacional privado*, vol. II, cap. XXXI (Comares, 2014).

national laws to the determination of damages where legal action has only been taken before Spanish courts seeking a judgment on the entire damage.

In order to avoid the fragmentation or patchwork of the applicable law, it has been proposed to apply the law of the victim's place of habitual residence, or the law of the tortfeasor's habitual residence (following the logic of the State of origin rule in Directive 2000/31/CE, 8 June 2000, on certain legal aspects of information society services, in particular electronic commerce, in the Internal Market ('Directive on electronic commerce').[125]

Nevertheless, the trend is the extension to conflicts issues of the existing case law by the CJUE regarding international jurisdiction under Brussels I bis Regulation and, therefore, the application of the law of the place of the victim's place of habitual residence to the entire damages caused because it is in this place where the centre of the person's life and its inherent rights are located.[126] Along similar lines, the Spanish Supreme Court has expressed its view in cases where a French printing house has been condemned because of the defamatory nature of the news published by a French newspaper, both in digital and printed version, in relation to two well-known Spanish football clubs, Barcelona FC and Real Madrid, which were mentioned as possibly using doping techniques. It is understood that the damage in its entirety is suffered in Spain, place of domicile of the persons concerned and where their fame and reputation is centred.[127]

## §2. Patent Law

*133.* The protection of patent rights follows the principle of territoriality which is only surpassed by the process of international co-operation or legal integration as it occurs in the EU.[128]

*134.* Due to the existence of a plurality of international agreements applicable on the matter, the protection of patent rights in Spain is articulated by means of conventional and internal rules, and, of course, EU Law.[129] In statutory law, there is a choice-of-law rule that jointly governs industrial and intellectual property (Article 10.4 CC).[130] According to Article 10.4 CC:

125. See Judgment TS 144/2013, 4 Mar. 2013, rejecting any liability of Google as provider of intermediation services in the information society.
126. STJUE 25 octubre 2011, eDate Advertising/Olivier Martínez, As. C-509/09 and C-161/10. See also E. Torralba Mendiola, *La difamación en la era de las comunicaciones: ¿Nuevas? perspectivas de Derecho Internacional Privado Europeo*, Indret 1/2012; J.J. Álvarez Rubio, *Derecho applicable a los derivados de la difamación*, Revista de Derecho de la Unión Europea, 22/2012, 137–151.
127. Judgments TS (Sala Primera de lo Civil)24 Feb. 2014, rec. nº 229/2011 (Real Madrid), TS de 7 Nov. 2011, rec. nº 183/2010 (Futbol Club Barcelona).
128. Judgments TS, 26 Sep. 1980; AT Cataluña, 22 Mar. 1985.
129. See M. Desantes Real, *Hacia un tribunal unificado y un efecto unitario para las patentes europeas en caso todos los Estados miembros de la Unión Europea. Consecuencias de la autoexclusión de España (Towards a unified court and a unitary effect for European patents in almost all the member states of the European Union. Consequences of Spain's auto-exclusion)*, 51–70 (REDI 2013).
130. Judgments TS, 21 Jul. 2000 and 22 Mar. 2000.

Intellectual and industrial property rights shall be protected within Spanish territory in accordance with Spanish law, without prejudice to the provisions of international treaties and conventions to which Spain is a party.

*135.* The expression 'rights of industrial property' includes patents and utility models, as well as trademarks and commercial trade names (as distinctive signs).[131] The conflict rule on this matter is not focused on intellectual property rights but in their protection, given the finality of these rights. The *lex loci protectionis* rule under Article 10.4 CC is applicable to the creation, modification, transmission, and extinction of these rights, as well as to issues related to the non-contractual responsibility derived from the infringement of such rights, though concerning the infringement the applicable rule is now contained in the Article 8 of Rome II Regulation.[132]

*136.* This rule must be considered in conjunction with Article 2 of the Patent Act 11/1986, 20 March,[133] Article 3 of the Trade Mark Act 17/2001, 7 December,[134] Article 4 of the Legal Protection of Industrial Design Act 20/2003, 7 July,[135] and Article 11 of the Legal Regime of Plant Variety Protection Act 3/2000, 7 January,[136] which determine the scope of protection of Spanish laws on industrial property.

*137.* Thus, Article 2 of the Patent Act sets out the scope of personal application of the Spanish substantial legislation on patents, determining who can obtain a patent according to the Spanish legislation.[137] Beneficiaries are:

- Natural or legal persons of Spanish nationality; non-Spanish citizens which reside in Spain or have a real and effective industrial or commercial establishment; foreigners of States that have ratified the Convention of the Union of Paris of 1883 on industrial property.
- Foreigners requiring protection on grounds of reciprocity.
- Spanish citizens and foreigners domiciled in Spain or having an effective establishment in a Member State of the Convention of the Union of Paris invoking provisions of this convention for the protection of industrial protection in Spain, provided that these rules are more favourable than Spanish domestic laws.[138]

---

131. Judgment TS 8 Nov. 1989.
132. See J. Carrascosa González, *Article 10.4*, M. Pasquau Liaño (ed.), Jurisprudencia civil comentada (Código civil) (Comares 2000).
133. BOE, 26 Mar. 1986, amended by 29 Apr. 2002 Act for the adaptation into Spanish law of the EC Directive on the legal protection of biotechnological inventions (BOE, 30 Apr. 2002).
134. BOE, 8 Dec. 2001.
135. BOE, 8 Jul. 2003.
136. BOE, 10 Jan. 2000, and correction, BOE, 8 Feb. 2000.
137. Wording is similar in the other mentioned acts.
138. C. Otero García-Castrillón, *Las patentes en el comercio internacional* (Dykinson 1997); J. Carrascosa González, *Ley aplicable a las patentes en DIPr Español*, Anales Rev. Facultad Derecho Univ. Murcia, n. 19, 2001, 7–48.

## §3. Copyright

*138.* As we have seen, copyright law is regulated along with patent law in Article 10.4 CC. The expression 'rights of intellectual property' includes copyright rights of a literary, artistic or scientific work (Article 1 of Intellectual Property Act).[139] This rule is complemented with the legislation contained in Articles 163–167 of the Copyright Act,[140] which sets out the scope of application of the Spanish material legislation related to protection of copyrights, without prejudice to EC regulation. Therefore, there is a complementary relation between Article 10.4 of the CC and Articles 163–167 of the Copyright Act.

*139.* The beneficiaries of such protection[141] are determined following two criteria:

(a) Spanish citizens, nationals of States of the EU and national foreigners of third States connected with the Spanish legal system by habitual residence in Spain or by the publication of the work in Spain.
(b) Other foreigners, on grounds of reciprocity.[142]

139. Judgment TS 7 Jun. 1995.
140. Royal Legislative Decree 1/1996, 12 April, BOE, 22 Apr. 1996, amended by 7 Jul. 2006 Act 23/2006 (BOE, 8 Jul. 2006).
141. Authors (Art. 163), Performers (Art. 164), Producers, Makers of Ordinary Photographs and Publishers (Art. 165), Broadcasting Organisations (Art. 166), Beneficiaries of Protection by *Sui Generis* Rights (Art. 167).
142. See, D. Moura Vicente, *Principios sobre conflictos de leyes en materia de Propiedad Intelectual*, CDT, Vol. 3, n. 1, 2011, 5–23; M. Sabido Rodriguez, *La creación intelectual como objeto de intercambios comerciales internacionales* (Cáceres: Univ. de Extremadura 2000); J. Carrascosa González, *La propiedad intelectual en el Derecho internacional privado español* (Comares 1994).

# Chapter 5. Company Law

## §1. Formation of a Company

*140.* Article 9.11 CC sets out the general choice-of-law rule on the law applicable to corporations: the *lex societatis*, applicable to all the internal affairs of a corporation, is determined by reference to the law of the State of the corporation's nationality. The law of the corporation's nationality governs legal capacity, incorporation, representation, transformation, dissolution and winding-up. The criteria for the attribution of Spanish nationality to corporations are to be found in Spanish Company law. Articles 8 and 9 LSC determine the system of attribution of Spanish nationality to all types of commercial companies. According to the wording of these provisions:

- All corporations (public limited corporations and limited liability corporations) having their registered domicile in Spanish territory, whatever the place where they were incorporated, will be Spanish and will be governed by the Spanish laws.
- Corporations (public limited corporations and limited liability corporations) which have their principal establishment or exploitation in Spanish territory must have their registered domicile in Spain.

*141.* For most opinions, Spanish law follows the effective or real seat theory.[143] Spanish law seeks to avoid the existence of pseudo-foreign corporations. A fraudulent or fictitious registered office outside Spain will not prevent the application of Spanish laws if the country most closely connected with the effective activity of the company is Spain, as evidenced by the location of the corporation's main place of business.[144]

*142.* Nonetheless, there are some opinions that reconcile the seat theory with the incorporation theory.[145] Although from the wording of the rule it seems possible to have a domicile in Spain, even in cases where the company has been incorporated in a foreign country, the attribution of legal personality requires the corporation's entry in the Register of Companies. Therefore, it implies the incorporation of the company according to Spanish law or the adaptation of the company's articles of incorporation to the Spanish law. However, case law by the ECJ requires that companies validly incorporated or constituted under the laws of another Member State of the EU must be recognized in Spain under the principles of mutual recognition of companies and free establishment of legal persons (Decisions ECJ, *Centros*, 9

143. See F.J. Garcimartín Alférez, *Derecho de sociedades y conflictos de leyes: una aproximación contractual* (EDR 2002).
144. See J. Carrascosa González, *Sociedades fantasma y Derecho internacional privado*, REEI, n. 27, 2014.
145. Judgment AP Madrid, 10 May 2010.

March 1999, C-212/97; *Überseering*, 5 November 2002, C-208/00; *Inspire Art*, 30 September 2003, C-167/01).[146]

*143.* Furthermore, the nationality of corporations may give way to positive conflicts of nationality, which will be solved in conformity with the rules in Article 9.9 CC, Spanish nationality prevailing.

## §2. Stocks and Stockholders

*144.* According to Article 9.11 CC, the *lex societatis*, as determined by nationality, governs, among other internal issues of the company, the corporation's internal composition and the governing corporate bodies, the acquisition and loss of the condition of shareholder, as well as shareholders' rights and obligations towards the corporation and among themselves.

*145.* Related to the condition of shareholder is the question of the loss of the shareholder status as a consequence of the transmission of stocks and shares. The transmission of stocks and shares implies the change of title over them. The *lex societatis* governs the validity and effects of the transmission.

## §3. Company Residence

*146.* As it has been previously stated, every company having its principal place of business in Spain must establish the social or registered domicile in Spain. Articles 8 and 9 LSC impose the obligation to make the registered domicile in Spain coincident with the place where the effective administration and management centre is situated or where the principal exploitation or establishment is located.[147]

*147.* In Spain, the international transfer or migration of the registered domicile means a change in the *lex societatis*. This situation is governed by Articles 92–103 LME (Act on the Structural Modifications of Commercial Companies 2009) which under certain requirements establishes the procedure to be followed in order to validly transfer the company seat or domicile to another country (Articles 95–103

146. See F.J. Garcimartín Alférez, *La Sitztheorie es incompatible con el Tratado CE. Algunas cuestiones de Derecho internacional de sociedades iluminadas por la Sentencia del TJCE de 19 de marzo de 1999*, Revista de Derecho Mercantil, n. 232, 645–686 (1999); *La sentencia Überseering y el reconocimiento de sociedades extranjeras: se podrá decir más alto, pero no más claro, Revista de Derecho Mercantil*, n. 248, 2003, 663–682; *La sentencia 'Centros': una visión a través de los comentarios*, REEI, n. 1, 2000, 1–23; S. Sánchez Lorenzo, *El Derecho europeo de sociedades y la sentencia 'Centros': la relevancia de la sede real en el ámbito comunitario*, AEDIPr, t. 0, 2000, 115–157; *id.*, *El derecho de establecimiento secundario de las sociedades ficticias en el ámbito comunitario*, in *Derecho de Sociedades. Libro homenaje al profesor Fernando Sánchez Calero*, Vol. I, 451–480 (McGraw-Hill 2002).

147. See P. Maestre Casas, *Nacionalidad y domicilio de las personas jurídicas en la nueva Ley de Sociedades de Capital*. in *Algunos retos que plantea la realidad social, económica y jurídica actual en los ámbitos societario y laboral*, 51–67 (M. Sabido Rodríguez (dir.), Aranzadi 2012).

LME) and conditions that must be satisfied in order to transfer seat or domicile into Spain by a foreign company (Article 94 LME).[148]

## §4. COMPANY LIABILITY

*148.* The *lex societatis* will determine the corporation's liability. It will also apply to the determination of the natural persons legally representing the corporation and the manner in which the corporation may result liable for acts done by its governing bodies or agents.[149]

*149.* A specific choice-of-law rule is established on voluntary representation. According to Article 10.11 CC:

> [I]f there is not an express submission, the law of the country where the powers are exercised will be applied to the voluntary representation.

*150.* In cases of responsibility derived from illicit acts, it is thought that the general solution would be to apply the *lex loci delicti commissi*, although the *lex societatis* may establish the personal responsibility of natural persons, company officials or agents, responsible for the corporation's behaviour.[150]

## §5. COMPANY MERGER

*151.* Article 9.11.II CC establishes that 'in the merger of corporations of different nationalities the respective personal laws shall be considered'. This rule, apparently simple, allows the distributive application of different legal systems, but is not operative, given the complexities of international mergers. Difficulties in the co-ordination of the different personal laws involved in a merger operation have been solved by Directive 2005/56/EC on Cross-border Mergers of Limited Liability Companies, which has been implemented in Spanish law by Articles 54–67 LME.

## §6. BANKRUPTCY OF A COMPANY

*152.* As pointed out above, all matters related to corporations fall under the scope of the *lex societatis*. Nonetheless, insolvency is subject to different connecting

---

148. See F. Martínez Rivas, *Traslado de sede social en la Unión Europea: del caso Daily Mail al caso Cartesio. Veinte años no son nada*, CDT, vol. 1, n. 1, 2009, 132–142; R. Miquel Sala, *Transformación transfronteriza: exigencias para el Estado Miembro de acogida. Comentario a la STJUE C-378/10 (Vale Építési Kft)*, CDT, Vol. 5, n. 2, 2013, 610–661.

149. Judgment AP León, 7 May 2008, applying the Portuguese *lex societatis* to the administrator's liability.

150. De acuerdo con la sentencia AP Valencia, 26 de junio de 2012, aun cuando no esté previsto por la lex societatis, la lex loci delicti puede imponer una responsabilidad directa de los socios o de los administradores de la sociedad por los daños causados a acreedores de la sociedad.

factors for choice-of-law purposes. In principle, bankruptcy does not imply the winding-up of a company, unless there is an express agreement of dissolution as a consequence of a judicial decision. It will be the lex societatis to govern the rules on dissolution, winding-up and termination of the legal person and, the appointment of a receiver and his powers.[151]

*153.* In order to determine the PIL regime applicable to insolvency proceedings, it must be distinguished as EU proceedings or non-EU proceedings. The first ones are governed by Council Regulation 1346/2000 of 29 May 2000 on insolvency proceedings. Community proceedings are those in which the centre of the debtor's main interests is located in the territory of a Member State. Regulation 1346/2000 tends to offer special protection to the creditor who has his habitual residence, domicile or registered office in the territory of a Member State.[152] Non-community proceedings would be those in which the centre of the debtor's main interest is not located in the Community. Non-community proceedings are governed in Spain by Act 22/2003, 9 July, on Bankruptcy,[153] which addresses PIL aspects in Articles 10 and 11 and in Title IX (Articles 199–230).

According to Article 10, Act on Bankruptcy 2003, Spanish courts shall have jurisdiction to open insolvency proceedings in two cases:

(a) Whenever the centre of the debtor's main interests is located in Spain.
(b) Whenever the debtor has an establishment within the Spanish territory.

Due to the primacy principle of community law, the scope of this rule is clearly restricted.

*154.* Article 4 of Regulation 1346/2000 establishes that 'the law applicable to insolvency proceedings and their effects shall be that of the Member State within the territory of which such proceedings are opened'. That is to say that proceedings opened in Spain will be governed by the Act 22/2003, except as otherwise provided in the Regulation. To those insolvency proceedings not covered by Regulation 1346/2000, Articles 200 through 209 of Act 22/2003 on Bankruptcy are applicable.

*155.* Regulation 1346/200 (Article 16) establishes as a principle that 'any judgment opening insolvency proceedings handed down by a court of a Member State which has jurisdiction pursuant to Article 3 shall be recognized in all the other Member States'. With regard to judgments coming from non–Member States, Article 220 of the Act on Bankruptcy sets out the conditions of effectiveness in Spain. The conditions are:

---

151. Judgment AP Madrid, 18 May 2009, Argentinean Company in process of winding-up owning immovable property in Spain: application of Argentinean Law. See F.J. Garcimartín Alférez, *Derecho internacional privado*, 340–342 (3rd ed., Civitas/Thomson-Reuters, 2016).
152. See L. Carballo Piñeiro, *Vis attractiva concursus in the European Union: its development by the European Court of Justice,* Indret. Revista para el análisis del Derecho, nº 3, 2010.
153. BOE, 10 Jul. 2003. Véase A.L. Calvo Caravaca, J. Carrascosa González, *Derecho concursal internacional* (Colex 2004); B. Campuzano Díaz, *Aspectos internacionales del Derecho concursal* (Laborum 2004).

- That the judgment refers to a collective proceeding based on the debtor's insolvency, in which debtor's goods and activities are submitted to the control or supervision of a foreign court or authority, in order to their liquidation or reorganization.
- That the jurisdiction of the foreign court or authority is based in one of the grounds contained in Article 10 of the Act or in a reasonable ground of similar nature.
- That the rights of the defendant are respected.
- That the judgment is not contrary to the Spanish *ordre public*.

## §7. Trust

*156.* The institution of the trust, developed by the common law, does not exist in Spanish Law, as is the case in most civil law jurisdictions, where the concept of the trust is unknown. Fiduciary contracts (*contrato de fiducia*) are possible to the extent permitted under the general principles of the Civil Code, but those contracts cannot be considered as functional equivalents to the trust. Spain has not adhered to the 1985 Hague Convention on the Law Applicable to Trusts and their Recognition. It is to be regretted that Spain has not followed the example of other civil law jurisdictions like Italy or the Netherlands, countries that have ratified the Hague Convention. The situation is even more regrettable if we take into account that the Brussels I bis Regulation on international jurisdiction and recognition and enforcement of decisions in civil and commercial matters, Regulation (EC) 1215/2012, makes a reference to the private international law rules of the forum to determine the domicile of the trust (Articles 7.6 and 63.3).[154]

*157.* Characterization of the trust in a civil law environment is a difficult task. The problem posed by an unknown institution reveals the deficiencies of classic conflict-of-laws rules, whose application depends on a previous characterization of the issue at hand. The Spanish conflict-of-laws system follows the rule of characterization according to the *lex fori* to select the applicable choice-of-law rule (Article 12.1 CC), but gives no guidance as to how to proceed in cases unknown to the *lex fori*. Even the search for a functional equivalent institution does not produce significant results.[155] The trust cannot be characterized as contractual. If a contractual characterization could be upheld the applicable law should be ascertained according to Article 10.5 CC, since the Rome Convention on the law applicable to contractual obligations and Rome I Regulation expressly exclude from its scope of

154. On this interrelationship between *forum* and *ius* as a strong reason for Spanish adhesion to the Hague Convention see M. Checa Martínez, *El trust angloamericano en el Derecho español*, 143–144 (McGraw-Hill 1998).

155. From the internal perspective, see I. Arroyo, *Trust y Ley civil*, 95 (RJC 1982); S. Camara Lapuente, *Operaciones fiduciarias o trusts en el Derecho español*, 1757 (RCDI 1999); J. De Arespacochaga, *El trust, la fiducia y figuras afines*, 118–129 (Marcial Pons 2000). For choice-of-law purposes see M.A. Asín Cabrera, *La ley aplicable al trust en el sistema español de Derecho internacional privado*, 2095–2096 (RGD, 1990); C. González Beilfuss, *El trust. La institución angloamericana y el Derecho internacional privado*, 58–60 (Bosch 1997); M. Checa Martínez, *supra*, 105–106.

application 'the constitution of trusts and the relationship between settlors, trustees and beneficiaries' (Article 1.2.g). A characterization pertaining to the law of corporations is not possible either. It is true that there may be functional similarities (functions of certain trust devices may be similar to those of corporations) and the concept of domicile of the trust is employed both by choice-of-law and international jurisdiction rules on trusts and corporations in a comparative private international law perspective. Even Brussels I bis Regulation uses the domicile of the trust as a special forum rule in Article 7.6, but similarities with jurisdictional criteria applicable to corporations are to be entirely rejected. Brussels I bis Regulation governs the domicile of corporations in Article 63.1 and the domicile of trusts in Article 63.3, but in quite a different fashion. Domicile of corporations is determined by alternative criteria based on corporation law (registered office, central administration, principal place of business), but the domicile of trusts is only to be ascertained by reference to the private international law rules of the forum, which in the case of Spain simply do not exist. The reason for this is that in Common law countries the concept of domicile of a trust is quite different from what could be expected in Civil Law countries (which would be something similar to a seat or registered office), on the contrary, the expression in Common law countries is just a reference to the place most closely connected with the trust and to the law that should govern the trust. Therefore, choice-of-law rules will determine international jurisdiction in a classical example of forum legis.

*158.* A characterization according to proprietary rights and remedies and the application of the *lex situs* for both movable and immovable property (Article 10.1 CC) might be appropriate in some cases to govern the relationships between settlor, trustee (legal owner) and beneficiary (equitable owner) over the trust estate and even in their relations with third parties (external relations). However, it would be insufficient for other cases and could even be misleading, since the internal relations in a trust cannot be reduced to property interests because personal rights and duties also stem from the trust. Sometimes the creation of a trust mainly poses questions of succession law (trust wills or living trusts with *mortis causa* provisions). Indeed, one of the most common situations in which a civil law jurisdiction court may confront a trust is the case of a living trust that includes provisions over movable or immovable property located in a civil law jurisdiction. If the trusts affects the rights of forced heirs under the *lex successionis*, the Spanish judge could treat the trust as a donation or gift and decide its reduction to conform to rules on forced shares of the law of the nationality of the deceased (Article 9.8 CC, which is still applicable in cases of persons who died prior to the entry into force of Regulation 650/2012 on 17 August 2015). A testamentary trust or will trust could be challenged on the same grounds. In any case, there is no univocal approach to trusts characterization for choice-of-law purposes, but instead the specific issue before the court determines which characterization should be made. If a general approach is necessary to solve conflict-of-laws issues regarding trusts, the principle of the most significant or closest relationship (as laid down in Article 7 of the Hague Convention) is the only safe guideline to determine the law applicable to those aspects of the trust which should not come under other choice-of-law rules.

# Chapter 6. Family Law

## §1. Unmarried Couples

*159.* The Spanish Constitution 1978 does not expressly recognize cohabitation or unmarried couples, but lays down a wide or plural concept of family relations under which constitutional protection can be given to those situations. Statutory sources on cohabitation are in force in different Autonomous Communities:

- In Catalonia, Act on Situations of Common Living and Mutual Help, 15 July 1998, now replaced by Article 234 Civil Code of Catalonia (Act 25/2010), (BOE 21 August 2010).
- In Aragon, Unmarried Stable Couples Act, 26 March 1999, now replaced by Tit. VI Decreto Legislativo 1/2011, de 22 Mars (Código del Derecho Foral de Aragón; BO. Aragón 29 Mars 2011).
- In Navarre, Equal Protection of Stable Couples Act, 3 July 2000 (BO. Navarra 7 July 2000, rect. BO. Navarra 29 September 2000).
- In Valencia, Unmarried Couples Act, 6 April 2001, (BOE 10 May 2001), not yet applicable as a result of its suspension following action by the Spanish Government before the Spanish Constitutional Court on grounds of unconstitutionality
- In the Balearic Islands, Stable Couples Act, 19 December 2001, (BOE 16 January 2002).
- In Madrid, Unmarried Couples Act, 19 December 2001, (BOE 5 March 2002).
- In Asturias, Stable Couples Act, 23 May 2002, (BOE 2 July 2002).
- In Andalusia, Unmarried Couples Act, 16 December 2002, (BOE 13 January 2003).
- In the Canary Islands, Unmarried Couples Act, 6 March 2003, (BOE 14 April 2003).
- In Extremadura, Unmarried Couples Act, 20 March 2003,(BOE 9 May 2003).
- In the Basque Country, Unmarried Couples Act, 7 May 2003 (BOE, 25 November 2011).
- In Cantabria, Unmarried Couples Act, 16 May 2005, (BO Cantabria, 24 May 2005).

These statutes can be divided into two groups, the first one (Catalonia, Aragon, Navarre, Balearic Islands, The Basque Country and Valencia) is expression of the competence of those Autonomous Communities to rule on civil legislation. The second group (Madrid, Asturias, Andalusia, Canary Islands and Extremadura) provides only a minimum degree of regulation applicable only because of the absence of Spanish statutory law dealing with unmarried couples. The scope of application of the statutes of the latter group of Autonomous Communities to unmarried couples, in the absence of other provisions, depends on the voluntary registration of the couple in a special administrative Register.

*160.* Decisions by the Spanish Constitutional Court have played a key role in the recognition and protection of the legal status of unmarried couples. Although Article

32 Spanish Constitution 1978 only mentions the right of man and woman to marriage, the constitutional jurisprudence, for example, *Decision of the Constitutional Court 222/1992*, 11 December 1992, holds that there is not just one single concept of family (matrimonial family), but that, on the contrary, other forms of family or family relations, i.e., different from the matrimonial family, can also be given protection under the constitutional policy of family protection set out in Article 39 Spanish Constitution. This Decision, and the previous *Decision 184/1990*, 15 November 1990, held that unmarried couples cannot be excluded from that protection, although the degree of legal protection for marriages and unmarried couples may differ since those two situations are not entirely equivalent, as long as the stronger legal protection afforded to married couples does not hinder or limit unreasonably the choice of other forms of family relations.[156]

*161.* The absence of a national statute on unmarried couples in Spain has led to the development of case law governing the effects of unmarried couples.[157] Spanish courts have had to face the lack of specific legal provisions and the need to answer the increasing number of cases dealing with unmarried couples. As a consequence, most of the legal regime applicable to unmarried couples in Spain has been developed by case law and criticism on this situation is that of unpredictability, since it is an area in a permanent state of change and development. The Spanish Supreme Court has dealt with a number of cases concerning unmarried couples, mainly in the areas of pension rights and division of property after separation or death. Basically, the Supreme Court holds the view that marriage laws are not applicable to unmarried couples, that resorting to legal analogy is not possible when trying to justify the application of the matrimonial property regime to the property of unmarried couples, in the absence of an agreement to that effect, that contracts between the members of the unmarried couple are permitted and that those agreements or contracts can make reference to the application of the rules on matrimonial property; that joint or common property may be a consequence of the tacit agreement of the parties as evidenced by their acts, and that protection can be given to the members of unmarried couples in case of separation on the basis of legal provisions on unjust enrichment.[158]

*162.* The public policy exception to the applicability of the foreign law designated by the conflicts rule cannot be invoked against unmarried couples. The Spanish Constitution (Article 39) also affords protection to other forms of family relations, i.e., different from marriage. Legislation passed in the Autonomous Communities of Catalonia, Aragon, Navarre, Balearic Islands, etc., is an expression of that policy of recognition towards unmarried stable couples. This affirmation is not

156. See Judgment of ECHR 8 Dec. 2009, *Muñoz Díaz v. Spain*: Spain is condemned because of the denial of a social security widow's pension in the case of a couple married according to Gipsy custom, which is not recognized in Spain as a valid form of marriage celebration.

157. Spain has ratified the 2007 Munich Convention on the recognition of registered partnerships, still not in force.

158. Decisions by Supreme Court 15 Jul. 1986, 11 Dec. 1992, 18 Feb. 1993, 22 Jul. 1993, 11 Oct. 1994, 27 May 1994, 30 Dec. 1994.

only applicable to different-sex unmarried couples but also to same-sex unmarried couples.

*163.* Issues of characterization are at the core of legal analysis in determining the law applicable to unmarried couples. Recourse to the conflicts rules on marriage or marital relations is possible by analogy, but such rules are inadequate to govern unmarried couples and their application would be against the will of the members of the unmarried couple, who decided not to be married and adopted other form of family relationship. The absence of a unitary characterization and regulation of the unmarried couple in Spanish law leads to a fractioning or scission of the applicable law, a process in which recourse may be made to the conflicts rules on contracts (Article 10.5 CC), personal status (Article 9.1 CC), extra-contractual obligations (Article 10.9 CC), proprietary rights (Article 10.1 CC) and successions (Article 9.8 CC).

*164.* The coexistence of different civil legislations concerning unmarried couples in Spain creates interregional conflict of laws that should be dealt with by reference to rules which apply to international conflict of laws (Article 16.1 CC), with the exception that the connecting factor based on nationality must be replaced by *vecindad civil* or civil vicinity. The State has an exclusive competence to govern choice-of-law rules (Article 149.1.8 CC) and that exclusiveness not only affects bilateral conflict-of-laws rules, but also unilateral choice-of-law rules. This is one of the reasons why the Equal Protection of Stable Couples Act, 3 July 2000, of Navarre was challenged before the Constitutional Court. The Act of Navarre laid down the rule in Article 2.3 that its scope of application covered all stable couples provided that at least one of its members were of the civil vicinity of Navarre. This unilateral rule governing the scope of application of the Act has been considered contrary to the exclusiveness of the State to govern choice-of-law rules (TC Judgment 93/2013, 23 April 2013). A similar problem could be found in the Catalonian 1998 Statute on this issue (now replaced by Article 234 of the Catalonian Civil Code where the unilateral rule on the scope of application has been suppressed).

*165.* Contracts entered into between members of an unmarried couple to govern their property relations will be subject to the conflicts rules in Article 10.5 CC. Rome I Regulation on the law applicable to contractual obligations is not relevant on this issue. Article 1.2 of Rome I Regulation excludes non-commercial contracts from its scope of application, such as contracts relating to wills and succession, rights in property arising out of a matrimonial relationship, rights and duties arising out of a family relationship, parentage, marriage or affinity, including maintenance obligations in respect of illegitimate children. Even if there is no express exclusion of the contracts to cohabitate, the exclusion of all contracts concerning matters of family law leads to the same result.[159]

159. A wide interpretation of the exclusion to cover all matters related to family law is held in the Giuliano/Lagarde Report on the Rome Convention on the law applicable to contractual obligations, DOCE, C282, 31 Oct. 1980.

*166.* The connecting factors used by Article 10.5 CC are mostly of a personal nature (common nationality, common habitual residence) and therefore are suitable to govern contracts within the context of family relations. The closing connecting factor based on the place of conclusion of the contract (*lex loci celebrationis*) is indeed rigid and may lead in certain circumstances to the application of a law only vaguely connected with a business contract, but in contracts to cohabitate the place of the contract will also in most cases be the place of common habitual residence of the members of the unmarried couple.

*167.* Conflicts between the laws of the different territorial units of Spain governing contracts to cohabitate are possible, since most Autonomous Communities statutes specifically rule such contracts. Those interregional conflicts of laws will also be subject to Article 10.5 CC, but the first connecting factor based on the common nationality of the members will be replaced by the common civil vicinity or *vecindad civil.*

*168.* In cases where there is no contract to cohabitate, specific statutory conflicts rules are non-existent (court cases are abundant but limited to internal situations for the moment). Consequently, the doctrine developed by legal scholars is the only help to be found in the process of determining the law applicable to unmarried couples in the absence of a contract to cohabitate. This situation should be solved by the Spanish legislator through the enactment of special rules to determine the applicable law to unmarried couples. The unification of these rules at the EU and in the international level is also desirable, but a considerable lapse of time will pass before the EU Regulation Proposal 2011 on the property consequences of registered partnerships will enter into force as an enhanced co-operation regulation applicable in the seventeen Member States that have expressed in 2016 their intention to be bound by such Regulation

*169.* Most scholars reject the idea that conflicts rules for marital relations or matrimonial property in Article 9.2 CC may also apply to unmarried couples by analogy. The rejection is based on the idea that marriage requires matrimonial consent and that in the absence of such consent the need to respect the free will of the members of the unmarried couple should exclude the possibility of applying matrimonial rules to their relations.[160] The rejection of a unitary approach based on the application of the conflicts rules on the effects of marriage has an important consequence, the applicable law must be determined through a fragmentary approach depending on the specific issue to be decided.[161]

160. See S. Sánchez Lorenzo, *Las parejas no casadas en el Derecho internacional privado*, 508–511 (REDI 1989); J.D. González Campos, *Derecho internacional privado. Parte especial*, 293 (6th ed., Eurolex 1996); I. Lázaro González, *Las Uniones de Hecho en el Derecho internacional privado español*, 344–346 (Tecnos 1999).

161. S. Sánchez Lorenzo, *supra*, 507–529; I. Lázaro Gonzalez, *supra*, 262.

*170.* One possibility is recourse to the law applicable to civil or personal status governed by Article 9.1 CC.[162] The application of this conflicts rule seems entirely justified in cases where the foreign law creates a legal institution of civil status (e.g., registered partnerships in the laws of the Nordic countries).[163] Personal status is subject to the personal law determined by nationality. Such a solution can be useful when both members share the same nationality. If that is not the case, the applicable law would be the law of the common habitual residence of the members, since residence is the connecting factor to be used when nationality is not applicable in the Spanish conflict-of-laws system (Article 9.10 CC). This solution would also be applicable to interregional conflicts with the exception that *vecindad civil* or civil vicinity would replace nationality. This conflicts rule would have the complementary advantage of its compatibility with the unilateral rules on scope of application in the Autonomous Communities statutes on the subject. That is, the law chosen by the conflicts rule (law of the common *vecindad civil* or common residence) should also comply with the unilateral scope of application requirement in the legislation of the Autonomous Community (at least one of the members of the couple must be of *vecindad civil*, or resident as the case may be, in that Autonomous Community).

*171.* A second possible approach would be the application of the conflicts rule on extra-contractual obligations in Article 10.9 CC, which governs the question by reference to the law of the place where the fact that is the cause of liability happened (*lex loci commissi*). Regulation 864/2007, Rome II, expressly excludes from its scope of application extra-contractual obligations arising out of family law relations or legal relations comparable to family law relations. The application of *lex locit commissi* will normally lead to the application of the law of the residence of the unmarried couple.[164] The actions seeking to indemnify or compensate one of the members for services rendered to the other during the existence of the unmarried couple are characterized in Spanish law under the rules on unjust enrichment. Consequently, the applicable law should be ascertained according to Article 10.9 CC on extra-contractual obligations. Article 10.9, third paragraph, CC governs the applicable law to unjust enrichment subjecting the question to the 'law by virtue of which the transfer of property value was made in favour of the enriched party', but this rule is not applicable to unmarried couples. In the case of services voluntarily made by one member of the unmarried couple for the benefit of the other, there is no previous legal relationship operating or requiring a transfer of property and therefore the applicable law to situations of unjust enrichment must be ascertained by reference to the general conflicts rule on torts, i.e., Article 10.9, first paragraph (*lex loci delicti commissi* rule). The same characterization would be applicable to maintenance obligations between members of the unmarried couple (this issue is outside the scope of application of the Hague Protocol on the law applicable to maintenance

---

162. J.M. Fontanelles i Morell, *Noves perspectives per una regulació de les unions de fet en el dret international privat espanyol*, in J.M. Martinell & M.T. Areces Piñol, *Uniones de Hecho*, 236–245 (Universidad de Lérida, 1998).
163. I. Lázaro González, *supra*, 361–362.
164. S. Sánchez Lorenzo, *supra*, 523.

obligations 2007, which is only applicable to maintenance obligations based on kinship or marriage).[165]

*172.* The legal regime applicable to property relations (existence of community of property or of a separation of property regime, determination of property assigned to the household, rights of one member over the property of the other, etc.) is also under the influence of the *lex rei sitae* in Article 10.1 CC, applicable to both movable and immovable property. The division of joint or common property (*comunidad de bienes* under Articles 392–406 CC) after separation will also be governed by the *lex situs* under Article 10.1 CC.[166]

*173.* The hereditary rights of the surviving member will be governed by the law applicable to successions. In Article 9.8 CC (still applicable to persons who died prior to 17 August 2015), the law applicable to both testamentary and intestate succession is governed by the law of the nationality of the deceased at the time of death. This law is applicable to movable and immovable property (principle of unity) and whatever might be the country where the property is situated (principle of universality). Gifts or donations made *inter vivos* between the members of the couple can be subject to actions seeking a reduction to comply with the heirs' indefeasible shares in case the decedent's law of nationality establishes rules on forced heirship. Gifts or donations *mortis causa* are characterized in Spanish law as succession matters and their substantial validity is subject to the law applicable to succession.

## §2. Marriage

### I. Validity (Capacity, Form)

*174.* Marriage is a constitutional right connected with the right of equality between men and women, which is also a principle of public policy (Article 32 Spanish Constitution). The right to marriage is open to heterosexual and same-sex relationships.[167] Same-sex marriage was made possible in Spain following reform of Article 44 Civil Code by Act 13/2005, in force from 3 July 2005, and this possibility is also applicable to foreign citizens getting married in Spain, even though the law of their nationality does not recognize same-sex marriages.[168]

---

165. *Ibid.*, 523.
166. *Ibid.*, 519.
167. See C. González Beilfuss, *El matrimonio de personas del mismo sexo en el Derecho internacional privado*, in *Estudios Jurídicos sobre persona y familia* (Comares 2009); S. Álvarez González, *Dimensión internacional del matrimonio entre personas del mismo sexo: lo que el ojo del legislador no vio*, in *Estudios del Derecho de familia y de sucesiones* (Universidad de Santiago de Compostela 2009).
168. Resolución Circular DGRN, 29 Jul. 2005, on Civil Marriages between persons of the same sex and Judgment TC (Pleno) 198/2012, de 6 de noviembre de 2012. See M. Checa Martínez, *Matrimonios del mismo sexo y Derecho internacional privado*, in *La reforma del matrimonio*, 389–417 (J.V.

A polygamous marriage is incompatible with Spanish public policy, although some favourable effects for the women concerned can be recognized.[169]

*175.* The celebration of marriage requires the consultation of multiple laws, since the applicable law is not confined to a single choice-of-law rule. There is a distinction between issues related to capacity and consent and issues related to formal validity.

*176.* Consent is an essential requirement for the validity of marriage and it is submitted to the spouses' personal law (Article 9.1 CC, as an issue related to civil status). For the same reason, requirements related to capacity are submitted to the personal law of each spouse, although the marital bond impediment is subject to the public policy exception in cases of polygamous or polyandrous marriages.

*177.* In relation to the form of marriage, the Spanish system conceives a solemn act that requires for its validity the manifestation of consent in a certain form and with the intervention of certain authorities in the presence of witnesses. These requirements do not preclude the admission of informal marriages if they are admitted in the place where the celebration took place and the spouses have their residence in that territory.[170]

*178.* The celebration of marriage is allowed in a plurality of forms, civil or religious. The validity of religious forms requires the existence of an agreement between the State and the confessional group (Evangelical, Hebraic, Islamic or Canon law marriages), but all forms have the same civil effects, the only distinction is the competent intervening authority. The control of capacity to marry is done in a different moment depending on the religious authority who is to intervene in the marriage, while for Evangelical and Hebraic it is done prior to the marriage, in the same way as it is done for the civil marriage (Article 56 CC), Canon and Islamic marriages benefit from a control done *ex post* (Article 63 CC). These religious forms, different from the Canon law celebration, are not possible where marriage between Spanish citizens is celebrated in a foreign country, because it is understood that the agreements with the different religious entities (Islamic, Hebraic and Evangelical) have a strict territorial scope of application.[171]

*179.* According to Article 49 CC, Spanish citizens can legally marry in or outside Spain. In the latter case, marriage can be celebrated according to the Spanish law (consular marriage foreseen in Article 51.3 CC) or in conformity with the law of the place of celebration (Article 49 CC).[172] A marriage celebrated in Spain, if at

---

Gavidia (dir), Marcial Pons, 2007); M. Soto Moya, *Uniones Transfronterizas entre personas del mismo sexo* (Tirant lo Blanch 2013).

169. Resolutions DGRN 8 Sep. 1995 and 24 May 2001.
170. Resolution DGRN, 2 Jan. 1998.
171. Instrucción DGRN 20 Feb. 1993.
172. See Judgment TS (Sala Civil), 20 Nov. 2011, validity of marriage in civil form in Mexico by Spaniards at a time when in Spain the Canon Law marriage was the only form of celebration available to Spanish Catholics.

least one of the spouses is Spanish, only admits the form of marriage regulated under Spanish domestic laws. If marriage is celebrated in Spain between foreigners, Article 50 CC allows the celebration of marriage in conformity with Spanish laws, as the law of the place of celebration, or in accordance with the national law of any of the spouses. In this way, foreigners can celebrate marriages in Spain according to the civil form foreseen by Spanish law, but also in the different religious forms admissible in Spain,[173] or in the form established by the personal law of any of the spouses, including consular marriage or religious forms admitted by those national laws. This makes possible the celebration of marriages between foreigners in Spain in all the religious forms permitted by their national laws, but not if one of the spouses is a Spanish citizen, since for Spaniards the only religious forms admissible are those 'legally foreseen by Spanish laws'.

*180.* Marriages celebrated in a foreign country between Spanish citizens or if any of the spouses is Spanish, will be valid if they are in conformity with the civil form foreseen by the law of the place of celebration, or with the religious forms admitted by the same law. The civil and religious forms admitted in Spanish law are also possible through a consular marriage (Article 51.3 CC). Consular marriage of a Spanish citizen in a foreign country in the presence of a foreign consular authority is admitted, provided that the Vienna Convention on Consular Relations is observed; moreover, international practice and customs, require that none of the spouses can be national of the State in which the consul exercises his/her functions and that at least one of the spouses must be Spanish citizen.[174]

## II. Dissolution

### *A. Annulment*

*181.* Article 107.1 CC (Act 11/2003, 29 September 2003) establishes that the nullity of marriage and its effects shall be determined according to the law applicable to its celebration. Therefore, the law applicable to nullity depends on the legal requirement of validity that has not been observed. If nullity is a consequence of lack of consent or capacity, the national law of the spouse whose consent or capacity is under scrutiny will be the governing law applicable to nullity.[175] If it is a question of form, laws applicable to the formal validity of marriage are applicable to nullity challenged on formal grounds. No matter what law governs nullity, in Spain the intervention of the Public Prosecutor (*Ministerio fiscal*) is required (Article 749 Civil Procedure Act (LEC), 1/2000, 7 January 2000).

*182.* The law that governs nullity is also applicable to the effects of nullity, including the existence of a 'putative marriage' (the Spanish Civil Code understands

173. Resolution DGRN, 4 May 1998. Judgment AP Barcelona, 20 Jun. 2006.
174. Resolution DGRN, 24 Feb. 2001.
175. See Judgment AP Cádiz 57/2012, 2 Feb. 2012 and comment by A. Font i Segura, REDI, 2103, 319–323.

that 'the declaration of nullity of a marriage does not invalidate the effects already produced with respect to offspring and to *bona fide* spouses', Article 79 CC).

### *B. Divorce*

*183.* In Spain, as in many other countries, there is a basic distinction between separation and divorce (only the latter implies dissolution of marriage). While separation, as a cessation of cohabitation, can be a separation of fact or judicially declared, divorce can only be the consequence of a judicial decision to that effect. Article 107.2 CC established the choice-of-law rule applicable to legal separation and divorce;[176] however, this conflict-of-laws regime for divorce was radically changed because of the entering into force of Regulation 1259/2010, Rome III, 20 December 2010, implementing enhanced co-operation in the area of the law applicable to divorce and legal separation, on 21 June 2012, in Belgium, Bulgaria, Germany, Spain, France, Italy, Latvia, Luxembourg, Hungary, Malta, Austria, Portugal, Romania, Slovenia and Lithuania. It should be reminded that its universal scope of application implies that Article 107.2 CC no longer could be applied by Spanish courts and to this effect Article 107.2 CC has been redrafted by Law 15/2015 (in force from 23 July 2015) only to affirm that separation and divorce will be governed by the choice-of-law rules of the EU.

*184.* Maintenance obligations between spouses require a different characterization, although, as a result of remission by Article 8 of the Hague Convention on the Law applicable to Maintenance Obligations, 2 October 1973, to the law applicable to the divorce, the lex causae used to be the same; however, Article 5 of the Hague Protocol 23 November 2007 has changed this situation by submitting the issue to the law of the place of habitual residence of the creditor, unless the other party objects that the law of the last common habitual residence of the spouses is the law most closely connected with the marriage. Also outside the scope of application of

---

176. Setting out that:

> [S]eparation and divorce shall be governed by the spouses common national law at the time of petition; in the absence of a common nationality, by the law of their common habitual residence in that moment, and, in the absence of a common habitual residence, by the law of the last common habitual residence of the spouses, provided that one of the spouses is still habitually resident in that State.

Nevertheless, Spanish law was applicable where one of the spouses is Spanish or is habitually resident in Spain in three cases:

(a) Where none of the connecting factors in Article 107 is applicable.
(b) In cases in which the petition has been filed by both spouses or by one of them with the consent of the other.
(c) If the applicable law does not recognize separation or divorce, or is discriminatory, or goes against public policy.

The scope of the law governing separation and divorce was usually understood by courts in an extensive way, covering causes or grounds for separation and divorce, effects of the petition, provisional measures and causes of dissolution of the matrimonial property regime.

divorce conflicts rules we may include the liquidation of the matrimonial property regime, custody of minors, effects upon the name and surnames, and social security matters.

## III. Legal Effects of Marriage

*185.* The applicable law designated by Article 9.2 CC will govern the so-called effects of marriage, which is a much wider concept than the matrimonial property regime, since those effects of marriage of a personal nature should also be considered under that legal category. This unitary solution to the personal and property effects of marriage avoids conflicts of characterization, but the expression 'effects of marriage' can be criticized for the reason that its origin can be traced back to Canon Law and includes those personal duties deriving from marriage (Articles 66–71 CC) whose enforceability would be against the principle of individual freedom of the spouses and are therefore not enforceable in the Spanish legal system.[177]

## IV. Matrimonial Property

### *A. Principal International Sources (Conventions)*

*186.* Spain is not a party to any multilateral international convention on the law applicable to matrimonial property, therefore the private international law sources remain within the frame of internal sources. The exception to this rule would be the rules on recognition and enforcement of foreign judgments, since Spain is a party to a good number of bilateral conventions that may be applicable to judicial foreign decisions on marital property. As to the Hague Convention on the Applicable Law to Matrimonial Property, Spain did not sign the Convention and there have been no attempts to adhere to it.

### *B. Principal Statutory Sources*

*187.* The Spanish statutory rules on conflict of laws can be primarily found in the Preliminary Title to the CC (Articles 8–16) enacted by Decree 1836/1974, 31 May,[178] but since 1974 many of its provisions have been modified, particularly in the field of the law applicable to the effects of marriage (Article 9.2), to matrimonial property arrangements (Article 9.3) and to the rights of the surviving spouse

177. For all those reasons some writers prefer the expression 'relations between spouses' to that of 'effects of marriage', see M. Amores Conradi, *Article 9, 2 y 3, Comentarios al Código civil y Compilaciones forales*, 2nd ed., vol. I, t. II, 182–185 (Edersa 1995); M. Amores Conradi, *La nueva ordenación ... , infra*, 39–42.

178. BOE, 9 Jul. 1974.

(Article 9.8) by means of the Reform of the Civil Code to Avoid Sex Discrimination Act 1990.[179]

### C. Evolution of PIL Rules with Respect to Matrimonial Regimes

*188.* Spanish choice-of-law rules on matrimonial property were subject to legislative reform on two occasions. The current regulation of the applicable law to matrimonial property regime in Articles 9.2 and 9.3 CC was laid down by the Reform of the Civil Code to Avoid Sex Discrimination Act, 15 October 1990. This regulation replaced the wording of Articles 9.2 and 9.3 CC as originally formulated in the Preliminary Title to the Civil Code, 1974.[180] Prior to this regulation, choice-of-law issues to matrimonial property regime were solved according to the original Article 1325 CC, 1889.

*189.* It should be added that the entry into force of the Spanish Constitution 1978 did have a direct impact on Articles 9.2 and 9.3 CC in force since 1974. Constitutional provisions granting the fundamental right of equal protection and no discrimination (Article 14) and equality of the spouses (Article 32.1) were partially against the connecting factor employed by the choice-of-law rules developed in 1974, since the husband's personal law was applicable as the closing connecting factor for both personal and property effects of the marriage. To solve the problem of constitutionality of the closing connecting factor of Articles 9.2 and 9.3 CC favouring the application of the husband's personal law, it was commonly held that the direct enforceability of the Constitution rendered this connecting factor inapplicable after the promulgation of the Spanish Constitution, even to marriages celebrated prior to 1978, since the constitutional provisions should also have to be retroactively applied.[181] It is true that in Spain no decision by the Constitutional Court was rendered directly on the issue, unlike the cases of Italy and Germany where the Constitutional Courts of both countries expressly declared the unconstitutionality of similar regulations in force in those countries, but the opinion of legal writers was almost unanimous.[182] Finally, the Spanish Constitutional Court (Decision of 14 February 2002) has expressly established that the former wording of Articles 9.2 and 9.3 of the Civil Code is unconstitutional and therefore is not applicable even for transitory choice-of-laws issues.

179. BOE, 18 Oct. 1990. Before this reform and since 1974, Art. 9.2 CC used the law of the nationality of the husband at the time of marriage as the connecting factor in cases of different nationality of the spouses. That solution has been held unconstitutional in a Decision of the Spanish Constitutional Court, 14 Feb. 2002 on grounds of sex discrimination according to Arts 14 and 32 of the Spanish Constitution, a decision that is relevant for transitory choice-of-law purposes.

180. M.A. Amores Conradi, *Las relaciones entre cónyuges en el nuevo Derecho internacional privado de la familia: valores jurídicos y técnicas de reglamentación*, ADC, 1987, 89.

181. See Judgment AP Barcelona 24 Mar. 2009.

182. M.A. Amores Conradi, *La nueva ordenación de la ley aplicable a los efectos del matrimonio*, Revista Jurídica de Castilla-La Mancha, 1991, 46–47 and comments to the decision by the TS, 6 Oct. 1986, REDI, 1987, 239; A. Borrás Rodríguez, *La Ley 11/1990 de 15 de octubre: de la no discriminación por razón de sexo a la discriminación entre ordenamientos jurídicos*, 272 (REDI 1991); A. Borrás Rodríguez, *No discriminación por razón de sexo: Derecho internacional privado*

*190.* The successive coexistence of different choice-of-law rules requires the determination of transitory rules for choice-of-law purposes. To this effect, the general prohibition of retroactive application of law means that the current wording of Articles 9.2 and 9.3 CC is applicable to marriages celebrated after 7 November 1990. As to marriages celebrated between 1974 and 1990 the applicable choice law rules should be those adopted in Articles 9.2 and 9.3 CC of the Preliminary Title to the Civil Code introduced by Decree 1836/1974, with the exception that the closing connecting factor based on the husband's personal law may no longer be applicable for the constitutional reasons outlined above. For marriages celebrated before 1974 the choice-of-law rule would be the original Article 1325 CC, 1889. In any case, as to the validity of matrimonial property agreements the applicable legal order must be that in force when the agreement was entered into.[183]

### D. *Main Choice-of-Law Rules*

*191.* In case the spouses have entered into a marriage agreement (*capitulación matrimonial* as set out at Article 1325 CC), the applicable law to matrimonial property is determined by Article 9.3 CC, redrafted by Act 11/1990, of 15 October, for the reform of the Civil Code to avoid sex-based discriminations. The content of Article 9.3 is as follows:

> The pacts or agreements by which the matrimonial property regime is stipulated, modified or substituted shall be valid if they conform to the law that governs the effects of marriage, or to the law of nationality or residence of the parties at the time of their conclusion.

*192.* Party autonomy for choice-of-law purposes is not expressly included in Article 9.3 CC. Therefore, the question is whether a choice-of-law clause would be admissible in a matrimonial property agreement. Of course, the spouses are free to draft the matrimonial property agreement in compliance with any of the laws mentioned in Article 9.3 CC, but that is an expression of material party autonomy, whose admissibility is undoubtedly recognized by Article 9.3 CC. The true question is the validity of a choice-of-law clause inserted in the matrimonial property agreement, i.e., party autonomy for a choice-of-law purpose. Such a hypothesis is also admitted by most Spanish legal scholars.[184] This means that, according to Article

---

*español*, 233 (ADC 1991); A. Borrás Rodríguez, *Non discrimination à raison de sexe et modification du droit international privé espagnol*, Rev. crit. dr. int. pr., 626 (1991); J.A. Carrillo Salcedo, *L'évolution du droit international privé espagnol depuis la réforme de 1974*, Travaux com. fr. dr. int. pr., 122 (1991–1993).

183. M.A. Amores Conradi, *La nueva ordenación … , infra*, 48–51. For case law on the transitory rules for choice-of-law purposes see decision of the AP of Malaga, 17 May 1995 and note by P. Maestre Casas, *REDI*, 1997, 260; also decision of the AP of Palma de Mallorca, 23 Dec. 1994, *REDI*, 1996, 302 and comments by R. Arenas García, 302.

184. M.A. Amores Conradi, *La nueva ordenación … , infra*, 53–54; M.A. Amores Conradi, *Articles 9.2 y 9.3, Comentarios al Código Civil y Compilaciones Forales, supra*, 187–188; M. Aguilar Benítez de Lugo, *Lecciones de Derecho civil internacional*, 165 (Tecnos 1996); M.P. Diago Diago, *Pactos*

9.3 CC, the spouses may choose the applicable law to the matrimonial property agreement by reference to the law applicable to the effects of marriage in the absence of a matrimonial property agreement (as determined by Article 9.2 CC), or to the law of the nationality or residence of any of the spouses at the time of the agreement.[185] This limitation on party autonomy – the possible choice is limited to the laws designated in Article 9.3 – is not satisfactory and concerns over choice-of-law clauses whose purpose is the evasion of the law otherwise applicable are not sufficient to justify the limitation imposed by Article 9.3 CC. But if, as most common opinion suggests, choice-of-law clauses are admitted in the matrimonial property agreement, with the aforesaid limitations as to the law that can be validly chosen, another question to be solved is the relationship between the choice of law included in an authentic document prior to marriage, as ruled in Article 9.2 CC, and a choice-of-law clause inserted in a matrimonial property agreement concluded after marriage under Article 9.3 CC. In such a case, the choice of law in the matrimonial property agreement would render the previous agreement to the law applicable to the effects of marriage almost useless, since all matrimonial property issues would be subject to the law chosen in the matrimonial agreement, and the agreement prior to the marriage would only govern the personal effects of marriage.[186]

*193.* In case spouses have not concluded any agreement with respect to their property (*capitulación matrimonial*), the applicable law to matrimonial property is determined by Article 9.2 CC, as it was redrafted pursuant to Act 11/1990, 15 October for the reform of the Civil Code to avoid sex-based discriminations:

> The effects of marriage shall be governed by the personal common law of the spouses at the time of marriage; where this is not applicable, by the personal law or law of residence of any of the spouses, chosen by both of them in an authentic document prior to the celebration of the marriage; in absence of this choice, by the law of habitual common residence immediately after marriage, and, in absence of such residence, by the law of place of celebration of the marriage.

*194.* The first connecting factor used by Article 9.2 CC is the 'common personal law of the spouses at the time of celebration of their marriage', personal law being determined by nationality. Only in case spouses are of a different nationality at the time of celebration of their marriage may the subsidiary connecting factors be applied, but always in a hierarchical way.[187]

---

*o capitulaciones matrimoniales en Derecho internacional privado*, 115–124 (Justicia de Aragón 1999); E. Rodríguez Pineau, *Régimen económico matrimonial. Aspectos internacionales*, 51–58 (Comares, 2002).

185. See Judgment TS 20 Nov. 2011.

186. M. Aguilar Benítez de Lugo, *supra*, 156.

187. Judgment AP Barcelona 29 Feb. 2012, Argentinean spouses who acquire Italian nationality and later they transfer their residence to Spain: the law applicable to matrimonial property and its liquidation is Argentinean Law. See F.J. Garcimartín Alférez, *Derecho internacional privado*, supra, 462–464.

*195.* The second connecting factor is party autonomy. The spouses may choose the applicable law to their matrimonial property relations, but their freedom will be limited. Those limitations come, first, from the subsidiary character of party autonomy as a connecting factor, since party autonomy can only be applied if the spouses are of a different nationality at the time of their marriage. Second, the laws that may be chosen by the spouses are limited either to the laws of the nationality or to the laws of habitual residence of any of the spouses. Third, the selection of the law by the parties must take place before the marriage and needs to be formulated in an authentic document. With respect to this stringent regime for party autonomy, one may wonder what reasons led the Spanish legislator to such a limited admission of party autonomy to govern the effects of marriage. In this respect, it is highly doubtful why the spouses are not allowed to choose the applicable law in cases where both of them are of the same nationality, since the interest in their integration in their habitual place of residence should favour the validity of such a choice of law.[188]

*196.* If the above-mentioned connecting factors are not applicable, because spouses are of a different nationality and have not selected the law prior to the marriage, the next connecting factor according to Article 9.2 is the place of habitual common residence immediately after marriage. The place of habitual common residence should not be criticized, but the time element to which the connecting factor is associated (i.e., the first place of common habitual residence), though quite common from a comparative perspective,[189] may in certain cases be clearly unreasonable, since it can lead to the application of the law of first common habitual residence of the spouses after marriage even in cases where the common life of the spouses shows a closer relationship with the law of some other place of residence after marriage. Such rigidity could have been avoided by using instead a more flexible formulation based on the idea of the closest relationship of the common life of the spouses, as is the case in Article 4.3 of the 1978 Hague Convention on the Law Applicable to Matrimonial Property Regimes, or by means of an escape clause centred around the same idea of favouring the application of the law most closely connected to the matrimonial life of the spouses.[190]

*197.* In cases where the preceding connecting factors are of no use, because spouses are of a different nationality, have not chosen the applicable law before the marriage and there has not been any habitual common residence immediately after marriage, the last connecting factor leading to the determination of the law that governs matrimonial property according to Article 9.2 is the place of celebration of the marriage (*lex loci celebrationis*). The reason supporting this rule seems to be the need for a final connecting factor that might be easily applied to cases that would be otherwise quite difficult to be solved by a single connecting factor. Nevertheless,

188. That is the criticism made by those who, admitting the need to respect the cultural identity of origin of the spouses, believe that the voluntary integration of spouses of the same nationality in the legal environment of their habitual place of common residence should be favoured by a more flexible regulation of party autonomy.

189. M. Revillard, *Droit international privé et pratique notariale*, 69–70 (Defrenois 1998).

190. M.A. Amores Conradi, *La nueva ordenación ...* , *infra*, 70.

the criticism as to the rigidity of the solution can also be put forward and again it is doubtful that its application in certain cases may not lead to absurd results; for instance, when the place of celebration of the marriage has been merely fortuitous and is in no way an expression of the legal and social environment most closely connected with the matrimony.

### *E. Scope of Application of these Rules*

*198.* Within the scope of the *lex causae* designated by Article 9.2 CC and as far as matrimonial property is concerned, this law should govern, in the absence of a matrimonial property agreement, the legal regime applicable to the matrimonial property relations between the spouses and its effects on third parties, the composition of the estate, the determination of common or separate property, the powers to dispose of and administer the estate wherever situated and the contractual responsibility of one of the spouses for debts incurred by the other.[191] The same issues would be under the applicable law chosen by the spouses in case they have entered into a marriage agreement inserting a choice-of-law clause in their agreement under Article 9.3 Civil Code. In any case, the applicable law will govern conditions of validity and effects of the matrimonial property agreement. It must be noted that the *lex causae* will govern the scope of party autonomy of the spouses to regulate their matrimonial property relations in a matrimonial agreement and, therefore, will also determine the imperative rules that cannot be excluded by agreement, as well as the rules to be applied to issues not covered by the matrimonial property agreement.

### *F. Interregional Conflict of Laws*

*199.* In Spain there may be conflicts of laws as a result of the coexistence of different civil legal orders.[192] Thus, the Spanish Civil Code is not the only regulation, but there are also regulations of matrimonial property in Catalonia, Aragon, Balearic Isles, Navarre, the Basque Country, and Valencia. These conflicts of laws shall be solved, according to Article 16.3 CC, in the following way

> The effects of marriage between Spaniards shall be governed by the Spanish law that is applicable according to the criteria set out in Article 9, and where inapplicable, by the Civil Code. In the latter case it shall be applied the separation regime of the Civil Code if pursuant to both personal laws of the spouses a separation regimen should be applied.

*200.* In order to find the law applicable to interregional conflicts of laws, the choice-of-law rules for international conflicts of laws are also applicable. This means that Article 9.2 CC is applicable to the matrimonial property regime if the

191. V. Simo Santoja, *Espagne*, in M. Verwilghen, *Régimes matrimoniaux, successions et liberalités*, vol. I, 717 (Editions de la Baconnière, 1979).
192. See *supra*, para. 12.

spouses have not entered into a property agreement, but the possibility of applying a foreign law is excluded, since Article 16.3 only refers to one of the Spanish laws that may be applicable.[193]

*201.* It should be added that according to Article 16.1 CC the civil vicinity or *vecindad civil* is the substitute for the connecting factor based on nationality, so that the first connecting factor arising out of Article 9.2 CC is the common civil vicinity or *vecindad civil* of the spouses. If such a common *vecindad civil* is absent, the possibility that the spouses may have chosen the law applicable to their matrimonial property relations comes into consideration, but this choice should have been made prior to the marriage and in an authentic document and only the choice of either the law of the *vecindad civil* or the law of the place of residence of any of the spouses will be valid. If there is not such a choice by the spouses, the law of the first habitual residence after marriage will be applied, and in case this connecting factor cannot be applied, i.e., because there was no common residence immediately after marriage, the applicable law will be that of place of the celebration of the marriage (*lex loci celebrationis*).

*202.* It is worth noting that in the case of different civil vicinity of the spouses and if the first habitual residence and the place of celebration of the marriage were abroad, Article 16.3 sets out a preference for the application of the legal regime included in the Spanish Civil Code, though in the case that both personal laws of the spouses, as determined by *vecindad civil*, adopt a separation of property regime (i.e., the case in Catalonia, Valencia and Balearic Isles), the rules of the Civil Code to be applied will be those on separation of property and not those on community of property. The fact that the Spanish Civil Code is the last connecting factor in Article 16.3 has been challenged on constitutional grounds because it does not respect a principle of equality among the different civil legal orders that coexist in Spain. However, a decision by the Spanish Constitutional Court, 8 July 1993, justified the preference given to the Spanish Civil Code for the reason that legal certainty would require a closing and objective connection factor.[194]

*203.* Article 16.3 CC deals only with cases in which both spouses are of Spanish nationality, but when just one of the spouses is Spanish and has a special *vecindad civil* not subject to the Spanish Civil Code, more difficulties are encountered in the existing choice-of-law rules. This case would also fall under Article 9.2 CC which may lead to the application of the Spanish law on grounds of being, not the common personal law of the spouses, since in this case one of them would be

---

193. For some comments on that Article see M.E. Zabalo Escudero, 'Article 16.3', *Comentarios al Código Civil y Compilaciones Forales, supra*, 1301–1315; C.I. Asúa González, *Algunas cuestiones en relación al régimen civil aplicable a los efectos del matrimonio entre personas de distinta vecindad civil: el párrafo tercero del Article 16 del Código Civil*, Revista Jurídica de Castilla-La Mancha, 73–88 (1991).

194. In a dissenting opinion, Magistrate J.D. González Campos insisted on the need for a different closing connecting factor that would have been compatible with the principle of equality between the diverse legal orders that coexist in Spain, in conformity with rules laid down in Art. 149.1.8 of the Spanish Constitution (BOE, 2 Aug. 1993).

a foreigner, but because the spouses could have chosen either the personal law or the law of residence of anyone of them in an authentic document prior to the marriage. In such a case, personal law could be understood as comprising also a special *vecindad civil*, insofar as Article 14.1 CC expresses that the question of being subject to the *Civil* Code or to special civil laws must be solved according to *vecindad civil*, and that Article 16.1 CC clearly states that the personal law will be that of the *vecindad civil*. However, if Article 9.2 leads to the application of Spanish law as the first habitual common residence after marriage or as the law of the place of celebration of the marriage it is highly questionable whether these connecting factors could give way to the application of a special civil legal order instead of the Civil Code.

*204.* The foregoing solutions to interregional conflicts of laws may also be applicable by foreign courts when the choice-of-law rule of the forum leads to the application of Spanish law, since that designation would be that of a multiple legal order. That is the case in the Hague Convention on the applicable law to matrimonial property regimes 1978 in force in France, The Netherlands and Luxembourg, which in Article 16 lays down the rule that the reference made to the law of a multiple legal order should be understood as made to the specific legal order designated by the rules of that country, what leads to the application of Articles 15 and 9.2 CC in order to single out the applicable legal order if the Spanish law is applicable under the Hague Convention.

## V. Spousal Maintenance

*205.* Maintenance obligations between spouses are subject to specific choice-of-law rules for maintenance and cannot be considered under the scope of the law applicable to the matrimonial property regime or the law applicable to divorce. This issue was governed by the Hague Convention on the Applicable Law to Maintenance Obligations 1973,[195] in force in Spain since 1 October 1986, and now is governed by the Hague Protocol 2007 on the law applicable to maintenance obligations (applicable in State members from 18 June 2011, as a consequence of a decision by the EU), submitting the issue to the law of the place of the habitual residence of the creditor, unless the other spouse objects that the law most closely connected with the marriage is the law of the last common habitual residence (Article 5). The universal scope of application of the Hague Protocol results in the inapplicability of the Spanish statutory conflict-of-laws rule for maintenance obligations in Article 9.7 CC, which has been redrafted by Law 26/2015 to include a simple reference to the Hague Protocol 2007 or the legal text that might substitute it in the future.

## VI. Custody of Minors

*206.* The issue of the protection of minors includes a variety of institutions such as parental custody, guardianship and other protective measures with the common

195. BOE, 16 Sep. 1986.

purpose of child protection. All these institutions of minor's protection used to be subject to the national law of the minor according the conflicts solution laid down in Article 9.6, paragraph 1 CC:

> [T]he guardianship and other institutions of protection of incapable individuals shall be governed by his/her national law.

*207.* However, the entry into force of the Hague Convention, 19 October 1996, on Jurisdiction, Applicable Law, Recognition, Enforcement and Co-operation in Respect of Parental Responsibility and Measures for the Protection of Children, having a universal scope of application replaced for most practical purposes Article 9.6 Spanish Civil Code, establishing as the basic conflict-of-laws solution the application of the *lex fori.*[196] Art. 9.6 CC has been redrafted by Law 26/2015 to include a mere reference to the application of the 1996 Hague Convention.

*208.* With respect to the prevention of child abduction by one parent the issue is subject to the 1980 Hague Convention on the Civil Aspects of International Child Abduction and to Regulation (EC) 2201/2003, on International Jurisdiction and the Recognition and Enforcement of Judgments in Matrimonial Matters and in Matters of Parental Responsibility, and also to the Spanish Minor Protection Act 1/1996, 15 January 1996.[197] The 1980 Luxembourg European Convention on Recognition and Enforcement of Decisions concerning Custody of Children and Restoration of Custody of Children should also be taken into consideration.[198]

## VII. Child Support

*209.* Maintenance obligations were subject to Article 9.7 of the CC, although this statutory choice-of-law rule was first substituted by the 1973 Hague Convention on Maintenance Obligations, on account of its universal or *erga omnes* scope of application, and now by the Hague Protocol 2007 on the law applicable to maintenance obligations.[199] To this effect Article 9.7 CC has been redrafted by Law 26/2015 to include only a remission to the Hague Protocol 2007.

## VIII. Legitimacy, Legitimization and Adoption

*210.* Article 9.4 CC has been entirely redrafted by Law 26/2015 on the system of protection of infancy and adolescence substituting the national law as connecting

196. Judgments AP Zaragoza 20 Apr. 2012 and AP Barcelona 9 Jan. 2013 comment by S. Álvarez González, REDI, (2013-2), 323–326.
197. BOE, 24 Aug. 1987; correction, BOE, 30 Jun. 1989. See P. Maestre Casas, *Sustracción y Restitución internacional de menores,* in *Nuevos conflictos del Derecho de Familia*, 499–542 (E. Llamas (coord.), La Ley 2009); C. Caamiña Domínguez, *La sustracción de menores en la Unión Europea* (Comares 2010).
198. BOE, 1 Sep. 1984.
199. See F. Garau Sobrino, *Las fuentes españolas en materia de obligaciones alimenticias ¿Hacia un Derecho internacional privado extravagante?*, CDT, vol. 3, no. 2, (2011), 130–144.

factor by the law of the place of habitual residence of the child. Article 9.4 CC now sets out that:

> The determination and character of natural affiliation shall be governed by the law of the habitual residence of the child at the time of the affiliation determination. In the absence of a habitual residence of the child, or if this law would not allow the declaration of affiliation, the national law of the child shall be applied.

*211.* With the expression 'character of the natural affiliation' the distinction between matrimonial (legitimacy) and non-matrimonial affiliation (legitimization) is avoided, because the legal effects of both sorts of affiliation are the same, and distinctions between legitimate and illegitimate affiliation are unjustified in Spanish law (Article 39.2 CE).

*212.* The Spanish legislator's choice in favour of the law of the child's habitual residence protects the interests of the child and also avoids the discrimination that would imply the application of any of the parents' law. This rule has been introduced in order to make the affiliation process easier since in most cases the situation will imply a minor residing in Spain and applying Spanish law to paternity actions filed before Spanish Courts will avoid the application of foreign laws in most cases. Of course, there will also be some cases of minors with habitual residence in a foreign country, being the domicile of the defendant in Spain the jurisdictional basis for the exercise of Spanish jurisdiction, The child's habitual residence, or in its defect, the national law of the child, governs the different kinds of affiliation and related presumptions, as well as evidentiary means, although certain requirements of procedural nature in the Spanish code of civil procedure (LEC) should also be followed. Spanish law admits the validity of biological means of evidence establishing paternity, and admission of this means of proof is characterized as pertaining to Spanish public policy, even against foreign applicable laws that do not admit this kind of evidence.

*213.* Adoptive affiliation is under the rule in Article 9.5 CC, which refers matters related to the granting of adoptions by Spanish authorities and recognition of foreign adoptions by Spanish Courts, to the International Adoption Act, 28 December 2007,[200] which contains specific rules of applicable law (Articles 18–24) and recognition of foreign adoptions (Articles 25–31), although the 1993 Hague Convention on Protection of Children and Co-operation in respect of Inter-country Adoption must also be taken into consideration.[201] Article 18.1 International Adoption Act 2007 states that requirements of an adoption to be granted by a Spanish judge will be governed by Spanish law. However, according to Article 19,

---

200. BOE, 29 Dec. 2007, amended by Law 26/2015 (BOE, 29 Jul. 2015). See A.L. Calvo Caravaca & J. Carrascosa González, *En torno a la Ley 54/2007 de 28 de diciembre, de adopción internacional: el ataque de los clones,* CDT, Vol. 2, no. 1, (2010), 73–139, http://www.uc3m.es/cdt.

201. BOE, 1 Aug. 1995. See also the Convention on cooperation in matters of adoption between Spain and the Russian Federation 9 Jul. 2014.

the national law of the adopted child should be observed in matters of capacity and necessary consents if the child is habitually resident outside Spain or if he does not acquire the Spanish nationality as a consequence of the adoption. The application of the national law of the adopted child is only justified where the Spanish authority considers that it enhances the possibilities of recognition of the adoption in the country of the nationality of the adopted child (Article 19.2 International Adoption Act 2007). Non-acquisition of the Spanish nationality as a result of adoption affects all individuals over the age of 18, because in such cases Spanish nationality is not automatically granted; instead, there is a right of option according to Article 19.2 CC.

Of particular interests are the situations of conversion from a Moroccan kafala to a Spanish adoption which may be granted by Spanish authorities without much control of the requirements for its recognition in Morocco. Thus, an adoption can be granted in Spain by Spanish authorities according to Spanish law over a minor of Moroccan nationality whose habitual residence is in Spain because previously a Moroccan kafala has been granted by Moroccan authorities in favour of two Spanish nationals.[202] This situation has led Morocco to complain publicly and to reiterate the need for more controls on the constitution of kafalas and its recognition in Spain, while Spain declared its willingness to give a clear solution to this issue in its adoption laws.[203] The International Adoption Act 2007 governs the recognition of kafalas in Spain in Article 34 (amended by Law 26/2015) which refers to the legal effects in Spain of foreign decisions on the protection of minors that do not create a filiation relationship (*status filii*), such as the Moroccan Kafala, and the new Article 34.2 imposes on the Spanish authorities in charge of the Civil Registry an obligation to control the validity of the foreign decision.

*214. In order to* expedite adoptions by Spanish citizens in a foreign country, the consular adoption is permitted whenever the receiving State of the Consul allows it and the adoptive child has his/her domicile in the consular demarcation. The consul will apply Spanish law (Article 17 International Adoption Act 2007).

*215.* Spanish legislation tries to guarantee the international validity and effectiveness of adoptions granted by Spanish courts. That is the reason behind the rule establishing that the judge may require, as long as it is so petitioned by the adopting parent or the State Attorney, the application of the laws of the nationality or habitual residence of the adoptive parent or the adopted child in relation to the necessary consent or authorizations for the adoption (Article 20 International Adoption Act 2007).

*216.* If the adoption is granted by a foreign authority, questions of recognition may arise. Article 26.1 International Adoption Act 2007 (amended in 2015) provides

---

202. For example, Judgment AP Barcelona 27 Jun. 2011. This solution should also be seen in light of the Decision of the ECHR 4 Oct. 2012, *Harroujd v. France*, in which the ECHR understood that the prohibition of adoption in cases of Kafala is not a violation of Art. 8 of the Convention.

203. See P. Diago Diago, *La Kafala islámica en España*, CDT, vol. 2 n. 1, (2010), 140–164; J.R. Verda y Beamonte, *Efectos jurídicos en España del acogimiento de derecho islámico («kafala»)*, Diario La Ley, n. 7393, 3 May. 2010.

the requirements for validity in Spain of an adoption constituted by foreign authorities when no international conventions are applicable. First, it should have been constituted by a competent foreign authority. Second, the adoption should not be against public policy. There is a need to emphasize the fact that Spain does not recognize adoptions made abroad by a Spanish adoptive parent if the effects of that adoption constituted in a foreign country do not substantially correspond with those of the Spanish legislation, in what is known as the 'effects equivalency test' (Article 26.2 International Adoption Act).[204] This rule prevents the recognition of foreign legal institutions as adoptions where the effects are not equivalent because the foreign institution does not create an affiliation bond between adoptive parent and adoptive child or because it does not require the dissolution of prior natural affiliations, or only give effect to a revocable affiliation.[205] This last obstacle can be solved if there is a waiver of the right to revoke the adoption before the minor is brought to Spain and waiver is made in an authentic act or before the Judge responsible for the Civil Registry (Article 26.2).[206] In the case of foreign adoptions which have lesser effects than those foreseen in Spanish Law ('simple adoptions', as opposed to full adoptions), these may have effects in Spain, but will not be registered in the Civil Registry as adoptions and shall not be enough to obtain Spanish nationality, although simple foreign adoptions can be transformed into full adoptions by Spanish authorities (Article 30).[207]

## IX. Guardianship

*217.* In most cases, the solution will be given by the 1996 Hague Convention on Jurisdiction, Applicable Law, Recognition, Enforcement and Co-operation in Respect of Parental Responsibility and Measures for the Protection of Children.[208] Article 9.6 of the Civil Code (amended in 2015) on the law applicable to the protection of minors only includes a reference to the application of the Hague Convention 1996, which is also applicable to the content of paternity (natural affiliation or adoption) and to the exercise of parental responsibility, as clearly stated in the reference made by the new Article 9.4 second paragraph, Civil Code (introduced in 2015):

> The law applicable to the content of filiation by nature or adoption, and to the exercise of parental responsibility, shall be determined according to the Hague Convention, 19 October 1996, on Jurisdiction, Applicable Law, Recognition,

204. See Resolutions DGRN 1 Dec. 2008, 28 Apr. 2010, 10 Feb. 2012, all in connection with adoptions under Ethiopian Law.
205. Resolution DGRN 14 May 1992, on adoptions in Morocco=Kafala. See M. Guzmán Zapater, *Adopción internacional: ¿Cuánto queda del Derecho internacional privado clásico?*, in *Mundialización y familia*, 83–120 (A.L. Calvo Caravaca & J.L. Iriarte Ángel (ed.). Colex 2001).
206. Resolutions DGRN 11 Mar. 1997, and 5, 14, and 16 Feb. 1998, about adoptions in Nepal, where the adoption of male individuals is revocable but female adoptions are irrevocable.
207. Auto AP Barcelona, 13 Jan. 2010.
208. Judgment AP Zaragoza, 20 Apr. 2012.

Enforcement and Co-operation in respect of Parental Responsibility and Measures for the Protection of Children.

## X. Pre-marital and Divorce Agreements

*218.* Pre-marital or post-matrimonial divorce agreements are possible in Spanish law. With regard to the effects of divorce upon the spouses the common opinion in scholarly writings and also in most recent case law is that such agreements are possible, as separate agreements or agreements included in a matrimonial property agreement. However, with regard to the effects of divorce upon the children of the spouses most opinions and case law reject their obligatory or compulsory character in the Spanish legal system. Nevertheless, Spanish private international law does not contain an express rule on pre-marital or post-nuptial divorce agreements. Article 9.2 CC only allows the choice of the applicable law to the effects of marriage prior to celebration when choice is made in an authentic document, but the rule does not, strictly speaking, include the law applicable to the effects of divorce. Article 9.3 CC includes the possibility of choice of law with regard to matrimonial property, subject to the limitations established at the same article, but it does not include the possibility of a choice of the law applicable to the effects of divorce. Therefore, the possibility of a pre-matrimonial or post-matrimonial divorce agreement was subject to the law applicable to divorce as ascertained by Article 107 Civil Code or, after 21 June 2012, by Regulation 1259/2010. Precisely, after Regulation 1259/2010 on the law applicable to separation and divorce entered into force, spouses have the possibility of selecting the applicable law to their divorce in a divorce agreement, subject to the conditions set forth at Articles 5–7 Regulation 1259/2010. Application of Regulation 1259/2010 may give way to an increase in the number of nuptial or divorce agreements, since making a selection of a law favourable to the validity of the agreement will secure the enforcement of the material contents of the nuptial agreement.

*219.* As regards promise of marriage, two material provisions of the Civil Code must be considered (Articles 42 and 43 CC). According to Article 42 of the CC:

> The promise of marriage does not produce the obligation to celebrate the act of marriage, nor to carry out what was stipulated in case of non-celebration. An enforcement claim will not be admitted.

But, Article 43 lays down the rule that:

> Non-compliance without good cause of a certain promise of marriage done by a person of full age or by an emancipated minor will only produce the obligation of compensation to the other party for the costs and the obligations incurred in consideration to the promised marriage.

Spanish legal scholars are inclined to treat the issue according to a family law and not to a contractual characterization, since non-performance does not generate obligations. However, from a conflict-of-laws perspective it seems we would be dealing with a case of non-contractual responsibility, close to cases of unjustified enrichment foreseen in Article 10.9 CC.

*220.* As pointed out above, divorce is only possible through a judicial declaration. But a separation in fact is admitted, and frequently implies the existence of agreements between spouses which affect different matters such as their personal situation, spousal support (or alimony), paternity relationships and so on. A majority of legal writers understand that these agreements do not admit a contractual characterization, and that instead a proper classification under family law should be preferred. From this perspective, we may understand that such agreements are governed by the law applicable to the effects of marriage which may be contractually modified. Agreements that affect the matrimonial property regime will be submitted to the law applicable to matrimonial property regime (Article 9.2 and 3 CC), and agreements that affect the offspring's situation will be submitted to the law that governs paternity relationships (Hague Convention 1996), etc.

## XI. Artificial Insemination, Surrogacy

*221.* The Human Assisted Reproduction Act 14/2006, 26 May 2006,[209] governs the techniques of assisted reproduction permitted in the Spanish legal system. There is no rule of applicable law in this Act, but due to the fact that this issue concerns the determination of filiation, it is reasonable to propose the application of the child's place of habitual residence, following the solution of Article 9.4 CC. However, attention should be given to the public policy characterization of these rules, so that a foreign law that does not conform to the techniques of assisted reproduction permitted under Spanish legislation can be dismissed.

*222.* More specifically, *with* regard to surrogacy, Article 10 of the already cited Act 14/2006 includes a strict prohibition and absolute nullity in relation to the contract of surrogacy, with or without exchange of money, by which a woman, the surrogate mother, gives up any parental rights in favour of the contractual party or of a third party. The affiliation of a child born by means of gestational surrogacy in a country where it is legal will ordinarily be subject to the law of the place of birth, but in Spain the application of Spanish law by means of the public policy exception, would lead to the nullity of the contract and the nullity of its effects with regard to the parental rights of the substituted mother and, therefore, because contracts of such nature will be null in Spain, to the non-recognition of the parental affiliation obtained by means of a surrogacy agreement in a foreign country.[210] In order to

209. BOE, 27 May 2006.
210. See S. Álvarez González, *Efectos en España de la gestación por sustitución llevada a cabo en el extranjero,* AEDIPr, T. X, 2010, 339–377; *id., Reconocimiento de la filiación derivada de gestación por sustitución,* De Bruselas a La Haya. Estudios sobre la unificación internacional y regional

resolve this recurring problem concerning Spanish heterosexual or same-sex couples that have decided to have a child by means of a surrogacy agreement in a foreign country, Instruction DGRN 5 October 2010,[211] made clear, somewhat surprisingly for most commentators, that surrogacy agreements to be performed in a foreign country are not contrary to Spanish public policy, and that foreign surrogacy affiliations determined by foreign judicial authorities should be recognized by Spanish Courts (by means of *exequatur* in cases of contentious foreign judicial decisions and by means of incidental recognition by the Civil Registry in cases of voluntary, i.e., non-contentious foreign judicial decisions). This Instruction was issued as a consequence of a very well-known case that was decided by Resolution of DGRN 18 Feb. 2009 in favour of the claim made by two Spanish men who had not been able to register their two sons born by means of a surrogacy agreement in California (USA) in the Spanish Consulate. However, this Resolution was annulled by Judge of First Instance no. 15 of Valencia (15 September 2010), later by AP Valencia (23 November 2010) and by Judgment STS (Sala Civil, Pleno) 6 February 2014 which decided definitively against the claimants.[212] The particular facts of the case taken to the Supreme Court, involving two men as parents, allows us to speculate on the narrow interpretation that could be given to the decision by the Supreme Court, although the decision speaks clearly of its potential application also to heterosexual couples. The decision allows for one parent to be recognized as such as long as he is the true biological parent, and only gives to the other committing parent a right of adoption, being the surrogate mother is the only legal mother possible under Spanish laws. Of course, prior to the decision by the Spanish Supreme Court there have been other decisions by the DGRN and Spanish courts accepting the registration of filiation by means of a surrogate motherhood contract in a foreign country.[213] The Spanish Supreme Court has had the opportunity (*Auto* 2 February 2015)

del Derecho internacional privado. Liber Amicorum Alegría Borrás, Marcial Pons: Madrid, (2013), 77–90; I. Heredia Cervantes, *La DGRN ante la gestación por sustitución*, Anuario de Derecho Civil, vol. 66, no 2, (2013), 687–715.

211. Instruction DGRN 5 Oct. 2010, on the Civil Registry regime of children born by surrogacy agreement (BOE 7 Oct. 2010). See A. Calvo Caravaca & J. Carrascosa González, *Notas críticas en torno a la Instrucción de la Dirección General de los Registros y del Notariado de 5 octubre 2010 sobre régimen registral de la filiación de los nacidos mediante gestación por sustitución*, http://www.uc3m.es/cdt; M. Guzmán Zapater, *Gestación por sustitución y nacimiento en el extranjero: hacia un modelo de regulación (sobre la Instrucción DGRN de 5 de octubre de 2010)*, AEDIPr, T.X, 2010, 731–743.

212. J.M. De Torres Perea, *Comentario a la STS de 6 de febrero de 2014 sobre maternidad por sustitución desde la perspectiva del interés del menor*, Diario La Ley, No 8281, 18 Mar. 2014; A. Hernández Rodríguez, *Determinación de la filiación de los nacidos mediante gestación por sustitución: ¿Hacia una nueva regulación legal en España?*, Cuadernos de Derecho Transnacional, vol. 6, núm. 2, 2014, 147–17; M.J. Parrón Cambero, *Vientre de alquiler: mater semper certa est, pater semper incertus est*, Diario La Ley, No. 8269, 12 Mar. 2014; M. Sáez-Santurtún Prieto, *La maternidad subrogada: estado actual de la cuestión a raíz de la STS de 6 de febrero de 2014*, Diario La Ley, No 8293, 15 Apr. 2004; J.A. Seijas Quintana, *Gestación por sustitución: el Tribunal Supremo deniega la inscripción de filiación de dos niños nacidos de una madre de alquiler*, Diario La Ley, No 8363, 28 Jul. 2014.

213. Juzgado de Primera Instancia de Pozuelo de Alarcón, 25 Jun. 2012; Resolutions DGRN 3 May 2011, 6 May 2011, 9 Jun. 2011, 27 Jun. 2011, 23 Sep. 2011. Filiation through surrogate motherhood has also been recognized for other purposes, such as maternity leave, in Judgments TSJ Asturias 20 Sep. 2012 and TSJ Madrid 18 Oct. 2012.

to review its previous decision of 6 February 2014 after the decisions by the ECHR 26 June 2014 in the cases *Mennesson v. France* (no. 65192/11) and *Labassee v. France* (no. 65941/11), and in the cases *Paradiso and Campanelli v. Italy* (27 January 2015), but the Court has decided that its previous ruling does not go against the ruling of the ECHR; the main reason for this holding is that Spanish law and the Spanish Supreme Court decision on the issue afford a sufficient level of family status protection that is considered enough to comply with Article 8 of the European Convention on Human Rights.[214]

Anyway, the situation in Spain is still quite open and subject to intense political debate on the opportunity and convenience of new regulation on the recognition of surrogate motherhood given the need of so many Spanish committing couples to have their children registered at the Civil Registry. From a sociological point of view, it seems that international surrogate motherhood has displaced international adoption as the preferred method of choice for infertile ccuples.

214. J. Flores Rodríguez, *Vientres de alquiler: más cerca de su reconocimiento legal en Europa (Comentario a la STEDH de 26 de junio de 2014, recurso nº 65192/11*, Diario La Ley, No. 8363, 18 Jul. 2014; J. Vela Sánchez, *Los hijos nacidos de convenio de gestación pueden ser inscritos en el Registro Civil español. A propósito de la sentencia del Tribunal Europeo de Derechos Humanos de 26 de junio de 2014*, Diario La Ley, No. 8415, 6 Nov. 2014.

# Chapter 7. Succession Law

## §1. *Lex Successionis*

*223.* Spain did not ratify the 1989 Hague Convention on the Law Applicable to Succession to Estates of Deceased Persons, nor did ratify the 1973 Hague Convention on International Administration of Estates, and therefore the applicable law was to be ascertained according to Spanish statutory choice-of-law rules. However, the situation has completely changed after 17 August 2015 when the EU Regulation 650/2012 on international successions entered into force, not only in matters related to the applicable law to the succession, but also to jurisdiction, and recognition and enforcement of judicial decisions; the Regulation also governs the recognition and enforcement of authentic instruments in matters of succession and the creation of a European Certificate of Succession.[215] However, the application of Regulation 650/2012 is only possible to the succession of persons that die after 17 August 2015, while Article 9.8 CC will still be applicable to the succession of persons who died prior to that date.

The principle of personality has been very important in Spanish conflict of laws rules regarding succession and therefore the main rule is the application of the national law of the deceased at the time of death, as stated in Article 9.8 CC:

> Succession to the estate of deceased persons is governed by the national law of the deceased, whatever may be the nature of the assets and whatever the country in which they are situated.

*224.* This solution leads to the application of a single law to movable and immovable property of the *de cujus* (principle of unity) and wherever that property may be located (principle of universality). The same rule applies to both testamentary and intestate succession, and is also applicable to succession contracts.

*225.* Contractual succession is referred to at Article 9.8 CC only marginally. The real scope of the particular provision relating to contractual succession is the solution of cases of mobile conflict. To this effect, the succession agreements concluded in conformity with the law of the nationality of the deceased at the time of the agreement remain valid even if another nationality is subsequently acquired. Exceptions to this rule are the rules on forced statutory shares in favour of certain relatives of the deceased. The law of nationality of the *de cujus* at the time of death is always to be applied to forced heirship. Succession contracts or agreements are forbidden in Spanish law (Article 1271 CC). However, this prohibition does not exclude the possibility of applying a foreign law that admits the validity of succession contracts. The prohibition of succession contracts does not amount to a public policy principle,

215. See J. Carrascosa González, *El Reglamento sucesorio Europeo 650/2012, análisis crítico*, (Comares 2014) and *Reglamento sucesorio europeo y actividad notarial*, *CDT*, Mar. vol. 6, n. 1, (2014), 5–44.

as evidenced by the fact that succession agreements are possible in the civil laws of Catalonia, Aragon and Balearic Islands.

*226.* In addition to the Spanish internal rules on succession in the Spanish Civil Code, there are other regulations on succession in force in the legal orders of some Autonomous Communities. The following are worth mentioning:

- Articles 411–465 Catalonia Civil Code (Act 10/2008);
- Articles 316–536 Aragon Foral Code (Act 1/2011);
- Compilation of the Civil Law of the Balearic Islands (6 September 1990);
- Compilation of the Civil Foral Law of Navarre (1 April 1987);
- Civil Foral Law of the Basque Country Act (25 June 2015);
- Civil Law Act of Galicia (14 June 2006).

This situation of coexistence of different civil legislations may lead to interregional conflict of laws that must be solved, according to Article 16 CC, with resort to the same choice-of-law rules applicable to international conflicts of laws (i.e., Article 9.8 CC), the exception being the fact that the connecting factor based on nationality must be replaced by civil vicinity or *vecindad civil*.[216] After entry into force of Regulation 650/2012, Article 9.8 will still be applicable to interregional conflict of laws, even in cases where the deceased died after 17 August 2015 because the EU Regulation is not applicable to interregional conflict of laws cases.

## §2. Scope of Application

*227.* The applicable law under Article 9.8 CC governs testamentary and intestate succession. A wide range of issues are subject to the law of the nationality of the deceased. Among such issues: the opening of the succession; the determination of heirs and legatees and their respective order and rights in the succession, including commorientes rules; the limitations on the testator's freedom to dispose of his/her estate resulting from rules on forced heirship or indefeasible shares (*legítimas*) in favour of some relatives and other reserves; the conditions and effects of the acceptance or rejection of the estate by the heirs, including hereditary transmission and estate acquisition; the administration of estates by testamentary executors designated by the testator, as well as their powers of administration and the rules for distribution of the estate among heirs;[217] however, Article 786 LEC 2000, allows the distribution of the estate to be done according to the rules set out by the testator even if such rules are different from those in the *lex successionis*, provided that the former are not against the interests of the forced heirs.

---

216. In general, as to conflict of laws in the interregional dimension see. J.D. González Campos & A. Borrás Rodríguez, *Spain*, in *European Succession Laws*, 321–322 (Jordan 1998); A. Font Segura, *La sucesión hereditaria en Derecho interregional*, 23–81 (ADC, 2000).

217. See J. Vallet de Goytisolo, *Normas de Derecho internacional privado aplicables en la transmisión y en la partición de la herencia*, 15–26 (RDN 1969); V.L. Simó Santoja, *infra*, 748–749.

Also under the *lex successionis* are to be determined the hereditary rights of the State in absence of heirs, a question characterized in Spanish conflict of laws as one pertaining to the realm of succession laws and not to property laws.[218]

The *lex successionis* also governs rules on *inter vivos* dispositions and the reduction of gifts *inter vivos*. The same characterization can be held about gifts or donations *mortis causa*, which under Spanish law are reserved the treatment of testamentary dispositions as to their substantial validity and effects (Article 620 CC).[219]

*228.* Outside the scope of the *lex successionis*, and therefore submitted to different choice-of-law rules and connecting factors, are the rights of the surviving spouse, which are governed, according to the last rule in Article 9.8 CC (Civil Code reform by Act 11/1990), by the law applicable to the effects of marriage. This solution was intended to be applied irrespective of the matrimonial property or the successoral characterizations of the rights of the surviving spouse, but always subject to the limitations imposed by the rules on forced heirship of the *lex successionis*, which should always prevail over the law applicable to the effects of marriage.[220] The application of only one law to the effects of marriage and to the hereditary rights of the surviving spouse seemed to be motivated by the legislator's desire to avoid possible adaptation problems between two different applicable laws (the law applicable to the effects of marriage and the law applicable to the succession of the deceased). Nevertheless, DGRN in Resolutions 11 March 2003 and 18 June 2003, quite rightly has made a very restrictive interpretation of the last rule in Article 9.8 CC interpreting that the rights of the surviving spouse referred to in Article 9.8 CC are exclusively those characterized as pertaining to the primary matrimonial property regime (such as, possibly a right of usufruct or a life interest over some property, as foreseen by matrimonial property rules), but not those rights of the surviving spouse which are of a hereditary nature or characterization, which will always be governed by the *lex successionis*. This seems to be a more rational and practical solution in both interregional and international conflict of laws hypothesis, since the hereditary rights of the surviving spouses are always interconnected with the hereditary rights of the other heirs to the succession, and the *lex successionis* cannot be subject to the laws of two different countries where there is only one estate to be divided, nor does it seem very realistic or practical to imagine the Spanish judge arriving at a mixed solution (adaptation) between the laws of two different countries. It can be said that the Spanish legislator established a complex solution to a quite theoretical problem, but doing so arrived at a solution that created more problems than it solved ('*hard cases make bad law*'), simply because it arrived at a result that consists in applying two succession laws to one estate, something with which Courts will have greater difficulties of application, is against the expectations of the interested parties, and is against the basic principles of unity and universality

218. A.L. Calvo Caravaca, *Article 9.8 CC*, in Comentarios al Código Civil y Compilaciones forales, *supra*, 372–373; A. Borrás Rodríguez, *La sucesión abintestato en ausencia de parientes llamado en el Derecho interregional español*, 895 (La Ley, 1988).

219. See Resolution of the DGRN from 6 Mar. 1997, *RAJ*, 1997, number 2033 and comments by M. Checa Martínez, REDI, 1998, 323.

220. See E. Zabalo Escudero, *Los derechos del cónyuge viudo* (Aranzadi 1993).

contained in Article 9.8 CC. We can add that the solution is quite far from the interests of an immigration country as Spain, because it complicates successions of foreigners in Spain and in most cases will have the effect of reducing the rights of their surviving spouses in mixed couples: reference by Article 9.8 to Article 9.2 means the application of the *lex materialis* of the first habitual residence of the marriage to the hereditary rights of the surviving spouse. If this place is Spain, Spanish succession laws only foresee a right of usufruct or life interest over a third of the estate, which is quite minimal when analysed in a comparative law perspective. The rule at Article 9.8 *in fine* can only be of some help in case of successions of Spanish citizens in Common Law countries, but only to give protection to the foreign spouse. Even though there are many reasons for a restrictive interpretation of Article 9.*8 in fine*, the Spanish Supreme Court has rendered a recent judgment (STS 28 April 2014) on this issue holding that the literal interpretation of that Article is the only possible interpretation as the only expression of the *voluntas legislatoris*, rejecting the restrictive interpretation made by the Dirección General de los Registros y del Notariado. This literal application of Article 9.8 *in fine* will be applicable to interregional conflict of laws and to successions opened before 17 August 2015, but in cases of successions to which the EU Regulation is applicable the rights of the surviving spouse will be subject to the *lex successionis*.

### §3. Testamentary Disposition

### I. Validity of Wills

*229.* The essential validity and effects of testamentary succession is governed by the *lex successionis* and this law is to be ascertained by reference to the law of nationality of the deceased at the time of death, as established in Article 9.8 CC, although the validity of a will granted according to the law of a previous nationality is also admitted, provided that it is not against the indefeasible shares of the forced heirs that result from to the law of the last nationality of the deceased. The indefeasible shares of the forced heirs laid down in Spanish law are not part of the Spanish public policy exception, since such shares differ greatly in Spain (different rules apply in Catalonia, Basque Country and Navarre). The issue was settled in a Supreme Court Decision from 15 November 1996, which excludes the *legítimas* from the public policy exception.

The entry into force of Regulation 650/2012 on successions allows the choice of the applicable law to the succession by the testator (*professio iuris*), but choice will be limited to the national law of the testator. It should be noted that the main connecting factor in the EU Regulation is the last habitual residence of the deceased, and that only through *professio iuris* the law of the nationality of the deceased will be applicable. The possibility of choice of the national law even before the entry into force of the Regulation 650/2012 was foreseen at the transitional provisions in Article 83 of the same EU Regulation, what means that the *professio iuris* rule has had an anticipated application.

The question of prohibitions of hereditary designation is also a matter under the *lex successionis*; some legal orders, including the Spanish, set out prohibitions against persons who may exert some undue influence over the testator, such as the notary, the priest or guardian of the testator (Articles 752–754 CC).

*230.* Renvoi of first degree is generally accepted in Article 12.2 CC and has been traditionally applied to successions. However, there is a growing trend in case law to reject renvoi. This is evidenced by the Decision of the Supreme Court 15 November 1996 (last will granted in Spain according to the laws of the State of Maryland), reaffirmed in Decision of 21 May 1999 (last will granted in Spain in conformity with English law). These were cases where testamentary succession and admission of renvoi could have jeopardized the principles of unity and universality of succession and led into a scission or fractioning of the applicable law as a result of the existence of movable and immovable property of the deceased located in different countries. In the reasoning of the Court, there was also consideration for the need to respect the testator's freedom to dispose of his estate according to the law of his nationality.[221] The principle of unity of the law applicable to the succession has been confirmed as the paramount principle with regard to the admission of renvoi in the latest decisions of the Supreme Court, 23 September 2002 and 12 January 2015, in which renvoi to Spanish law was admitted taking into consideration that all immovable property of the deceased was located in Spain and that Spain was also the place of the last domicile of the deceased, therefore leaving the whole of the succession subject to Spanish law after having accepted renvoi from English conflict of laws.[222]

*231.* Formal validity of testamentary dispositions must be ascertained in conformity with the choice-of-law rules in the 1961 Hague Convention on the Applicable Law to the Form of Testamentary Dispositions, in force in Spain since 10 June 1988.[223] The 1973 UNIDROIT Washington Convention on a Uniform Law to the Form of International Wills has not been ratified.[224] The universal scope of application of the Hague Convention renders Article 11 CC, a general choice-of-law rule applicable to formal validity, inapplicable to testamentary dispositions. Article 3 of

221. As to Decision of the TS, 15 Nov. 1996 see E. Rodríguez Pineau, *Estates in Spain. Inheritance According to Spanish Conflict Rules. A Judgement of the Spanish Tribunal Supremo*, IPRax, 1998, 135; E. Rodríguez Pineau, REDI, 1997, 265. For comments on Decision of the TS, 21 May 1999, see E. Rodríguez Pineau, REDI, 1999, 757; M.A. Amores Conradi, *Cuadernos Civitas de Jurisprudencia Civil*, 1130 (1999).

222. See J.L. Iriarte Ángel, *Reenvío y sucesiones en la práctica española*, in *Perspectivas del Derecho sucesorio europeo*, 111–136 (R. Viñas & G. Garriga (coord.), Marcial Pons 2009); S. Sánchez Lorenzo, *Algunos problemas del régimen jurídico de los actos inscribibles relativos a ciudadanos británicos*, Revista Crítica de Derecho Inmobiliario, 1999–2025 (2006); M. Virgós Soriano, *Derecho de sucesiones y reenvío: la respuesta del sistema español*, Anales de la Academia Matritense del Notariado, 181–210 (2004).

223. BOE, 17 Aug. 1988.

224. International Institute for the Unification of Private Law, *Washington Convention on a Uniform Law to the Form of International Wills 1973*, Washington DC, 27 Oct. 1973, www.unidroit.org/english/conventions/1973wills/1973wills-e.htm, 27 Oct. 1973.

this Convention also allows the application of statutory choice-of-law rules or other rules of the States party to the Convention which may lead to the validity of the will, which means the validity of the Consular Last Will established in Article 734 CC.[225] The entry into force in Spain of the Hague Convention also meant the ineffectiveness of Articles 732 (specific choice-of-law rule on the validity of holograph wills) and 733 CC (prohibition of joint last wills granted in a foreign country), issues now entirely under the scope of the Hague Convention.[226]

Outside the scope of application of the Hague Convention are the choice-of-law rules for interregional conflicts of laws concerning formal validity of wills, a subject-matter in which there are some relevant differences in the legal orders that coexist in Spain. For example, the civil laws of Aragon, Navarre and Galicia accept the validity of joint last wills granted outside those territories, although the issue is characterized as a matter of capacity and not as one of formal validity and, consequently, is subject to the testator's personal law or *vecindad civil*.[227] However, also within the scope of the Hague Convention are some matters of capacity, since Article 5 lays down the rule that provisions limiting the admissible forms of testamentary disposition based on age, nationality or other personal circumstances of the testator will be regarded as matters of form.

## II. Revocation of Wills

*232.* According to Article 9.8 CC, a last will granted in conformity with the law of the nationality of the deceased at the time of drafting remains valid even if nationality is subsequently changed. Exceptions to this rule are the rules on forced shares, an issue to which the law of nationality of the deceased at the time of death is always to be applied. With this limitation concerning the rules on forced heirship, the revocation of a previous will can be done according to the law of the decedent's nationality at the time of granting of a new will.

## III. Interpretation

*233.* The construction of the will is also a question under the scope of the *lex successionis* as determined by Article 9.8 CC. The law of the nationality of the

225. See J.D. González Campos & F.J. Garcimartín Alférez, *Article 11*, in *Comentarios al Código Civil y Compilaciones forales*, *supra*, 800–802.

226. See J.C. Fernández Rozas & S. Sánchez Lorenzo, *supra*, 506; Prior to the entry into force of the Hague Convention see A. Álvarez Rodríguez, *Reflexiones acerca del testamento ológrafo otorgado por un español en Francia*, 1233 (RGD 1988).

227. See M.E. Zabalo Escudero, *Derecho interregional de sucesiones en España*, Revista valenciana d'estudis autónomics, no 54, (2010), 220–241; M.E. Zabalo Escudero. *El testamento conjunto en Derecho internacional privado. Especial referencia al testamento mancomunado aragonés*, 6351 (RGD 1989); M.E. Zabalo Escudero, *Dos recientes leyes aragonesas en el ámbito civil (sucesiones y parejas de hecho)*, 305 (REDI 1999); J.J. Forner Delaygua, *Forma de las disposiciones testamentarias: Reforma del Código Civil español y de la legislación catalana*, 271 (REDI 1992); J.D. González Campos & A. Borrás Rodríguez, *supra*, 313–314; M. Requejo Isidro, *Ley local y forma de los actos en el Derecho internacional privado español*, 361–364 (Eurolex 1998).

testator governs the rules that courts must follow in the interpretation of the words included in the will and the circumstances under which a reference to extrinsic evidence is admitted to disclose the testator's intention. To this effect, the same law will be applicable to both movable and immovable property and whatever might be the country where the property is located.

# Part III. Annex: International Civil Procedure

## Chapter 1. Sources of ICP

*234.* International civil procedure (ICP) essentially includes international jurisdiction (i.e., jurisdiction on private international cases) and the recognition and enforcement of foreign resolutions. Beyond these notions, there are other issues of international litigation, such as service of documents, taking of evidence, etc. Some of these issues are included in another area, called international legal co-operation.[228] National and international rules on all these issues are numerous.

*235.* Spanish statutory rules on international jurisdiction are included in Articles 21 et seq. of the LOPJ 1985.[229] International Jurisdiction in civil matters is governed by the new Articles 22–22 *nonies* LOPJ 1985, as redrafted by the reform of LOPJ in 2015 (Law 7/2015, 21 July). Therefore, the problem of international jurisdiction has not, until the last decades, been treated in an appropriate fashion by both jurisprudence and academia. It used to be considered a matter of lesser importance when compared to choice-of-law problems. However, the enactment of the international jurisdiction criteria of the Judicial Power Act (LOPJ) 1985, and the entry into force in Spain of the Brussels and Lugano Conventions led to the development of extensive legal writing,[230] which has predominated over choice-of-law issues during the last decades in Spanish legal writing. In addition, case law increasingly reflects the importance of international jurisdictional issues, as evidenced by the growing number of decisions of lower and upper courts that deal with this issue.

*236.* The statutory Spanish rules on recognition and enforcement of foreign judgments were originally included in Articles 951 et seq. of the Spanish Civil Procedure Act 1881 (former LEC).[231] Quite recently, the new Act of International Judicial Cooperation in Civil Matters (Law 29/2015, 30 July) has derogated Articles 951

228. See D.P. Fernández Arroyo, *Derecho internacional privado (una mirada actual sobre sus elementos esenciales)*, 37–39 (Advocatus, 1998).
229. A.L. Calvo Caravaca & J. Carrascosa González, *Competencia judicial internacional: régimen de producción interna en Derecho internacional privado español*, DeCITA, No. 4, 2005, 519–542.
230. See the seminal article of M.A. Amores Conradi, *La nueva estructura del sistema español de competencia judicial internacional en el orden civil: Article 22 LOPJ*, 113 (REDI, 1989)
231. A.L. Calvo Caravaca & J. Carrascosa González, *Efectos en España de sentencias dictadas en procedimientos contenciosos*, DeCITA, No. 4, (2005), 543–570.

et seq. LEC 1881 after being in force for more than a century and has introduced a new legal regime in Articles 41–61 on the recognition and enforcement of foreign decisions. With regard to international child abduction new procedural rules can be found in Articles 778 *quater* to 778 *sexies* LEC 2000 as a result of the modifications introduced by the Ley de Jurisdicción Voluntaria (Ley 15/2015, 2 July).

*237.* In spite of the relevance of the mentioned national rules, it is obvious that the Spanish ICP system has been displaced by the 'Brussels system'. First, the 1968 Brussels Convention on Jurisdiction and the Enforcement of Judgments in Civil and Commercial Matters[232] entered into force in Spain in 1991. Actually, Spain ratified a version of this Convention,[233] elaborated especially for the admission of Portugal and Spain to the EC. The Brussels Convention was 'communitarized' by Regulation 44/2001 (now Regulation Brussels I bis 2015/2012), in force in all Member States, since 1 March 2002, except Denmark, although its rules were extended also to Denmark as a consequence of the entry in force (on 1 July 2007) of the Agreement between the EC and the Kingdom of Denmark on jurisdiction and the recognition and enforcement of judgments in civil and commercial matters on 19 October 2005. Second, the 1988 Lugano Convention on the same matters[234] has also been in force in Spain since 1994, now replaced by the 2007 Lugano Convention.[235] Third, Regulation 2201/2003 concerning jurisdiction and the recognition and enforcement of judgments in matrimonial matters and the matters of parental responsibility (Brussels II *bis*), repealing Regulation No. 1347/2000 is in force in all EU Member States, except Denmark, from 1 August 2004. Regulation 4/2009 on jurisdiction, applicable law and recognition and enforcement of judicial decisions on maintenance obligations is also in force from 18 June 2011 (Brussels III). Finally, Regulation 650/2012 on international successions governs international jurisdiction and recognition and enforcement of foreign judments in cases where the deceased died after 17 August 2017. All these rules diminish considerably the number of cases that fall under the scope of application of national rules.

*238.* Additionally, the statutory system on international jurisdiction (dated from 1985, although heavily redrafted in 2015) has been remarkably influenced by the Brussels Convention. That is to say, even before Spanish accession to the EC, the basic principles of the Brussels Convention were already present in the Spanish system of international jurisdiction for civil matters. The influence of Brussels I bis has also been extended to Spanish rules on lis pendens with the introduction of new rules in Articles 37–40 Law 29/2015 on International Judicial Cooperation in Civil Matters which clearly resemble those contained in Brussels I bis in relation to lis pendens with third states.

---

232. BOE, 28 Jan. 1991; correction, BOE, 30 Apr. 1991.
233. Signed at San Sebastián, Spain, 26 May 1989. The subsequent version of 1996 followed the accession of Austria, Finland and Sweden (1998 OJ C 27, 1).
234. BOE, 20 Oct. 1994; correction BOE, 10 Jan. 1995 (1988 OJ (L 319) 9).
235. Besides EU Member States, Lugano Convention is in force in Iceland, Norway and Switzerland.

*239.* The PIL system also includes plenty of international conventions related to ICP. Most of them are bilateral conventions exclusively focused on the recognition and enforcement of foreign resolutions. Nevertheless, there are also some conventions that include rules on international jurisdiction: bilateral conventions between Spain and Romania (1997) and Spain and El Salvador (2000). There are also several conventions on specific matters[236] in force in Spain, which contain rules on jurisdiction.

---

236. Especially on very specific types of torts (such as nuclear accidents) and international carriage issues (transportation of goods by road, railroad, air and maritime bills of lading). Jurisdiction in cases of international carriage by sea has been governed by the Law 14/2014 on Maritime Navigation (Arts 468 y 469), but always without prejudice to the international conventions and EU Regulations in force in Spain.

## Chapter 2. The Principle of *Lex Fori*

*240.* Whenever a Spanish court assumes jurisdiction over a PIL issue, the *lex fori* governs all matters relating to procedure. It is a principle of universal application[237] with a long-standing tradition in Spain. In fact, the Supreme Court recognized this principle in decisions of 31 January 1921 and 19 December 1930. In the latter decision, the Supreme Court clearly states that:

> Application of the formal statute of lex terrae or lex loci is clear in all that regards procedural matters and it is the rule by which our procedural civil law is governed ...

*241.* In the Spanish legislation, the *lex fori regit processum* rule was expressly established in the Preliminary Title to the CC in Article 8.2.[238] Currently, this rule was replaced by Article 3 LEC (Act 1/2000, 7 January 2000), which sets out that:

> Besides the exceptions contained in Treaties and International Conventions, civil procedures in Spanish territory are governed exclusively by Spanish procedure law.

*242.* This rule's generality and inflexibility is obviously inadequate to the reality of international civil litigation today, and for these reasons it has been thoroughly criticized.[239] Particularly, it must be taken into consideration that this rule refers to civil procedure in Spain, and thus it does not cover that, in the context of international litigation, it is likely that some procedural acts may have to be conducted necessarily in another forum with the help of international co-operation. Thus the wording employed by the former Article 8.2 of the CC was much better, because it referred to 'proceedings conducted in Spanish territory'.[240]

*243.* Moreover, Article 3 does not provide for any exception to the scope of the *lex fori* rule, even though it is obvious that some important issues can hardly be governed by such principle. The new statute should have at least determined which issues are not characterized as procedural in order to determine the applicable law. Issues related with legal capacity, legal standing of the parties and representation, as well as those related to certain aspects of evidence, require special solutions.[241]

---

237. See E. Castellanos Ruiz, *La ley aplicable al proceso y el Article 3 de la LEC 1/2000*, 240 (AEDIPr 2001).
238. See A.L. Calvo Caravaca, *Régimen del proceso civil con elemento extranjero y asistencia judicial internacional*, 5095 (RGD 1986); M.D. Adam Muñoz, *El proceso civil con elemento extranjero y la cooperación judicial internacional* (Aranzadi 1995).
239. E. Castellanos Ruiz, *infra*, 242; P.P. Miralles Sangro, *Régimen del proceso civil con elemento extranjero y asistencia judicial internacional*, in E. Pérez Vera (ed.), *supra*, 385–386.
240. See E. Castellanos Ruiz, *infra*, 243–247, who holds the view that that the provisions of Art. 3 new LEC are 'undesirable, unfair and clumsily made'.
241. J.C. Fernández Rozas & S. Sánchez Lorenzo, *supra*, 281–287.

## Chapter 3. International Jurisdiction

### §1. General Principles

*244.* The Spanish national system of international jurisdiction contained in the LOPJ is based on various general principles. Article 117.3 of the Spanish Constitution sets the initial standard for the development of a system of international jurisdictional, stating that:

> The exercise of jurisdictional authority in all types of procedures, judgments and the execution of judgments corresponds exclusively to judges and courts determined by the law, taking into account its rules on jurisdiction and procedure.

*245.* This article has been interpreted as implying a self-restraint of jurisdiction. It prevents courts from exercising jurisdiction in cases where there is no rule establishing jurisdiction of the Spanish Courts. Such a conclusion is important, because it represents a radical change from the long-standing Spanish tradition of what scholars defined as 'Spanish jurisdictional imperialism',[242] developed upon the interpretation of Articles 51 and 70 of the former LEC 1881, by which Spanish courts could validly exercise jurisdiction in all cases. However, in the system now in force, the wording of Article 117.3 combined with the constitutional principles of legal certainty and legality exclude an 'imperialist' approach. Article 21.1 LOPJ confirms this with much more precision establishing that any intervention of Spanish judges and courts will be in conformity with what is 'established in the present Act and international treaties and conventions in force in Spain'.

*246.* Some scholars have associated this principle of jurisdictional self-restraint with the constitutional principle that establishes 'the right to a predetermined judge established by the law' (Article 24.2).[243] According to some authoritative interpretations, this fundamental right is the reason why *forum non conveniens*[244] cannot be accepted in Spain. This conclusion is also the motivation of an attitude of great antagonism in Spain towards the eventual application of such doctrine in the Draft Convention on Jurisdiction and Enforcement of Judgments, which was discussed in The Hague Conference on Private International Law from 1992 through 2001.[245]

---

242. A. Miaja de la Muela, *El imperialismo jurisdiccional español y el Derecho internacional, Mélanges C. Fragistas*, vol. I-B (Thessaloniki, 1968), 89; D.P. Fernández Arroyo, *Compétences exclusives et compétences exorbitantes dans les relations privées internationales*, R. des C., 2006.
243. M.A. Amores Conradi, *La nueva estructura ...*, *infra*; J.D. González Campos, *La competencia judicial internacional. Aspectos generales*, in E. Pérez Vera (ed.), *supra*, 316–317.
244. J.D. González Campos, previous note, 318–319.
245. A. Borrás Rodríguez, *Una nueva etapa en la Conferencia de La Haya de Derecho internacional privado: la elaboración de un convenio sobre competencia judicial y ejecución de sentencias en materia civil y mercantil*, Responsa Iurisperitorum Digesta, vol. III, 2002, 60–61.

Yet, other scholars believe that Article 24.2 of the Spanish Constitution only intended the prohibition of special courts ex post facto.[246]

*247.* Another principle of special relevance is the right to judicial protection (*tutela judicial efectiva*) established in Article 24.1 Spanish Constitution. This rule has generated more decisions of the Constitutional Court than any other.[247] PIL cases have not been an exception. On the contrary, there is an international dimension in the protection included in Article 24.1.[248] *Decision TC 61/2000*, 13 March 2000, is based on such principle and granted legal protection to an American citizen who sought relief in Spain in order to change some measures taken by an American court regarding the custody of a minor. His claim was denied by both the first instance court and the Provincial Court. But the Spanish Constitutional Court established that 'given the circumstances, it was necessary to guarantee a reasonable access to justice'.[249]

*248.* Finally the wording of Articles 22–22 nonies LOPJ allows us to confirm the existence of a principle of proximity or minimum contacts test in the determination of the jurisdiction of Spanish judges and courts in international cases. This means that, in order to exercise international jurisdiction, the case must have a reasonable connection with Spain. Thus, the traditional 'imperialist' attitude that prevailed in this area is definitely over. This principle is also related with the principle of openness of the Spanish legal system to other legal systems, established in the Preamble and Articles 16.3, and 93–95 of the Spanish Constitution.[250]

## §2. Exclusive Fora

*249.* Article 22 LOPJ reproduces entirely Article 16 of the 1968 Brussels Convention (also similar to Article 22 of Regulation (EC) 44/2001 and Article 24 Regulation 1215/2012). This means that Spanish courts have exclusive jurisdiction over cases related to:

- Rights in rem in real property or tenancies of real property, if the property is situated in Spain.
- The constitution, validity, nullity or dissolution of corporations or other legal persons, as well as the agreements or decisions of their organs, if the company or the legal person has its domicile in Spain.

---

246. M. Virgós Soriano & F.J. Garcimartín Alférez, *supra*, 61. See Judgments TS 6 Feb. 1992 and TC 1/1996.
247. See F. Rubio Llorente (ed.), *Derechos fundamentales y principios constitucionales*, 261–383 (Ariel 1995).
248. F.J. Garcimartín Alférez, *Sobre el fundamento de la cooperación jurídica internacional*, in *Cooperación jurídica internacional*, 65–68 (Escuela Diplomática 2001).
249. I. Heredia Cervantes, *Competencia de los tribunales españoles para modificar decisiones extranjeras (Comentario a la STC 61/2000, de 13 de marzo)*, Derecho Privado y Constitución, 14, 2000, 185.
250. See *supra*, para. 5, and J.D. González Campos, *La competencia judicial …* , *supra*, 317–318.

- The validity or nullity of entries in Spanish public registers.
- The registration or validity of patents and other rights required to be deposited or registered, if the deposit or registration has been applied for or has taken place in Spain.
- The recognition and enforcement in Spanish territory of foreign judicial resolutions and arbitral awards.

*250.* The entry into force in Spain of the Brussels Convention in 1991 substituted by Regulation (EC) 44/2001, made Article 22.1 LOPJ almost inapplicable. In fact, since Article 24 of Regulation (EC) 1215/2012 is to be applied without considering the domicile of the parties, the possibilities for the application of Article 22 are almost non-existent. One exception could be the new rule on temporary leases of real property in Article 22 (introduced in the 2015 reform); this rule could be applied to cases in which the property is not located in Spain or the rest of the EU.

*251.* Nevertheless, it must be noted that prior to the entry into force of the Brussels system in Spain, the 'exclusive' character of these fora had no relevance, as opposed to what occurs in the Brussels system rules. In the Brussels system, these rules may 'send' a case to any of the Member States, so that the establishment of a hierarchy among the different categories of fora and the exclusive character of some of them is of great importance. In the Brussels system, if jurisdiction exclusively corresponds to a State (Article 16 of the Brussels and Lugano Conventions; Article 22 of Regulation (EC) 44/2001), and Article 24 of Regulation 1215/2012, the other states' courts cannot proceed under any circumstance and must reject the case of their own motion (Articles 19 Brussels and Lugano Conventions, Article 25 of Regulation (EC) 44/2001 and Article 27 Regulation 1215/2012). On the contrary, the national system rules of international jurisdiction are unilateral and, as such, only bind Spanish courts. Thus, for Spanish courts applying the jurisdictional rules in LOPJ, the distinction between exclusive or concurrent jurisdiction is of no importance, as long as any of the fora may confer jurisdiction on the Spanish courts.

*252.* Nevertheless, Article 22 LOPJ still has some significance for recognition and enforcement of judgments, because it grants an 'exclusive' character to all subject matters included in Article 22 LOPJ and this may prevent the recognition and enforcement of foreign judgments which may have been rendered against the exclusive character of the Spanish jurisdiction.

## §3. General Fora

*253.* The different general criteria used by LOPJ to grant jurisdiction to the Spanish courts are, domicile of the defendant situated in Spain (Article 22 *ter*), or voluntary submission by the parties, tacitly or expressly, to the jurisdiction of the Spanish courts (Article 22 *bis*).[251]

*254.* The influence of the Brussels system can also be seen in the Spanish general fora. Domicile of the defendant in one of the Member States is the general spatial requirement for the application of Regulation (EC) 1215/2012 (Article 5), but also a general forum (Article 4). In cases in which the defendant is domiciled in Spain, Spanish courts will have jurisdiction according to Article 22 *ter* LOPJ, only if the issue is outside the scope of application of Regulation (EC) 1215/2012. However, Article 22 *bis* LOPJ is not applicable to sustain jurisdiction of Spanish courts in cases of tacit submission by the parties, because Article 26 of the Regulation has a universal scope of application.[252]

## §4. Special Fora

*255.* Besides these general rules of jurisdiction, there are specific international jurisdictional rules applicable to some issues. Thus, according to Articles 22 *quarter*, 22 *quinquies*, and 25 LOPJ,[253] Spanish courts have jurisdiction in the following subject matters:

– Declaration of absence or decease, if the missing person had his last domicile in Spain or were of Spanish nationality
– Incapacity and protective measures over the person or property of minors and incapacity of natural persons, if they are habitually resident in Spain.
– Matrimonial matters:[254] here the new Article 22 *quarter* c) has reproduced all the different available fora at Article 3 Regulation 2201/2003 (Brussels II *bis*) seeking to unify the grounds for jurisdiction in cases of separation and divorce to which Regulation Brussels II bis is applicable with those applicable to matrimonial property.
– Affiliation proceedings and parent-child relationships, protection of minors and parental responsibility if the child is habitually resident in Spain at the time of the claim, or if the plaintiff is of Spanish nationality or is habitually resident in Spain, at least for six months prior to the filing of the claim

251. With respect to the admissibility of the express or tacit submission by the parties according to Art. 22.2 LOPJ 1985, see M.A. Amores Conradi, *La nueva estructura* … , *infra*, 139–140 and comments by R. Arenas García to the decision of the AP of Baleares, 18 Jul. 1995, REDI, 1996, 266. See also Judgment TS, Civil Chamber, 12 Jan. 2009, and commentary by *of* D.P. Fernández Arroyo, Rev. crit. dr. int. pr., 2009, 756–765.

252. Judgment TS, 16 May 2008.

253. Article 22 *sexies* LOPJ (amended in 2015 and formerly Art. 22.5 LOPJ) determines that Spanish courts can decide the adoption of protective and provisional measures to be enforced in Spain, regarding persons or assets located in Spain. See AP Barcelona, 31 Mar. 2010, pointing out the distinction between jurisdiction on the merits and jurisdiction on interim measures.

254. With respect to legal separation, divorce and nullity of marriage, as well as to parental responsibility, account must be taken of Regulation (EC) No. 2201/2003.

- Adoption: in situations determined by the Law of International Adoption (Law 54/2007, 28 December).[255]
- Maintenance, if the maintenance creditor or debtor is habitually resident in Spain, or if the maintenance claim is accessory to a claim of civil status or parental responsibility, where the Spanish courts have jurisdiction over the latter claim
- Succession, if the deceased had the last habitual residence in Spain or if the deceased were of Spanish nationality at the time of death and the assets were located in Spain. Here, the reform has been clearly restrictive with regard to the second alternative forum; while in the former wording of this rule the location in Spain of real property was sufficient to confer jurisdiction upon Spanish courts, now the rule requires the Spanish nationality of the deceased and cumulatively the location of the assets (in plural) in Spain.
- Contractual obligations, if the obligation in question has been performed or is to be performed in Spain.
- Non-contractual obligations, if the place where the harmful event occurred is located in Spain.
- In disputes arising out of the operations of a branch, agency or other secondary establishment, if the branch, agency or secondary establishment is situated in Spain.
- Consumer contracts, if the consumer or the other contracting party is habitually resident in Spain; the latter only will be in a position to file a claim in Spain where the consumer is habitually resident in Spain.
- Insurance, if the insurer, the policyholder or the beneficiary is domiciled in Spain.
- Movable property, if property is located in Spain at the time of the claim.
- Individual contracts of employment, if Spain is the State where the employee carries out his or her work, or where the contract was concluded, or if the defendant is domiciled in Spain or has a branch, an agency, a delegation or any other representation in Spain, or if both the employer and the employee are of Spanish nationality, regardless the place of conclusion of the contract and the place where the employee carries out his or her work.

255. Act 54/2007, 28 December, on international adoption (BOE, 29 Dec. 2007, amended in 2015)), includes PIL rules in Title II. In regard to jurisdiction, Art. 14 establishes Spanish jurisdiction for the constitution of adoption whenever any of the parties (the person who wishes to adopt or the person to be adopted) has, at the time of making the request for adoption, either Spanish nationality or Spanish habitual residence. The same criteria are established regarding jurisdiction to declare the the nullity of an adoption, adding the cases in which the adoption was constituted by a Spanish authority (Art. 15.1). In these cases, Spanish courts also have jurisdiction to convert a 'simple' adoption into a full adoption, an adoption that creates a permanent parent-child relationship (*adopción plena*) (Art. 15.2). According to Art. 17, except when the State of reception opposes, consuls of Spain have jurisdiction to constitute an adoption if the person who wishes to adopt has Spanish nationality and the person to be adopted has habitual residence in the jurisdiction of the consul.

## Chapter 4. Recognition and Enforcement of Foreign Judgments

*256.* As pointed out above, the statutory Spanish rules on recognition and enforcement of foreign judgments were originally included in Articles 951 et seq. of the 1881 Spanish Civil Procedure Act (former LEC). The new Spanish Code on civil procedure (new LEC), Act 1/2000, 7 January, in force since January 2001, contained no provisions on recognition and enforcement of foreign decisions, but included a provision in the final dispositions of Act 1/2000 for the enactment of an Act on International Judicial Co-operation for Civil Matters, which would address that issue, among other issues in the area of international civil co-operation. The new Act on International Judicial Cooperation in Civil Matters (Law 29/2015, 30 July) has entered into force on 20 August 2015 and the rules on enforcement and recognition under the 1881 Civil Procedure Act have been derogated after being in force for more than a century (the final provision of the new LEC also makes a reference to a new Act on Voluntary Jurisdiction, which has been enacted as Law 15/2015, 2 July, and has entered into force on 23 July 2015).

*257.* Therefore, the new rules in Articles 41–61 of Law 29/2015 on International Judicial Cooperation in Civil Matters are applicable, except when conventional (multilateral or bilateral conventions) or EU rules (such as Regulation 1215/2012, Brussels I bis, Regulation 2201/2003 Brussels II, Regulation 4/2009 Brussels III, and Regulation 650/2012 Brussels IV) apply.[256] Nevertheless, even if a treaty may be applicable, the new rules in Articles 52–55 Law 29/2015 on the judicial procedure of exequatur may be necessary if the convention does not contain rules on the procedure for recognition.

*258.* For the recognition of foreign judgments, the system provided in the old LEC 1881, required a previous exequatur procedure that had to be filed in the Spanish Supreme Court. But the Act 62/2003 and successive reforms later[257] have changed that and since then exequatur applications have had to be filed before the courts of first instance. Article 52 of Law 29/2015 establishes the jurisdiction of either the domicile of the person against whom the recognition or enforcement is sought or the domicile of the person to whom the effects of the judgment are referred. In absence of that, the judge of the first instance of the place of enforcement has jurisdiction. However, commercial judges (*Juzgados de lo Mercantil*) have jurisdiction on the recognition and enforcement of judgments and other foreign decisions on commercial matters, under the same criteria (Article 52.2). Finally, also under the same criteria, the Civil and Criminal Chambers of the Superiors Courts of

256. S. Sánchez Lorenzo, *El nuevo sistema de reconocimiento y ejecución de resoluciones en el Reglamento (UE) 1215/2012 ('Bruselas I bis')*, La Ley (Unión Europea), no. 25, 2015, 5–16. For the application of EU Regulations in relation to decisions from Gibraltar courts, Spain concluded a bilateral agreement with the UK on 19 Apr. 2000 by which the Gibraltar decisions must be certified by a competent authority in London (post-boxing agreement), see M. Checa Martínez, *El régimen de la cooperación judicial civil internacional con Gibraltar: fin de una controversia*, 281–289 (RCEA 2002).

257. *Act 62/2003, 30 December* (BOE 31 Dec. 2003).

Justice (highest court of each autonomous community) have jurisdiction on the recognition of foreign arbitral awards, and their decision is final; once the arbitral award is recognized, the judge of first instance has jurisdiction on its enforcement. The exequatur procedure in Law 29/2015 requires that foreign judgments be final and that they were rendered in a contentious procedure (Article 41) this excludes decisions in matters where there is no dispute. The exequatur is a written procedure which begins by the introduction of a claim accompanied with the original foreign decision or a certified authentic copy duly legalized or apostilled. The claim must be served on the defendant, who must have the possibility of being a part in the procedure and make opposition to the exequatur within thirty days of being served with the claim; the Ministerio Fiscal or Public Prosecutor shall also be a part in these exequatur proceedings (Article 54). Appeal to the Provincial Court (Audiencia Provincial) against the decision given by the Court of First Instance is possible for both parties and the appeal decision can be subjet to further appeal (*recurso de casación*) before the Spanish Supreme Court (Article 55).

*259.* Article 46 (Law 29/2015) establishes the requirements that must be complied with for the recognition of a foreign judgment: (a) the foreign judgment cannot be contrary to Spanish public policy; (b) aforeign judgment given in default of the defendant, who was duly served in sufficient time for his defence, can also be recognized;[258] (c) the foreign judgment must have been rendered by a competent jurisdiction according to reasonable jurisdictional factors. It is evident that such a requirement is not complied with if the foreign judge has ruled on issues characterized as pertaining to the exclusive jurisdiction of the Spanish courts. In addition, scholars agree that the establishment of some fora of protection for the weaker party (workers, consumers, the insured party, minors, etc.) implies the control of the jurisdiction of the court of the State of origin of the decision; (d) there must be no contradictions between the foreign judgment and a Spanish judgment, a previous foreign judgment of a third State that could be recognized in Spain, or a pending procedure in the Spanish courts.

258. Decision AP Madrid, 25 Feb. 2011.

## Chapter 5. International Arbitration

*260.* Spain is a party to the 1961 Geneva European Convention on International Commercial Arbitration.[259] Spain is also a party to the 1958 New York Convention on the Recognition and Enforcement of Foreign Arbitral Awards.[260] As Spain did not exercise its right to make a reservation under Article I.3, the Convention has a universal scope of application; i.e., it applies regardless of the country of origin of the arbitral award.

*261.* Eleven years after the ratification of the New York Convention, Spain enacted the Arbitration Act 36/1988 (*Ley de Arbitraje*), which included rules on recognition and enforcement of foreign arbitral awards (Articles 56 et seq.). Due to the universal character of the New York Convention, application of national statutory rules was in fact impossible.[261] Act 36/1988 was repealed by Act 60/2003, 23 December,[262] which was drafted following the 1985 UNCITRAL Model Law on International Commercial Arbitration.[263] Article 46.2 of the new act orders the application of the 1958 New York Convention to the recognition and enforcement of foreign awards, without prejudice to the application of other more favourable international rules. As Article III of the New York Convention refers to national systems of recognition in order to establish the procedural rules, Articles 52–55 Law 29/2015 on exequatur in the new Law on International Judicial Cooperation for Civil Matters are applicable to the procedure for the recognition of a foreign arbitral award.[264] The same reference to the procedure applicable to the recognition of foreign judicial decisions is established in Article 46.2 of Act 60/2003.[265]

---

259. BOE, 4 Oct. 1975.
260. BOE, 11 Jul. 1977. In addition, several of the bilateral conventions on recognition and enforcement of foreign judgments in force in Spain, also apply to arbitral awards.
261. Decisions TS, 11 Feb. 1981, 13 Oct. 1983, etc.
262. BOE, 26 Dec. 2003. Amended by Act 11/2011, 20 May (BOE, 21 May 2011). The reform does not affect the recognition and enforcement of foreign awards.
263. See D.P. Fernández Arroyo, *Arbitraje comercial internacional* and *Eficacia de las decisiones arbitrales extranjeras en materia de contratos internacionales*, in *Curso de contratación internacional*, 43–71, 987–1006 (2nd ed., A.-L. Calvo Caravaca & J. Carrascosa González (eds), Colex 2006).
264. AP Madrid, 1 Apr. 2009; AP Burgos, 27 Apr. 2009.
265. See A.L. Calvo Caravaca & J. Carrascosa González, *Derecho internacional privado*, 729–742 (16th ed., Vol. I, Comares 2016); C. Esplugues Mota, *Algunas breves reflexiones sobre el arbitraje comercial internacional en la nueva Ley española de arbitraje de 2003*, DeCITA, No. 2, 2004, 363–374; M. Gómez Jene, *El arbitraje internacional en la Ley de arbitraje de 2003* (Colex 2007).

# Selected Bibliography

§1. PUBLICATIONS

AAVV. *Pacis Artes. Obra Homenaje al Profesor Julio D. González Campos.* Madrid: UAM/Eurolex, 2005.

AAVV. Borrás, A. & Garriga, G. (eds.). *Adaptación de la legislación interna a la normativa de la Unión Europea en materia de cooperación civil. Homenaje al Prof. Dr. Ramón Viñas Farré.* Madrid: Marcial Pons, 2012.

AAVV. Carrillo Salcedo, J.A. & Espinar Vicente, J.M.ª (coords.). *Elisa Pérez Vera. Opera Selecta, Estudios de Derecho Internacional.* Madrid: UNED, 2012.

AAVV. Esplugues Mota, C. & Palao Moreno, G. (eds.). *Nuevas Fronteras del Derecho de la Unión Europea. Liber amicorum José Luis Iglesias Buhigues.* Valencia: Tirant lo Blanch, 2012.

AAVV. *Entre Bruselas y la Haya. Estudios sobre la unificación internacional y regional del Derecho internacional privado. Liber amicorum Alegría Borrás.* Madrid: Marcial Pons, 2013.

Abarca Junco, P. (ed.). *Derecho internacional privado.* Madrid: UNED, 2013.

Albaladejo, M. & Díaz Alabart, S. (eds.). *Comentarios al Código civil y Compilaciones forales.* vol. 1. 2nd ed. Madrid: Edersa, 1995.

Calvo Caravaca, A.L. & Areal Ludeña, S. (eds.). *Cuestiones actuales del Derecho mercantil internacional.* Madrid: Colex, 2005.

Calvo Caravaca, A.L. & Blanco-Morales Limones, P. (eds.). *Globalización y Derecho.* Madrid: Colex, 2003.

Calvo Caravaca, A.L. & Carrascosa González, J. *Derecho internacional privado* (16th ed.; 2 vols: vol. II with other authors). Granada: Comares, 2016.

Calvo Caravaca, A.L. & Carrascosa González, J. (eds.). *Curso de contratación internacional.* 2nd ed. Madrid: Colex, 2006.

Calvo Caravaca, A.L. &. Carrascosa González, J. (eds.). *Estudios sobre contratación internacional.* Madrid: Colex, 2006.

Calvo Caravaca, A.L. & Carrascosa González, J. (eds.). *Derecho del comercio internacional.* Madrid: Colex, 2012.

Calvo Caravaca, A.L. & Castellanos Ruiz, E. (eds.). *El Derecho de familia ante el siglo XXI: aspectos internacionales.* Madrid: Colex, 2004.

Calvo Caravaca, A.L. & Fernández de la Gándara, L. *Derecho mercantil internacional.* 2nd ed. Madrid: Tecnos, 1993.

Calvo Caravaca, A.L. & Iriarte Ángel, J.L. (eds.). *Mundialización y familia.* Madrid: Colex, 2001.

Espinar Vicente, J.M. *Tratado elemental de Derecho internacional privado.* Madrid: UAH, 2008.

Esplugues Mota, C. (ed.). *Derecho del Comercio internacional.* 6th ed. Valencia: Tirant lo Blanch, 2015.

Esplugues Mota, C., Iglesias Buhigues, J.L. & Palao Moreno, G. *Derecho Internacional Privado.* 9th ed. Valencia: Tirant lo Blanch, 2015.

Fernández Arroyo, D.P. *Derecho internacional privado (una mirada actual sobre sus elementos esenciales).* Córdoba: Advocatus, 1998.

Fernández Rozas, J.C. & Sánchez Lorenzo, S. *Derecho internacional privado.* 8th ed. Pamplona: Thomson-Civitas, 2015.

Fernández Rozas, J.C. et al. *Derecho de los negocios internacionales.* 4th ed. Madrid: Iustel, 2013.

Garau Sobrino, F.F. *Lecciones de Derecho procesal civil internacional.* 2nd ed. Palma de Mallorca: UIB, 2008.

García Velasco, I. *Derecho internacional privado (reflexiones introductorias).* Salamanca: Cervantes, 1994.

Garcimartín Alférez, F.J. *Derecho internacional privado.* 3rd ed. Pamplona: Thomson-Civitas, 2016.

González Campos, J.D. *Derecho internacional privado. Introducción.* Madrid: UAM, 1984.

González Campos, J.D. et al. *Derecho internacional privado. Parte especial.* 6th ed. Madrid: Eurolex, 1995.

Rodríguez Benot, A. (ed.). *Manual de Derecho internacional privado.* 2nd ed. Madrid: Tecnos, 2015.

Tomás Ortiz de la Torre, J.A. *Derecho internacional privado. Parte General.* Madrid: UCM. Vol. 1. 1992. Vol. 2. 2nd ed., 1990.

Virgós Soriano, M. & Garcimartín Alférez, F. *Derecho procesal civil internacional. Litigación internacional.* 2nd ed. Madrid: Thomson-Civitas, 2007.

## §2. Texts and Materials

Abarca Junco, P. et al. *Prácticas de Derecho internacional. Ejercicios y materiales de apoyo.* 7th ed. Madrid: Colex, 2013.

Álvarez González, S. et al. *Legislación de Derecho internacional privado.* 18th ed. Granada: Comares, 2015.

Borrás, A. et al. *Legislación básica de Derecho internacional privado.* 25th ed. Madrid: Tecnos, 2015.

Calvo Caravaca, A.L. & J. Carrascosa González, J. *Práctica procesal civil internacional.* Granada: Comares, 2001.

Calvo Caravaca, A.L. & J. Carrascosa González, J. *Legislación de Derecho internacional privado comentada y con jurisprudencia.* Granada: Colex, 2002.

Calvo Caravaca, A.L. & J. Carrascosa González, J. *Formularios procesales civiles internacionales.* 2nd ed. Granada: Comares, 2011.

Esplugues Mota, J.C. et al. *Legislación básica del comercio internacional.* 5th ed. Valencia: Tirant lo Blanch, 2011.

Fernández Rozas, J.C. & De Miguel Asensio, P. *Derecho internacional privado. Textos y materiales*. 6th ed. Pamplona: Aranzadi, 2016.

Forner Delaygua, J. et al. *Materiales de Derecho del comercio internacional*. Valencia: Tirant lo Blanch, 2006.

Iriarte Angel, J.L. et al. *Derecho internacional privado*. 13rd ed. Pamplona: Thomson-Aranzadi, 2015.

Maestre Casas, P. et al. *Aplicación práctica del Derecho internacional privado: casos y soluciones*. 4th ed. Salamanca: Ratio Legis, 2015.

Sánchez Lorenzo, S. (ed.). *Legislación de los negocios internacionales*. Madrid: Tecnos, 2008.

## Selected Bibliography

# Index

*The numbers here refer to paragraph numbers.*

## Index

www.ingramcontent.com/pod-product-compliance
Lightning Source LLC
Chambersburg PA
CBHW071352230926
51846CB00002B/519
*9789041182692*